LAMENTATIONS IN ANCIENT AND CONTEMPORARY CULTURAL CONTEXTS

Society of Biblical Literature

Symposium Series

Victor H. Matthews,
Series Editor

Number 43

LAMENTATIONS IN ANCIENT AND
CONTEMPORARY CULTURAL CONTEXTS

LAMENTATIONS IN ANCIENT AND CONTEMPORARY CULTURAL CONTEXTS

Edited by

Nancy C. Lee

and

Carleen Mandolfo

Society of Biblical Literature
Atlanta

LAMENTATIONS IN ANCIENT AND CONTEMPORARY CULTURAL CONTEXTS

Library of Congress Cataloging-in-Publication Data

Lamentations in ancient and contemporary cultural contexts / edited by Nancy C. Lee and Carleen Mandolfo.
    p. cm. — (Society of Biblical Literature symposium series ; no. 43)
    Includes bibliographical references and indexes.
    ISBN: 978-1-58983-357-9 (paper binding : alk. paper)
    1. Bible. O.T. Lamentations—Criticism, interpretation, etc. 2. Laments in the Bible. 3. Elegiac poetry—History and criticism. I. Lee, Nancy C. II. Mandolfo, Carleen.
    BS1535.52.L36 2008b
    224'.306—dc22   2008022774

16 15 14 13 12 11 10 09 08   5 4 3 2 1
Printed in the United States of America on acid-free, recycled paper conforming to ANSI/NISO Z39.48-1992 (R1997) and ISO 9706:1994 standards for paper permanence.

Contents

Laments from the Sudan, New Orleans, and Iraq

"Nyambol," Sudanese Rap Song, *Ceasefire* (2000)
Emmanuel Jal and Abdel Gadir Salim (P. Borg)

(Nuer)
E ngah? E ngah?
E Nyambol, Nyambol e:
Nyamabom leijde!

(English translation)
Who is it? Who is it?
It's Nyambol, Nyambol, that's who:
She is a survivor!

Nyambol was in misery,
Nyambol was only 13 years old....

"A Lament for New Orleans" (14 September 2005)
Clyde Fant

How like a widow sits the city
once so beautiful!
She weeps bitterly in the night,
with tears on her cheeks,
Because there is none to comfort her....
In her streets the flood bereaves;
in the sodden houses it is like death.
The leaders and elders of the city have fled,
but the poor are trapped within her levees....

Weep, weep for the great city!
Orators of platitudes, politicians of promises,
  it is you who betrayed her

... You channeled her rivers
and harnessed her waters, but for yourselves!
... You brought the might of the waves
and the winds to her very doors.
The poor, those who dwelt in the lowest places,
who lived in miserable shanties of wood,
termite-ridden and forlorn,
where none but the hopeless would dwell:
You have murdered them,
and their corpses drift in the brackish floods,
but their cries have gone up to God! ...

JAMAL KHAMBAR, KURDISH IRAQI (27 FEBRUARY 2007)

There was nobody to cry
There was nobody to shatter my silence
I was as lost as a child in the bosom of the universe
And there was nobody guiding me to find my homeland
At the last moment, the flute started to speak....

PREFACE

This anthology of scholarly essays and original lament poetry marks a culmination of nearly ten years of work by participants in the Society of Biblical Literature session originally called Lamentations in Ancient and Contemporary Contexts, inaugurated in 1999. Co-proposed by Nancy Lee and Tod Linafelt, it was, to our knowledge, the first scholarly group of its kind in the history of the SBL that devoted itself to "lament" (to Lamentations, other biblical and extrabiblical lament texts, including Psalms, and consideration of lament poetry in today's cultures). From the outset, the group welcomed and heard all of the above, from interdisciplinary perspectives, and even issued a "call to poets" as well as the usual call for papers. Perhaps it was because we were drawing to the close of the most violent century in human history, because tragic events around the world continue unabated, or because in the larger history of biblical scholarship lament was rather neglected that the work of this group has found a welcome and steady audience. This groundbreaking anthology on lament is the first volume of its kind to be published and includes a number of the most noted scholars of Hebrew Bible.

Beginning in 1999, the SBL Lament session focused on the scholarship of those who had recently completed commentaries or monographs on the book of Lamentations, that text having received a surprising surge of attention in recent years; a number of these authors have summarized their works in the first section of this volume. Other biblical lament texts and a rich array of studies from different cultural contexts pressed upon us the need to change our name to Lament in Sacred Texts and Cultures to reflect our founding aim. The second two sections of this volume include papers that address these areas.

The second section moves to studies of particular lament texts in the Hebrew Bible, such as the Psalms and Second Isaiah. The third section moves to the phenomenon of lament in cross-cultural contexts, with illustrations from the ancient Near East, to the Middle Ages, all the way to the present. Essays critically examine lament's forms, functions, artistries, strong participation of women, and lament genres' ability to address the painful realities of HIV-AIDS. The essays herein evidence the extraordinary breadth of how lament—both timeless and adaptable, with diverse faces—has ranged through human history, bounded over and through cultures and religions, from oral forms to the great written laments of Sumeria, even to popular rap music today. The contributors here are truly international, hailing from or representing in their work the cultures and spiritual traditions from over a dozen countries or regions.

Perhaps it is fitting that Walter Brueggemann closes out the volume, as he has influenced many of us with his persistent commitment to the importance of lament through the years. His essay is both a retrospective (more than an echo of his "Costly Loss of Lament" in 1986) and a prospective (in light of unrelenting human suffering all around) that throws light upon a larger path for continuing forward. We are grateful for the common cause we all share, and while we will differ in our understandings and interpretations, we press on to bring scholarship into relevant discourse with the needs of the world. We express our great thanks to all those participants in the Lament group and those who work on this through other disciplines, whether represented herein or not, for all have contributed to this important enterprise. Our special thanks to Catherine Zweig for her invaluable editorial assistance and bibliographic work. We also are most grateful to Kent Richards, Matthew Collins, Victor Matthews, Leigh Andersen, and Bob Buller for their support through the SBL.

Nancy C. Lee, Chicago, Illinois
Carleen Mandolfo, Waterville, Maine

Abbreviations

AB	Anchor Bible
ABR	*Australian Biblical Review*
AJT	*Asia Journal of Theology*
ANET	*Ancient Near Eastern Texts Relating to the Old Testament*. Edited by J. B. Pritchard. 3rd ed. Princeton: Princeton University Press, 1969.
AOAT	Alter Orient und Altes Testament
ASOR	American Schools of Oriental Research
BaghF	Baghdader Forschungen
Bib	*Biblica*
BibInt	*Biblical Interpretation*
BibOr	Biblica et orientalia
BibSac	*Bibliotheca Sacra*
BJS	Brown Judaic Studies
BKAT	Biblischer Kommentar, Altes Testament
BZAW	Beihefte zur Zeitschrift für die alttestamentliche Wissenschaft
CBET	Contributions to Biblical Exegesis and Theology
CBQ	*Catholic Biblical Quarterly*
ConBOT	Coniectanea biblica: Old Testament Series
DJD	Discoveries in the Judaean Desert
EI	*Eretz-Israel*
EncJud	*Encyclopaedia Judaica*. 16 vols. Jerusalem: Keter, 1972.
FAT	Forschungen zum Alten Testament
FOTL	Forms of the Old Testament Literature
HBT	*Horizons in Biblical Theology*
HCOT	Historical Commentry on the Old Testament
HJAS	*Harvard Journal of Asiatic Studies*
HSM	Harvard Semitic Monographs
HUCA	*Hebrew Union College Annual*
IBC	Interpretation: A Bible Commentary for Teaching and Preaching
Int	*Interpretation*
JANESCU	*Journal of the Ancient Near Eastern Society of Columbia University*
JBL	*Journal of Biblical Literature*
JHS	*Journal of Hellenic Studies*

JQR	*Jewish Quarterly Review*
JSNTSup	Journal for the Study of the New Testament Supplement Series
JSOT	*Journal for the Study of the Old Testament*
JSOTSup	Journal for the Study of the Old Testament: Supplement Series
JTSA	*Journal of Theology for Southern Africa*
KAT	Kommentar zum Alten Testament
LBH	Late Biblical Hebrew
NCB	New Century Bible
OBO	Orbis biblicus et orientalis
OBT	Overtures to Biblical Theology
OTG	Old Testament Guides
OTL	Old Testament Library
RB	*Revue biblique*
RBL	*Review of Biblical Literature*
RGG	*Religion in Geschichte und Gegenwart.* Edited by Kurt Galling. 7 vols. 3rd ed. Tübingen: Mohr Siebeck, 1957–1965.
RTR	*Reformed Theological Review*
SBH	Standard Biblical Hebrew
SBLAcBib	Society of Biblical Literature Academia Biblica
SBLDS	Society of Biblical Literature Dissertation Series
SBLEJL	Society of Biblical Literature Early Judaism and Its Literature
SemeiaSt	Semeia Studies
SJ	Studia judaica
SJOT	*Scandinavian Journal of the Old Testament*
SBT	Studies in Biblical Theology
TTS	Trierer theologische Studien
TBü	Theologische Bücherei
TQ	*Theologische Quartalschrift*
TRE	*Theologische Realenzyklopädie.* Edited by G. Krause and G. Müller. Berlin: de Gruyter, 1977–.
UF	*Ugarit-Forschungen*
VT	*Vetus Testamentum*
WMANT	Wissenschaftliche Monographien zum Alten und Neuen Testament
WTJ	*Westminster Theological Journal*
YNER	Yale Near Eastern Researches
ZAW	*Zeitschrift für die alttestamentliche Wissenschaft*

Part 1
The Biblical Book of Lamentations

On Writing a Commentary on Lamentations

Adele Berlin

Of the making of commentaries there is no end, to paraphrase Ecclesiastes, and the many recent commentaries on Lamentations prove the point.[1] Indeed, as long as the Bible is studied, no commentary will ever be the last, for each new commentary is an expression of engagement with the text at a particular moment in time, reflecting the state of scholarship, the needs of the audience, and the choices of the commentator. Because they reflect the state of biblical scholarship, commentaries reveal quite a lot about scholarly trends. At the same time, a commentary is a very personal creation, the expression of a relationship between a biblical book, a given interpreter, and the targeted audience. The result is, in each case, a slightly different application of generally accepted ways of interpreting the Bible.

On its most basic level, a commentary is like a tour guide leading the reader on a guided tour through a biblical book. Whether the tourists have been there before or are seeing it for the first time, the guide must answer three questions: What needs to be pointed out to the reader? How much explanation is required and of what type should it be? What overall impression should the reader be left with about the meaning of this book and its place within the Bible? As simple as this sounds, there are judgments to be made at every turn. The author of a commentary is not required to be innovative, but to provide the state-of-the-art information. Indeed, commentaries are more alike than different. Nevertheless, the urge is always to say something new or at least to present the book as it has never been presented before. So in the end, a commentary is more than a tour guide; it is a work of interpretative art.

---

1. See the recent commentaries and studies, all dating from after 1990 and several after 2000, by Chip Dobbs-Allsopp, Erhard Gerstenberger, Delbert Hillers (revised), Tod Linafelt, Nancy Lee, Kathleen O'Connor, Iain Provan, and Johan Renkema, which were available to me in published and/or prepublication form. I would add now Jill Middlemas, *The Troubles of Templeless Judah* (Oxford: Oxford University Press, 2005), which contains a long section on Lamentations (171–228).

My commentary on Lamentations was commissioned by the Old Testament Library series of Westminster John Knox Press, a series aimed at a scholarly and semischolarly audience made up mostly of students in graduate schools and/or Christian seminaries, academics, and clergy.[2] However, while the press is linked to the Presbyterian denomination and the target audience is largely Christian, this is not a Christian commentary. That is, it does not relate Lamentations to the New Testament or to Christian belief or practice. Indeed, the volumes in the OTL series are authored by a religiously diverse group of men and women, Jews, Catholics, and Protestants, because the purpose is to offer the best of current academic, rather than sectarian, interpretation.

As is usual, the format was set by the publisher. I was fortunate to be able to offer my own translation (some commentaries are based on existing translations made by people other than the commentator, sometimes resulting in a tug of war between the translation and the commentator). I regret, however, that the Hebrew text does not accompany the translation and commentary. This omission is standard practice, but it deprives the knowledgeable reader of a crucial part of the study of the text. In some sense, it allows the reader to forget that there is a Hebrew text. The best I could do was to convince the press to include the letters of the Hebrew alphabet to mark the alphabetical acrostics in four chapters.

I am not enamored of massive commentaries; the reader loses the view of the forest and often cannot even see the tops of the trees. The length of the commentary should be in proportion to the length of the biblical book. A biblical poem, like the proverbial picture, may require a thousand words to explain it, but there is such a thing as interpretative overkill. A commentary should not, cannot, be comprehensive. It should say just enough to give a sense of the author's perspective on the book's meaning and significance without weighing down the reader with all that has been said about it before. Commentaries are not histories of interpretation, although more thought ought to be given to the place of the history of interpretation within a commentary. In the early twentieth century series like the International Critical Commentary devoted significant space to the history of interpretation, beginning from ancient times, through medieval and modern times, with both Christian and Jewish representation. All that fell away in commentaries from the middle of the twentieth century, when the sources cited leapt from ancient Near Eastern texts to twentieth-century authors, bridging a silence of almost two thousand years as if entire streams of pre-modern interpretation did not exist. A middle course has emerged in more recent years, wherein commentators offer a selection from a range of ancient, medieval, and modern forerunners to support their case—in some cases cherry-picking to support their arguments and in other cases to indicate the span of possible interpretations, now

---

2. Adele Berlin, *Lamentations: A Commentary* (OTL; Louisville: Westminster John Knox, 2002).

that "the one correct meaning" is no longer sought with such assurance as it used to be (although most commentators still aim to present what they consider to be the best reading of a given verse or chapter, and ultimately the best understanding of the book as a whole).

In matters of text criticism and philology I treaded lightly since these are areas that have now been replaced as the central focus in many newer commentaries. The focus now is on the broader aspects of the meaning of the whole rather than on its parts, as can be seen from the shrinking amount of space given over to specific phrases and verses and the growth of introductions and summations of larger sections of the text. The trend now is against the dissection of the text in order to lay bare its textual and linguistic problems and in favor of viewing the text as a coherent whole. The effect is to suppress, to some extent, discussion of textual anomalies and, concomitantly, to limit the more technical aspects of the enterprise, thereby making the work more accessible to an audience not trained as professional biblicists.

Past commentaries on Lamentations, as on Psalms, have had a heavy dose of form criticism which I essentially dismissed as having gone as far as it could go. It does not seem to matter much whether the funeral dirge or the communal lament dominates in Lamentations, although I acknowledge the similarities to these genres as well as to the Mesopotamian lament literature. Rather than rehash the discussions of the generic antecedents of Lamentations, to which I had little to add, I preferred to emphasize the generic innovation of Lamentations and other post-586 B.C.E. laments for the destruction of the temple and Jerusalem. I call this new genre the "Jerusalem lament" and include in it Pss 74, 79, 102, 137, and others.[3] Although this genre obviously has forerunners, it is essentially a new poetic form for a new occasion, a development within exilic and postexilic biblical literature.

My approach is largely literary, but the implication of that approach has changed through the years. While literary approaches used to be mainly concerned with the structure and formal properties of the text, they are less so now. Accordingly, I avoided describing the formal attributes of biblical verse, such as parallelism, word patterning, and so forth. The reader who wants to see how to chart the so-called meter of Lamentations and its parallelisms can find this information elsewhere. Nor does a literary approach mean taking the text only as an aesthetic object, although I continue to appreciate the aesthetic accomplishments of the poet and try to point them out. To understand a piece

---

3. See Adele Berlin, "Psalms and the Literature of Exile: Psalms 137, 44, 69, and 78," in *The Book of Psalms: Composition and Reception* (ed. Peter W. Flint and Patrick D. Miller; Leiden: Brill, 2005), 65–86. Jill Middlemas, *The Troubles of Templeless Judah*, considers a similar group of psalms and Lamentations to be the product of post-586 Judah, as opposed to literature written in exile, and examines them for distinctive Judean thought.

of literature, one must understand the conceptual world that is being expressed, and that, more than anything, is what I attempted to do. I will present here a brief summary of three major aspects of the conceptual world that informs Lamentations: the paradigm of purity, the political paradigm, and the concept of mourning.

The larger Judean worldview that undergirds and informs the poetry of the book is the theology of destruction and exile, the same general theology that informs Deuteronomy, namely, that exile is the punishment for disobeying God's commandments. But while Deuteronomy is didactic in tone, with dire warnings, Lamentations no longer warns but laments the carrying out of the punishment. It is centered on suffering and mourning, and on the cry, unanswered, for a response from God. Why immortalize this moment of destruction and its con-comitant suffering? Not only because it is an enormous human tragedy, or the most horrendous national catastrophe in the history of Judah, but because, ironi-cally, it proves that Deuteronomic theology is true. And by so doing, it points to the continuation of the covenant between God and Israel. Destruction and exile are not the end of the relationship between God and Israel. Deut 30:1–5 envisions the return after the destruction: "When all these things befall you ... and you take them to heart amidst all the nations to which the Lord your God has banished you" (NJPS). It is that moment of banishment that Lamentations captures, the moment of "taking to heart," and implicit in it is the idea of return (see also Deut 4:27–31). To be sure, the promise of return is far from realized in Lamentations, and little optimism is expressed in it, but at certain moments the book seems to look beyond the destruction, to hold out hope for the future. In the end, though, despair overcomes hope. Past and future have little place in the book. It centers on the "present"—the moment of trauma, the interminable suffering. The book is not, in essence, a theological argument, although it is based on a certain theologi-cal view of the world. It is not an explanation of suffering but a re-creation of it and a commemoration of it.

More specifically, the theology of destruction is based on what I call the paradigm of purity and the political paradigm. The paradigm of purity says that moral impurity defiles the land, and, there being no ritual to expiate this type of impurity, the land will spew out its inhabitants. This is the theological under-standing of the exile, the act whereby the land of Israel rejects its inhabitants. The concept of the defilement of the land from moral impurity lies behind much of the imagery of Lamentations. Several passages from the Torah (Lev 18:24–28; Num 35:33–34) and the prophets (Ezek 22:1–4) express this idea, as does Ps 106:34–41:

> they worshiped their idols ... they shed innocent blood ... so the land was pol-luted with bloodguilt. Thus they became defiled by their acts.... The LORD was angry with his people, and he abhorred his inheritance. He handed them over to the nations; their foes ruled them.

Lamentations partakes of the same imagery and the same paradigm of moral defilement of the land, and many of the seemingly disconnected images of the book cohere around it, especially and obviously the ones of the sexually immoral woman. These images are not used only, or even primarily, because they are violent and shocking (although they are certainly effective in that regard), but because they have a central role in the paradigm of moral impurity (since one of the leading causes of moral impurity is sexual immorality). That role is both literal, in that the view was that immoral behavior pollutes the land in a literal sense, and figurative, in that the prophets made the morally impure woman (that is, the sexually wanton woman) into a metaphor for Israel. The paradigm of moral impurity is invoked continually in Lamentations, and the failure to recognize it leads to the misconstrual of the use of sexual imagery in the book.[4]

A different but related type of metaphorization may also occur, wherein the terms for ritual impurity are applied to moral impurity. (Ritual and moral impurity are usually distinct phenomena.) We find this most clearly in Lam 4:15, where the ritually impure leper (Lev 13:45) is the symbol of the morally impure leaders. The poet makes this comparison for the purpose of conveying the untouchability—the utter rejection—of those who have sinned. Some interpreters also see this type of metaphorization in 1:9 and 17, where Zion is compared to a menstruant (נדה). I argue in the commentary that 1:9 is probably not a reference to menstruation and that in any case exegetes have misunderstood the nature of menstrual impurity. Menstruation, like other genital discharges, causes ritual impurity, but there is no immorality or disgust associated with it (Lev 15:19–24). Nevertheless, it is clear that elsewhere in the Bible ritual impurity can *symbolize* moral impurity. In Ezek 36:17 the menstruant serves as a symbol of moral impurity: "their ways were in my sight like the impurity of the נדה." Ezra 9:11 refers to the defilement of the land as נדה. However, it should be stressed that this is not the plain sense meaning of נדה but a metaphorized use. There is nothing immoral about a menstruating woman. Only in a culture where the concept of impurity was thoroughly understood and accepted could the prophets and poets use it in this way. The modern reader needs to appreciate the pervasiveness of the purity/impurity system in biblical thought in order to appreciate its use in Lamentations.

The second paradigm used to explain the destruction, the political paradigm, does not come from the sphere of religion but from the sphere of law and international politics. It is based on the relationship between suzerain and vassal, best known through the ancient Near Eastern treaties and reflected also in the Assyrian and Babylonian annals. This is the model for the covenant between God, the sovereign, and Israel, who owes loyalty and allegiance to God. Deuteronomy is the book that most obviously frames the covenant in terms of a treaty (but cf. also Exod 20–23 and Lev 26). As is typical in these treaties, Deut 28 contains curses—the

---

4. For a fuller discussion, see Berlin, *Lamentations*, 19–21.

consequences for disobeying the stipulations of the treaty, which constitutes rebellion against the suzerain. The language of Deut 28:45–68 bears much resemblance to the descriptions of the war and siege in Lamentations: "The LORD will bring a nation against you from afar.... It shall shut you up in all your towns.... you shall eat your own issue, the flesh of your sons and daughters.... you shall be torn from the land.... The LORD will scatter you among the people" (NJPS). The treaty model helps us to understand why it is God, not the Babylonians, who is responsible for the destruction. It was with God that Israel made the covenant, and it is God, therefore, who is the offended suzerain. Like a human suzerain, he attacks the rebellious country, defeats it, and deports (portions of) its population. The Babylonians do not come into this theological picture at all, except as the vehicle through which God acts. Both the paradigm of purity and the political paradigm converge in their view that exile is the ultimate punishment for the most serious offenses, moral and/or political. It is, therefore, easy to understand how prophets and poets could fuse the two paradigms together, as they are fused in Lamentations.

The most central theme of Lamentations is mourning, which emerges in the very first image, the widowed city seeking comfort (1:1–2), and is pervasive throughout the book. Mourning is not only a set of customs or rituals relating to death, it is an abstract religious concept that had an important place in Israelite cultic thought. The book of Lamentations incorporates the concept of mourning in a number of ways.

From the work of Gary Anderson we learn that mourning is associated with the absence of sacrificing.[5] Since sacrifice and praise of God are parallel activities, it follows that joy is associated with praising God, as is often expressed in the Psalms (e.g., Pss 34:3; 35:21). The mourner, who cannot participate in public joy, is not permitted access to the temple, and his cultic double, the lamenter in psalms of lament, does not praise God during his time of trouble; rather, he hopes to be able to praise God in the future, after he has been delivered from trouble (see, e.g., Ps 71:20–24).

In his inability to praise God, the mourner is like the dead, and indeed, mourning is closely associated with death and Sheol. Sheol is not only the place where the dead reside; it is the place where the lamenter feels himself to be—the place experienced while in a state of mourning or lamenting. Only when the lamenter is delivered from his trouble does his state of mourning end, at which time he goes to the temple to sacrifice and/or utter praise to God. Psalm 86:12–13 is one example: "I will praise you, Lord my God, with my whole heart, and may I honor your name forever. For your loyalty overwhelms me, in that you have delivered me from the depths of Sheol" (see also Pss 9:14–15; 71:20; Jonah 2:2–10). Anderson makes the point that references to death and Sheol in psalms

---

5. *A Time to Mourn, a Time to Dance: The Expression of Grief and Joy in Israelite Religion* (University Park: Pennsylvania State University Press, 1991).

of lament are not simply metaphoric expressions for how bad the psalmist feels. They are, rather, religious concepts being re-enacted in the psalms. Descent to Sheol, the nadir of the earth (Amos 9:2), is the structural inversion of the temple, the symbolic entry-way to heaven. To be in Sheol is to be at the furthest remove from God. Death and mourning, as a religious concept, means to be cut off from God, just as life and joy mean to be in God's presence.

It should become immediately clear that within this conceptual worldview, the destruction of the temple—a permanent and national denial of access to God—becomes a prime occasion for public mourning. The destruction is a national death and all Judeans are mourners. This death is not only a political death, the end of an independent Judah, but also a religious death, in that access to God's presence is cut off (both for those who remained in Judah and those who were exiled to Babylonia). The notion of exile reinforces the distance from God and the temple, so it is natural that exile becomes the new Sheol. Lamentations incorporates this sense of mourning. In addition to being a literary or symbolic manifestation of the concept of mourning, it is likely that the book was used in rituals of public mourning that were instituted to commemorate the temple's destruction. Moreover, it perpetuates the state of mourning. The book holds out no comfort, and denies the existence of a comforter, thereby making the cessation of mourning impossible. Lamentations is a plea for comfort in the form of access to God. The plea throughout the book is that God should hear, see, remember, pay attention, and, at its climax, that he should "take us back" (5:21), but the plea is never answered, God remains silent, and so, in this book, the state of mourning cannot end.

Turning to more obviously literary phenomena, I was especially concerned to understand metaphors, the vehicle through which poetry expresses its view of the world. Surprisingly little work of value has been done on biblical metaphor.[6] I did not wish to theorize about biblical metaphor but to understand it in action, to explicate the metaphors in Lamentations. The overarching metaphors, like the city as a widow, as a betrayed lover, and as a mother bereaved of her children, are well-known, although they continue to be moving because they humanize and feminize the plight of the city with graphic intensity. More unexpected, and less-often commented on, are the smaller metaphors, like "Zion's roads are in mourning" (1:4), a personification of part of the city mourning for the entire city,

---

6. The best general works are, to my mind, Luis Alonso-Schökel, *A Manual of Hebrew Poetics* (Rome: Pontifical Biblical Institute, 1988), 95–141; and Meir Weiss, *The Bible from Within* (Jerusalem: Magnes, 1984). Consider also Herbert J. Levine, *Sing Unto God a New Song* (Indianapolis: Indiana University Press, 1995); William P. Brown, *Seeing the Psalms. A Theology of Metaphor* (Louisville: Westminster John Knox, 2002); Adele Berlin, "On Reading Biblical Poetry: The Role of Metaphor," in *Congress Volume: Cambridge, 1995* (VTSup 66; Leiden: Brill, 1997), 25–36; and now the recent book by Andrea Weiss, *Figurative Language in Biblical Prose Narrative* (Leiden: Brill, 2006).

now empty of festival pilgrims. This equation of emptiness and mourning reinforces the image of the mourning widow as the empty city at the beginning of the
chapter. Metaphors based on ancient realia call for an explanation for the modern
reader, so images from the realm of battle and siege—nets, yokes, siege works
(1:13–15)—receive some comment. Some images are shocking to the modern
reader, who takes them for innovative, like the cannibalism of mothers during
the starvation of the siege (2:20; 4:10), but this is a common trope of siege literature. Not that this makes the image any less effective, for conventional literature
(and much of the Bible is conventional in its literary forms of expression) can still
have strong impact. Indeed, we should abandon the modern notion that innovation trumps conventionality. There is plenty of creativity within the conventional
forms and images of the Bible.

Even the meaning of common idioms is not always obvious, and the commentator's job is to explain them. "The baby's tongue stuck to his palate from
thirst" (4:4) is, I think, a masterly use of a phrase that means a person cannot
utter a sound (as in Ezek 3:26; Job 29:10; Ps 137:6). The image is not simply of
a dry mouth or parched throat; the baby here is too weak from starvation even
to cry, a most unnatural state for a hungry baby and a sign of extreme physical
condition of the infant, who lies listlessly at his mother's breast, which has ceased
making milk. More puzzling is the unusual combination in the phrase "Where is
grain and wine" (2:12) that the children ask their mothers. The more usual combination is "bread and wine," the staple foods, or "grain and juice of grapes" the
raw materials for bread and wine. Here, I concluded, "grain and wine" stand for
the foodstuffs that can be stored for long periods. The children are asking whether
there is anything left in the storehouses. The implication is that all the supplies in
the city have been used up.

On the macro-level, I wanted to convey the "feel" of each chapter and locate
it in a literary context. Like many other interpreters, I take the five chapters as
five independent poems, although they are unified in that all of them relate
to the destruction. I see them as poetic expressions of different aspects of the
destruction, or as describing the destruction from different perspectives. Chapter
1 focuses on Jerusalem, the destroyed city, in the aftermath of the destruction,
when she is pictured in her mourning, her shame, and her desolation. The tone
is one of despair, depression, degradation, shame, and guilt. The destruction is
complete and the reader stands among the ruins. Chapter 2 takes the reader back
to the moment of destruction, with all its physical and theological force, as at the
behest of God, the buildings come tumbling down—architectural imagery pre-
dominates. The picture is full of anger and fury—God's anger at the city and the
poet's anger at God. The chapter focuses on God, the perpetrator of the destruction. The anger of God overshadows the guilt of Jerusalem. Chapter 3 portrays
the process of exile, with its alternating moods of despair and hope. The speaker
is a lone male, a Job-like figure trying to come to terms with what has happened.
His view is personal but at the same time representative of the people. Chapter

4 focuses on the people, reliving the siege and the suffering that accompanied it—the toll it took on the inhabitants of the city. The chapter paints a picture of utter degradation, painted with words demarking the washing out of color from the technicolor portrait of health and luxury to the black and white figures suffering from starvation and lack of all material benefits. Chapter 5 is the prayer of the Judean remnant, weakened and impoverished by foreign subjugation, deprived of king and temple, pleading with God not to abandon them forever, barely clinging to hope that God has not abandoned them altogether.[7]

I want to stress that these "settings" for each chapter are fictive settings intended to convey their literary mise-en-scène. They are not to be taken as historical; that is, I do not suggest that chapter 2 was actually written by an eye-witness to the siege, or chapter 3 by a real exile, or chapter 5 by a person in Judah after 586 B.C.E. A fine poet can give voice to an experience even though he did not experience it himself, can make us feel that not only he, but we, too, were there. It is all too easy to fall into the trap of mistaking a literary representation for a historical one, but it should be resisted. It is widely assumed that Lamentations was written in Judah or Jerusalem, because it is so focused on that city. While that position has a certain logic, and I have no alternative to offer, it is not out of the question that an author living in exile could have written all or parts of this book. What strikes me about the combination of the five perspectives in the five chapters is how broad is their representation of the circumstances and the results of the destruction, as if to undermine the current attempts by some scholars to make a sharp distinction between exilic and Judean literature. Wherever it originated, Lamentations ultimately became the property of all Jews, both those in Judah and those in exile.

For the most part, I have been describing the areas in which my commentary differs from most that preceded it. That is not to say that it is completely different, however, since it also includes discussion of date and authorship, philological, grammatical and textual problems, comparative ancient Near Eastern tropes, and issues arising from a consciousness of the literary expression of gender. Commentary-writing is a conservative enterprise. To be sure, the commentary genre changes over time, but for the most part, the changes do not eradicate all the signs of the genre. The writing of biblical commentaries has been with us for a very long time. Let's hope it will continue.

---

7. See Berlin, *Lamentations*, 7, and the introductions to each chapter.

Lamentations from Sundry Angles:
A Retrospective

F. W. Dobbs-Allsopp

The assignment is to provide a summary statement of my own past work on the biblical book of Lamentations, which includes a dissertation, a commentary, and a half-score of journal articles, essays of various sorts, dictionary entries, and reviews written over a period of a decade or so.[1] It is with some general discomfort that I have accepted the assignment—for the most part, I am content to let my work stand on its own, as originally articulated, flaws and all. Yet since I am (apparently) also temperamentally incapable of straightforward restatement, in the summary reprise that follows I accentuate what I continue to find valuable in this work, teasing out along the way some of its broader implications, with the ambition that the restatement itself thereby may make some (small) positive contribution of its own. One of the chief advantages of maintaining a relatively

---

1. F. W. Dobbs-Allsopp, *Weep, O Daughter of Zion: A Study of the City-Lament Genre in the Hebrew Bible* (BibOr 44; Roma: Pontifical Biblical Institute, 1993); idem, review of Paul Wayne Ferris Jr., *The Genre of Communal Lament in the Bible and the Ancient Near East, CBQ* 56 (1994): 103–4; idem, "The Syntagma of *bat* Followed by a Geographical Name in the Hebrew Bible: Reconsideration of Its Meaning and Grammar," *CBQ* 57 (1995): 451–70; idem, "Tragedy, Tradition, and Theology in the Book of Lamentations," *JSOT* 74 (1997): 29–60; idem, "Albright Fellows' Reports 1997–1998: Commentary on the Book of Lamentations," *ASOR Newsletter* 48/3 (1998): 19–20; idem, "Linguistic Evidence for the Date of Lamentations," *JANES* 26 (1998): 1–36; idem, "Lamentations," in *Eerdmans Dictionary of the Bible* (ed. David Noel Freedman, Astrid B. Beck, and Allen C. Myers; Grand Rapids: Eerdmans, 2000), 785–87; idem, "Darwinism, Genre Theory, and City Laments," *JAOS* 120 (2000): 625–30; idem, introduction and critical notes to Lamentations for *The New Oxford Annotated Bible: New Revised Standard Version* (ed. Michael D. Coogan et al.; New York: Oxford University, 2001), 959–68; idem, "The Rape of Zion in Lam 1:10," *ZAW* 113 (2001): 77–81 (with T. Linafelt); idem, "The Enjambing Line in Lamentations: A Taxonomy (Part I)," *ZAW* 113 (2001): 219–39; idem, "The Effects of Enjambment in Lamentations (Part 2)," *ZAW* 113 (2001): 370–85; idem, *Lamentations* (IBC; Louisville: Westminster John Knox, 2002); idem, "R(az/ais)ing Zion in Lamentations 2," in *David and Zion: Biblical Studies in Honor of J. J. M. Roberts* (ed. Bernard Frank Batto and Kathryn L. Roberts; Winona Lake, Ind.: Eisenbrauns, 2004), 21–68.

narrow textual focus over an extended period of time is that you can come at the interpretive task from a variety of perspectives and with a variety of issues in mind. It is in these sundry angles and the multiplex issues illuminated and exposed where I find that my own work matters most to me, and it is here, as well, beyond matters of detail (which are never inconsequential), that I think this work, individually and as a whole, most merits ongoing attention. The discussion is organized around five broad rubrics and concludes with some brief reflections on what still remains to be done—or, at least, what I would like to do, all other things being equal.

1. GENRE

In the process of revising his Anchor Bible commentary on Lamentations,[2] Delbert R. Hillers came to think that the biblical book had more in common with the Mesopotamian city laments than he previously allowed.[3] In the revised commentary, Hillers fully embraces the notion of a connection between the two bodies of literature[4] and, more specifically, proposes the existence of an Israelite city-lament genre: "A 'city-lament' genre would be an abstraction made, for the sake of discussion, to refer to a common theme: the destruction of city and sanctuary, with identifiable imagery specific to this theme, and common sub-topics and poetic devices."[5] The central thrust of my own dissertation work was to elaborate and extend Hillers's analysis. I add considerably to the repertoire of features shared by these compositions,[6] isolate biblical passages outside of Lamentations (especially in the so-called "oracles against the nations") that also exhibit related imagery, topoi, and the like,[7] and situate the discussion, far more intentionally, with regard to genre and genre theory.[8] Two principal findings of the study merit underscoring. The five poems that constitute the biblical book of Lamentations, both as entities in their own right and as a collection, participate in or manifest awareness of a genre of laments that mourn the fall and destruction of ancient cities and their chief sanctuaries, a genre which is most prominently (and perhaps even aboriginally) attested from ancient Mesopotamia (e.g., city laments, *balag*s, *eršemma*s), but which also appears, if only vestigially, at Ugarit (e.g., *KTU* 1.15.

---

2. *Lamentations* (AB 7A; Garden City, N.Y.: Doubleday, 1972).

3. *Lamentations*, xxviii–xxx

4. *Lamentations* (AB 7A; 2nd. ed.; Garden City, N.Y.: Doubleday, 1992), 32–39.

5. Ibid., 36.

6. *Weep, O Daughter of Zion*, esp. 30–96.

7. Ibid., 97–156.

8. Ibid., esp. 15–22; cf. Dobbs-Allsopp, "Darwinism"; "Genre," in Freedman, Beck, and Myers, *Eerdmans Dictionary of the Bible*, 493–94.

I.1–8), elsewhere in the Bible (e.g., Ps 78:56–72),[9] and even in Greek literature of various periods.[10] That is, Lamentations and these other laments for destroyed cities share a common literary genre. This is the study's most positive conclusion. No literary interpretation of Lamentations can (fully) ignore these larger genre relations. Less specific but potentially of much broader significance is the study's engagement with genre itself. Genre is absolutely critical to any intelligible reading of literature from the past—textual understanding simply cannot take place without some implicit knowledge of the genre conventions that are in play at any given moment. The evaluation and estimation of ancient literary genres is not an unproblematic undertaking. It is beset, as it always must be as a form of hermeneutical inquiry, by present-day interests and parochial theoretical commitments, and thus is potentially a never-ending and necessarily contestable exercise.[11] Moreover, as a tool of interpretation, genre analysis may be put to various and manifold ends. Nonetheless, attending to issues of genre, no matter the challenges, is integral to any and every act of literary interpretation. Surprisingly, outside of the rather narrow confines of form criticism,[12] it is still a subject too often overlooked by biblical scholars.[13]

2. Date, Language, Artifact

The question of date receives routine attention in most modern commentaries on Lamentations. Nothing surprising here. Of more interest is what passes for evidence of date. Since this collection of nonnarrative poems is wholly devoid of references to historically identifiable figures or events, scholars have felt compelled to deduce chronological implications from literary features (such as change in form or viewpoint) and the like that of themselves are not amenable to such calculations.[14] There is one aspect of Lamentations that is tractable chronologi-

9. Edward L. Greenstein, "Qinah 'al hurbam 'ir umiqdaš besifrut hayisraèlit ha-qedumah," in *Homage to Shmuel: Studies in the World of the Bible* [Hebrew] (ed. Zipora Talshir, Shamir Yonam and Daniel Sivan; Jerusalem: Ben Gurion University, 2001), 88–97.

10. Margaret Alexiou, *The Ritual Lament in Greek Tradition* (Cambridge: Cambridge University Press, 1974).

11. See esp. Adena Rosmarin, *The Power of Genre* (Minneapolis: University of Minnesota Press, 1985); cf. Dobbs-Allsopp, "Darwinism."

12. And the conceptualization of this method of reading is not without problems; see Tremper Longman III, "Form Criticism, Recent Developments in Genre Theory, and the Evangelical," *WTJ* 47 (1985): 46–47; Dobbs-Allsopp, "Genre," 493–94.

13. David Damrosch's *The Narrative Covenant: Transformations of Genre in the Growth of Biblical Literature* (San Francisco: Harper & Row, 1987) has often been overlooked. More recently, Carol A. Newsom, in her *The Book of Job: A Contest of Moral Imaginations* (Oxford: Oxford University Press, 2003), also calls for more attention to genre in the study of biblical literature (esp. 32–71).

14. Dobbs-Allsopp, "Linguistic Evidence," esp. 1–10.

cally—its language. Language changes through time, and if there is a large enough sample of a particular language, then those changes can be tracked and diachronic distinctions discerned.[15] The historical study of Biblical Hebrew is now long-standing and two diachronic dialects are widely acknowledged: Standard Biblical Hebrew (SBH), the dialect of Genesis–Kings and the Iron II extrabiblical Hebrew inscriptions; and Late Biblical Hebrew (LBH), the dialect of Ezra-Nehemiah and Chronicles and the Second Temple period more generally.[16] In a long article published in the *Journal of the Ancient Near Eastern Society*,[17] I situate the language of Lamentations relative to this larger diachronic understanding of Biblical Hebrew, arguing that it reflects a transitional stage between the two dominant phases of the language,[18] and thus likely dates to sometime in the sixth century B.C.E.[19]

---

15. The field of historical linguistics is predicated on the reality of language change; see Hans Henrich Hock (*Principles of Historical Linguistics* [Berlin: de Gruyter, 1986], 1), who begins his discussion of linguistic change by citing Gen 11:6–8.

16. For extended references to the broader scholarly discussion, see Dobbs-Allsopp, "Linguistic Evidence," esp. 1–2 n. 4; idem, "Late Linguistic Features in the Song of Songs," in *Perspectives on the Song of Songs—Perspektiven der Hoheliedauslegung* (ed. Anselm C. Hagedorn; BZAW 346; Berlin: de Gruyter), esp. 27 n. 2.

17. Dobbs-Allsopp, "Linguistic Evidence."

18. "The term 'transitional period,' " writes Avi Hurvitz (*A Linguistic Study of the Relationship between the Priestly Source and the Book of Ezekiel* [CahRB 20; Paris: Gabalda, 1982], 161), "implies that while it no longer includes all of the linguistic elements which typified the earlier period, at the same time it is still lacking some of the characteristic features of subsequent periods." Lamentations possesses clearly identifiable late features (e.g., מדינה "province"), though their total number is relatively small compared to the classic LBH sources, and even fewer are those features that are used to the exclusion of their SBH counterparts (e.g., אני instead of אנכי). There are multiple cases in which the corresponding SBH and LBH features appear simultaneously (e.g., אשר and ־שׁ). And still a considerable number of SBH features are used to the exclusion of their opposite in LBH (e.g., בת־יהוה instead of בת־האלהים). Ezekiel (see Hurvitz, *Linguistic Study*; Mark F. Rooker, *Biblical Hebrew in Transition: The Language of the Book of Ezekiel* [JSOTSup 90; Sheffield: JSOT Press, 1990]), Jonah (George M. Landes, "Linguistic Criteria and the Date of the Book of Jonah," *ErIsr* 16 [1982]: 147–70), and possibly other biblical books (e.g., Jeremiah, Second Isaiah) as well share this same general typological profile. The chronological boundaries of this stage of the language are necessarily permeable and fuzzy. SBH did not simply cease to exist after the Babylonian destruction of Jerusalem. Indeed, the language of Lamentations and the like represent synchronic snapshots of SBH evolving toward LBH, a process that would have been gradual, encompassing a number of generations. Nonetheless, the early sixth-century Arad and Lachish ostraca provide convenient chronological markers for the latest phases of classical SBH, with a mature LBH likely emerging sometime in the middle of the fifth century (cf. Jan Joosten, "The Distinction between Classical and Late Biblical Hebrew as Reflected in Syntax," *HS* 46 [2005]: 327–39, 338)—although substantive extrabiblical evidence for Hebrew is lacking until the later Dead Sea Scrolls.

19. The linguistic evidence itself is not susceptible of such fine-grained, chronological estimation (Dobbs-Allsopp, "Linguistic Evidence," 36 n. 208). A sixth-century date for Lamentations follows, more positively, from typological comparison (e.g., situating the language

The finding is of intrinsic interest, of course, as it is always beneficial to know the chronological horizons of a given text where possible. But there is a larger value to this kind of study as well. It spotlights the artifactual nature of literature.[20] That is, language arts are themselves, at every point, products of specific, local human cultures. They are historical. Not only the language used (which is obviously in focus in this particular instance), but literary tropes of every kind, imagery, diction, even ideologies, all exist as a matter of course in time and through space (no matter the difficulties in fixing on them from any singular perspective). In Lamentations, for example, the very use of the city-lament genre bespeaks a certain age—ancient—and place—the Near East. Its deconstruction of the Zion tradition is patently belated,[21] and even the commonplace trope of elders sitting at the gate (Lam 5:14) ultimately refracts the architectural realia of Iron Age cities in the southern Levant—the city gate and its supporting structures were often lined with built-in benches.[22] Such artifactuality is the warp and woof of the poet's art and will need to factor in any accounting of this art (see more below). It is also a datum in its own right, something given from history, something potentially relevant to all acts of historical imagining and reconstruction. The recent debates in the field over history, historiography, and the use of the Bible in historical reconstruction have mostly failed to consider the kind of artifactuality I have in mind here.[23] The so-called "minimalists," for example, ignore the diachrony of Biblical Hebrew, rendering their own versions of history highly improbable, and, in places, even laughable—the presumption of a single (late) period of origin for all or even most biblical literature is simply incompatible with the range, amount, and kind of diachronic linguistic variation in evidence.[24] And there have only been a handful of attempts to probe the artifactuality of biblical literature more fully, beyond purely linguistic interests, in the service of a more

---

within known chronological horizons; see n. 16 above) and extralinguistic considerations (e.g., the dates of the Babylonian destruction of Jerusalem [586 B.C.E.] and the rebuilding of the temple [ca. 520 B.C.E.]—there is no mention of the latter in Lamentations; the likelihood that Second Isaiah alludes to the book of Lamentations, see Patricia Tull Willey, *Remember the Former Things: The Recollection of Previous Texts in Second Isaiah* [SBLDS 161; Atlanta: Scholars Press, 1997]; Benjamin D. Sommer, *A Prophet Reads Scripture: Allusion in Isaiah 40–66* [Stanford, Calif.: Stanford University Press, 1998]).

20. See Delbert R. Hillers, *Poets before Homer: Collected Essays on Ancient Literature* (ed. F. W. Dobbs-Allsopp; Winona Lake, Ind.: Eisenbrauns, forthcoming).

21. Dobbs-Allsopp, "R(az/ais)ing Zion."

22. Philip J. King and Lawrence E. Stager, *Life in Biblical Israel* (Louisville: Westminster John Knox, 2001), 234–36.

23. For a balanced overview of the debate, with bibliography, see John J. Collins, *The Bible after Babel* (Grand Rapids: Eerdmans, 2005), 37–51.

24. Avi Hurvitz, "The Historical Quest for 'Ancient Israel' and the Linguistic Evidence of the Hebrew Bible: Some Methodological Observations," *VT* 47 (1997): 301–15; Martin Ehrensvärd, "Once Again: The Problem of Dating Biblical Hebrew," *SJOT* 11 (1997): 29–40.

precise historical understanding.[25] More should and can be done. By triangulating from textual and material artifacts known outside of the Bible to the artifactuality of the Bible we have the capacity for realizing a richer, far more articulate (however maximal or minimal) rendering of the history in and through which the Bible emerged.

3. Enjambing Lines

In 2001 I called attention to what I termed the "enjambing line" in Lamentations.[26] At some point I had noticed that in the secondary literature scholars often specified parallelism as warrant for any number of textual emendations and other interpretive gambits. And yet parallelism, as a line-level trope and interlinear linking device, is rare in Lamentations (except in the last poem, Lam 5). Most of the couplets (bicola) in Lam 1–4 in fact are nonparallel in nature. Rather, as often as not, the syntax carries over in one fashion or another from one line to the next, though the couplets themselves remain strongly end-stopped (as common throughout biblical verse). Robert Lowth, in fact, had assumed that these were not really couplets at all but unusually (for biblical verse) long lines.[27] But the phenomena of continuation of syntax from one line to the next is known as enjambment and is fairly commonplace in literature of all ages.[28] In the essay, which was published in two parts, I articulate and map the various kinds of enjambing lines in evidence in Lamentations and then try to say something of how an awareness of enjambment bears upon the reading of this poetry at a variety of levels.

The consequences of Lamentations' enjambing kind of line are not insignificant. First, if most of the lines in the first four poems of this poetic collection are in fact not parallelistic, then there can be little warrant for scholars' habitual recourse to parallelism as a chief explanatory trope, especially in places of textual difficulty. Of course, parallelism is not unknown in Lam 1–4, and thus will always

---

25. Gary Knoppers's "The Vanishing Solomon: The Disappearance of the United Monarchy from Recent Histories of Ancient Israel" (*JBL* 116 [1997]: 19–44) is the best example of what this kind of study can achieve; see also Baruch Halpern, *David's Secret Demons: Messiah, Murderer, Traitor, King* (Grand Rapids: Eerdmans, 2001), 57–72; William G. Dever, *What Did the Biblical Writers Know and When Did They Know It?* (Grand Rapids: Eerdmans 2001), esp. chs. 3 and 4 (although with a distinct polemical edge).

26. "Enjambing Line"; "Effects of Enjambment."

27. *Lectures on the Sacred Poetry of the Hebrews* (3rd ed.; London, 1788; repr., London: Routledge, 1995), 121–39; idem, *Isaiah: A New Translation* (London, 1778; repr., London: Routledge, 1995), xxviii–xxix.

28. Terry V. F. Brogan and Clive Scott, "Enjambment," in *The New Princeton Encyclopedia of Poetry and Poetics* (3rd ed.; ed. Alex Preminger and Terry V. F. Brogan; Princeton: Princeton University Press, 1993), 359–60.

be potentially relevant as a guide to understanding individual couplets. But it simply is not dominant or prominent in these poems, and therefore cannot and should not be assumed to be such.[29] Second, that parallelism is not prominent in this instance underscores in a quite stunning way that parallelism *qua* parallelism cannot be the differentia of biblical Hebrew verse—since by definition, then, Lam 1–4 would not count as verse.[30] And in this Lamentations is not unique. Almost a third of the post-Lowthian corpus of biblical verse is made up of nonparallelistic lines.[31] To be sure, these enjambing lines most commonly are played against a parallelistic norm, but their existence demands a theoretical reckoning all the same. Last, enjambment, as a phenomenon made visible at line boundaries, itself calls attention to the importance of the line as a fundamental structural unit in Hebrew verse. It is usually the couplet (and, to a lesser extent, the triplet) to which scholars devote most of their attention. And justifiably so, as the organization of biblical poems commonly involves an arrangement of couplets and triplets. But the line itself—the constitutive element of the couplet and triplet—is also crucial. Indeed, far more so than most acknowledge.[32] Readings of Hebrew poems can only be enhanced by more sustained attention at the level of the biblical Hebrew verse line.

4. LITERATURE, HISTORY, AND THEORY

In a 1999 essay entitled "Rethinking Historical Criticism,"[33] I sketch out an orientation to the literary study of the Bible that attempts to value theory and literary practice, on the one hand, and historical awareness, on the other. The piece is long and substantial. The handiest summary appears in the accompanying abstract:

The present paper seeks to provide a programmatic introduction to some of the major themes of historicist literary study and to explore how this body of work may help biblical scholars rethink historical criticism as a specifically literary

---

29. A related point: not all parallelism is of a kind. Its use in the Bible is multifaceted and often complex, both in realization and in effect, and frequently involves a good deal more than the semantic saying of what was just said only differently. Getting to know the stylistic *Tendenz* of a specific corpus of poems, including how parallelism is typically wielded—or not—and to what end, is crucial to any deep and thoroughgoing appreciation of said corpus.

30. Esp. Dobbs-Allsopp, "Enjambing Line," 238; see also David L. Petersen and Kent Harold Richards, *Interpreting Hebrew Poetry* (Minneapolis: Fortress, 1992), 14.

31. See Stephen A. Geller, *Parallelism in Early Biblical Poetry* (HSM 20; Missoula, Mont.: Scholars Press, 1979), 6, 30, 295–96, 379; Michael P. O'Connor, *Hebrew Verse Structure* (Winona Lake, Ind.: Eisenbrauns, 1980), 129–32, 409–22; Wilfred G. E. Watson, *Classical Hebrew Poetry* (JSOTSup 26; Sheffield: Sheffield Academic Press, 1984), 332–36.

32. In fact, I believe the line is *the* fundamental unit of biblical verse. It is the one element that differentiates verse and prose. Verse is written in line, prose is not.

33. *BibInt* 7 (1999): 235–71.

method of study and reading. It advocates a program of literary study in which biblical historical criticism, with its strong insistence on the need to historicize and the various philological practices it uses to accomplish this feat of historicization, continues to play a central and essential role, but recognizes, as well, the pressing need to rethink and retheorize the objectivist and foundationalist assumptions which have informed and motivated historical-critical practices in the past, and to facilitate the integration of the full panoply of literary methods, theories, and strategies of reading currently employed by literary scholars.[34]

One of the reviewers, liking the essay, commented that given its theoretical bent they would like to see the theory put into action. I responded to the editor that I would be glad to accommodate the request, although it would likely not come in the way the reviewer had envisioned—as I was not really articulating a methodology per se—and at any rate I would need another thirty or so pages, which I doubted they would want to give me. I did not get the extra thirty pages. My most recent piece on Lamentations,[35] a contribution to the Festschrift honoring J. J. M. Roberts, may be viewed in any number of ways, but there I did try more or less self-consciously a kind of "thick" reading that attended to theoretical matters as well as offered an intentional kind of literary reading and at the same time engaged philological and historical matters in a way customary of "historical-critical" scholarship—a reading, that is, of the type I call for in "Rethinking Historical Criticism."

This piece, too, is long. Its principal aim is to tease out how the Lamentations poet rethinks and refigures the old Zion tradition, which could not be maintained in the face of the catastrophic events surrounding the Babylonian destruction of Jerusalem. The poem's opening movement (2:1–8) depicts Yahweh's assault on Jerusalem. The city, temple, and supporting mythologies are all razed. What survives the verbal carnage of these verses is the uneasy figuration of Yahweh as enemy (esp. 2:4, 5) and the literary image of personified Zion. It is in the latter (esp. 2:13–19, 20–22), on my reading, that the poem seeks to counterfeit the Zion tradition. In raising (the figure of) Zion, "preserving her person(a), and provoking her voice, even as her material vestments of municipality and her once enlivening mythologies are razed, the poem incarnates within its readership a potentially life-bequeathing memory of hope."[36] The argument of the essay—my teasing out of the twin themes of Zion *razed* and Zion *raised*—is embedded within and, in part, enacted as part of a larger, informing reading of the poem as a whole. That is, the literary reading is itself integral to the argument at every step. I use the footnotes to reference secondary literature, as usual, but also to negotiate textual and philological matters and to assay pertinent historical and cultural information. These

---

34. "Rethinking Historical Criticism," 271.
35. "R(az/ais)ing Zion in Lamentations 2."
36. Ibid., 21–22.

last bits are critical to the entire project. They underscore the fact that reading texts from the past is always inevitably a troubled, contested and reconstitutive undertaking. Textual witnesses do not always agree, philological anomalies routinely arise, imagery as a culturally-laden artifact is forever in need of further elaboration, specification, identification. Making such aspects of the reading act visible, especially when the literature being read is held sacred by various communities, stands a better chance of forestalling totalizing postures and the foundationalism that they so often (seem to) inspire. Theory is most explicitly engaged in the second half of the essay, as I use a Levinasian leavened idiom ("other," "trace," "vocativity") to help explicate the force and significance of the poet's Zion raising gestures (e.g., Zion's coming to voice). Theory enables (quite literally) thought. We can conceptualize at all only because we have theories to provide the necessary framework and vocabulary for cognition. It is not, for example, that Lamentations cannot be read without Levinas. It can and it surely has. Rather, it is if not Levinas then with whom or by what? One of the burdens of "Rethinking Historical Criticism" was to show that theory matters. Part of the showing was the sustained theoretical reflection itself, resisting the strong pull toward exemplification. But there are other ways to show that theory matters. One is to put it to work on behalf of a specific act of interpretation. This, in small and large ways and with respect to "theories" in the plural, is one aim of "R(az/ais)ing Zion." My success and the benefits that accrue from these particular theoretical encounters, of course, are not givens and are open, as they must be, for readerly adjudication.

5. Lamentations: A Commentary

The commentary is a peculiar genre of scholarship that does not lend itself so readily to easy summing. In one respect, all commentaries, as a matter of course, treat a certain range of introductory matters (e.g., authorship, date, place) and furnish comment, in varying degrees of detail, on the texts of a particular corpus. Specific biblical commentary series differ in audience, focus, format, and so on. The Interpretation series, of which my volume on Lamentations is a part,[37] identifies its main audience as "those who teach, preach, and study the Bible in a community of faith" and aims to offer interpretation "that takes serious hermeneutical responsibility for the contemporary meaning and significance of the biblical text" and that has as its main point of focus for comment and exposition "whole portions or sections of text" rather than "individual verses and words." My own contribution takes shape within these broad parameters.[38]

---

37. *Lamentations.*

38. So, for example, philological and text-critical matters, however unavoidable when reading texts from the past, generally do not receive sustained attention or full documentation.

One of my ambitions for the volume was to write for the church in a way that was mindful of and accessible to other interested constituencies. I believe that church and academy must continually seek (where appropriate) to embed its own (parochial) discourses in ever larger arenas of thought and conversation. Ideas, even and especially those motivated by religious conviction,[39] if they are to have any large significance, need to be moved and framed in ways that allow them to gain a hearing in and contribute to what is nowadays a manifestly pluralistic and open public conversation.[40] Consequently, my own interpretive work (and this commentary in particular) "draws consciously and routinely on the best of critical thinking wherever it may be found, and it seeks to achieve in tone and pitch a discourse open to and engaged with the extraecclesial world." I remain convinced that the Bible, as well as other literature from the ancient Near East, has much to contribute to intellectual discourse on a whole host of issues, including most crucially matters that bear on our notions of human flourishing and well-being (i.e., ethics).[41]

In the introduction,[42] I treat the range of expected issues, but dedicate most of the space to two large topics: (1) relevant literary features, especially genre, Lamentations' nonnarrative, lyric (broadly defined)[43] medium, and a consideration of the kind of larger discourse staged by this group of poems; and (2) theology, a special focus of the Interpretation series more generally. My foregrounding of literary matters means to press the claim that whatever more the Bible is, and however it is put into play and to what ends, it is a collection of literary texts and thus, at bottom, requires being read as such. This is especially the case with regard to Lamentations. Its nonnarrative, lyrical and highly poetic medium crucially shapes the kind of discourse enacted. Indeed, I suspect that Lamentations' mostly lackluster reception in the past has had a great deal to do with readers' general failure to fully appreciate this poetry's underlying medium. My initial discussion of theology also takes its cue and works itself out from Lamentations' poetic medium. In my view, the "theology of Lamentations is occasional, pluralistic, equivocating, and fragmentary. Nowhere are there specific

---

39. One of the chief gains of postmodernity is that religious discourse is no longer (automatically) ruled out of bounds. See, for example, John D. Caputo, *On Religion* (London: Routledge, 2001).

40. This is the principal burden of Jeffrey Stout's recent *Democracy and Tradition* (Princeton, N.J.: Princeton University Press, 2004).

41. *Lamentations*, ix; see also F. W. Dobbs-Allsopp, "Brief Comments on John Collins's *The Bible after Babel*," *JHS* 6 (2006): 16–17. Online: http://www.arts.ualberta.ca/JHS/Articles/article_54.pdf.

42. *Lamentations*, 1–48.

43. See F. W. Dobbs-Allsopp, "Psalms and Lyric Verse," in *The Evolution of Rationality: Interdisciplinary Essays in Honor of J. Wentzel van Huyssteen* (ed. F. Leron Shults; Grand Rapids: Eerdmans, 2006), 346–79.

themes systematically developed or theological arguments set out in detail, and the poems steadfastly resist all attempts to superimpose on them a single unify-ing theological perspective."[44] Moreover, the themes selected for emphasis do not normally find a central place in more traditional and systematic theologies. My pose is explicitly postmodern, and I mine theological and nontheological sources alike in my effort to craft a way of thinking theology that may make claims and win interest beyond theology.

The commentary itself is composed of five essays, each offering a reading of Lamentations' component poems.[45] The focus stays trained chiefly on the poems themselves, though attention is also given throughout to how the indi-vidual poems interrelate and to the possible meanings and counter-meanings that these interrelations inspire and invite. The essays may be read individually, or, contrary to common expectation for this genre, as a part of a larger whole—in fact, one of my intentions was to craft a discourse specially congenial to a holistic, linear reading. But, however encountered, individually or holistically, the reading propounded in the volume remains only a reading. My reading. It is offered in the knowledge and with the happy expectation that others, too, will put forward their own readings of Lamentations, readings that may or may not contest my own. Pluralism and diversity is endemic to all hermeneutical undertakings and the poetry of Lamentations, itself so rich and dense, will always outdistance every attempt to comprehend it.

SOME CONCLUDING REFLECTIONS

The revival of interest in Lamentations, beginning in earnest with the publica-tions (in English) of commentaries by Hillers, Claus Westermann, and especially Iain Provan in the early 1990s,[46] shows no sign of letting up (as underscored by the present collection of essays). And even after more than a decade, I seem still to be only just getting into these wonderfully stimulating poems. Much remains to do, as, I suppose, will always be the case. Four broad areas hold special appeal for me: close readings, history and philology, text criticism, and translation. As others have observed, there is still a surprising scarcity of good, persuasive close readings of biblical poems. I have taken an initial run at such readings with respect to the poems in Lamentations, but they will repay many more close encounters of this kind. Outside of individual articles dedicated to specific

---

44. Ibid., 23–24.

45. Ibid., 49–154.

46. Hillers, *Lamentations* (2nd ed.); Claus Westermann, *Lamentations: Issues and Inter-pretation* (Minneapolis: Fortress, 1994); Iain Provan, *Lamentations* (NCBC; Grand Rapids: Eerdmans, 1991).

issues,[47] the commentaries by Hillers and W. Rudolph remain the principal loci of philological work on Lamentations.[48] Hillers's revisions in this area, in fact, were not substantial, meaning that there is still a need to gather and present the results of research in this area from the last forty years, and the possibility, as well, to generate additional insights, to reconsider long-standing philological cruxes. Prior to the recent publication of the first fascicle of *BHQ*,[49] text critical matters had not been engaged substantially since Rudolph's 1938 article, "Der Text der Klagelieder."[50] Here, too, even allowing for the advances achieved with *BHQ*, more remains to be done. Text criticism is itself part and parcel of the larger literary project.[51] It cannot be undertaken in the absence of consideration of other literary matters and literary interpretation itself cannot even be pursued without texts to interpret, texts that are themselves produced by the machinations of text criticism. Finally, translation is uniformly under-theorized and practiced with general indifference in the field.[52] In particular, the need for verse translations of biblical poems which themselves read as poems in the target languages is dire.[53] Perhaps the overriding point pressed in my commentary is the need to engage Lamentations *as poetry*. It is difficult to make this point for readers unfamiliar with Hebrew, since the most widely available and used translations are themselves so abysmal literarily.[54]

---

47. E.g., Thomas F. McDaniel, "Philological Studies in Lamentations, I and II," *Bib* 49 (1968): 27–53, 199–220.

48. Hillers, *Lamentations* (2nd ed.); Wilhelm Rudolph, *Das Buch Ruth, Das Hohe Lied, Die Klagelieder* (2nd ed.; KAT 17; Gütersloh: Mohn, 1962); cf. Hans Gottlieb, *A Study on the Text of Lamentations* (Aarhus: Aarhus Universitet, 1978).

49. *Megilloth* (fasc. 18 of *Biblia Hebraica Quinta*; Stuttgart: Deutsche Bibelgesellschaft, 2004).

50. *ZAW* 56 (1938): 101–22; cf. Bertil Albrektson, *Studies in the Text and Theology of the Book of Lamentations* (Lund: Gleerup, 1963); Frank Moore Cross, "4QLam," in Eugene C. Ulrich et al., *Qumran Cave 4.XI: Psalms to Chronicles* (DJD XVI; Oxford: Clarendon, 2000), 229–37.

51. See G. Thomas Tanselle, "Textual Study and Literary Judgment," in *Textual Criticism and Scholarly Editing* (ed. G. Thomas Tanselle; Charlottesville: University of Virginia, 1990), 325–37.

52. Cf. Edward L. Greenstein, *Essays on Biblical Method and Translation* (BJS 92; Atlanta: Scholars Press, 1989); Simon B. Parker, "Toward Literary Translations of Ugaritic Poetry," *UF* 22 (1991): 257–70.

53. Translation, of course, may be pursued toward a multiplicity of ends (see Lawrence Venuti, ed., *The Translation Studies Reader* [London: Routledge, 2000]). The achievement of fully realized, aesthetically satisfying renderings of biblical poems into verse is only one such end.

54. A chief challenge to the would be translator of Lamentations is accommodating the pronounced formality and ritualistic nature of these poems, which are integral to how they mean but perennial stumbling blocks for readers more accustomed (in taste and skill) to narrative and fiction. Perhaps the most successful formal rendering of Lamentations is still John Donne's (in *The Complete Poetry of John Donne* [ed. J. T. Shawcross; New York: Doubleday,

Other projects focusing on Lamentations can be imagined. The four just sketched obviously arise out of one set of peculiar interests—my own. They may suffice nonetheless to signal the bright future that awaits Lamentations study in this new century. This remains, as Hillers would have said, a biblical book that will repay close study.

1967], 371–83)—though obviously the literary gains in this instance are offset by interpretive losses due to the state of biblical knowledge during Donne's day.

VOICES ARGUING ABOUT MEANING

Kathleen O'Connor

Lamentations and the Tears of the World contains two parts: commentary on each of the book of Lamentations' five chapters (part 1) and theological reflections that arise from the commentary (part 2).[1] Lamentations arises from a massive catastrophe. Although there is some disagreement among interpreters about which catastrophe, tradition associates it with Babylonian invasion of Jerusalem in 587 B.C.E. That invasion, as well as the one before it (597) and one after it (582), destroyed Israel's world. The 587 siege of the city was the worst and the most decisive. The siege lasted two years during which young and elderly died of hunger and men died in battle. When the Babylonians finally broke through the city walls, they killed many, destroyed symbolic buildings—the king's palace and the temple where God had chosen to dwell, and they deported many of the notable citizens to Babylon. Lamentations is probably the work of survivors who remain in occupied Jerusalem.

Lamentations is a work of art by survivors, metaphoric and symbolic, rather than a precise account of events.[2] Because the book transposes disaster into the realm of art, it both evokes historical events and leaves them vague so as to make it difficult to date the book accurately.[3] But it is precisely the book's poetic openness that enables it to address disaster beyond its own historical confines. Its five poems are largely grim, hard-edged expressions of loss, of outrage, of desires for revenge. Only in chapter 3 does hope burst through, tentatively, unsteadily, and briefly. Yet even before considering *what* Lamentations says, it conveys meaning by *how* it says it.

---

1. Maryknoll, N.Y.: Orbis, 2002.

2. On Lamentations as a work of survival, see Tod Linafelt, *Surviving Lamentations: Catastrophe, Lament and Protest in the Afterlife of a Biblical Book* (Chicago: University of Chicago Press, 2000).

3. On ambiguity of dating see Ian Provan, *Lamentations* (NCBC; Grand Rapids: Eerdmans, 1991).

POETIC STRUCTURES: VOICES

Lamentations is a book of voices, of stunning, intermingling, and clashing testimonies by survivors of the city's fall. Each poem contains two voices, except for the last poem that contains only the voice of the community. By voices, I mean the literary device of multiple speakers. But voice is also a metaphor. To have voice signifies the human capacity to act in the world, in this case, by bringing pain to speech. Elaine Scarry writes that profound physical pain silences the capacity to speak and write about emotional pain.[4] Judith Herman argues that traumatic emotional pain closes down personhood.[5] It silences the voice. The voice is the self re-emerging. To acquire a voice means to gain identity, to come into the truth of one's history, and to become a moral agent. Lamentations poetic voices are acts of survival; they express resistance to death and a resilient grasp on life.

The multiple voices of Lamentations reach no unanimity about the causes of the tragedy or how to respond to it. In a haunting biblical echo of the spontaneous shrines that grew up in New York City after September 11, each poetic voice presents a limited view of the suffering that belongs to the whole community. I imagine the book as a public performance of speakers in which survivors stand up, each in turn, to tell of their particular pain and to demand God's attention. Together the voices possess only the raw harmony of common wounds, even as they offer competing and irreconcilable opinions of the disaster.

Then there is the problem of the "Missing Voice," the absence that looms over the book, the voice for which all the others yearn, and the only fully authoritative voice in the Bible. Lamentations is a "house for sorrow"[6] because God's voice is missing. The speaker in chapter 3 quotes God (3:57), but God never appears as a character. The Bible provides other divine responses to laments, for example Job 38–39 and Jer 12:4–6 and 15:19–21. These other responses suggest that divine silence in Lamentations is purposeful, that God's silence shows brilliant poetic restraint by the book's composers. On the one hand, divine silence means that human voices receive no mediation, no resolution. God's silence leaves each voice, each testimony, standing, unrefuted, and unresolved. But on the other hand, because God is silent, Lamentations honors human voices of suffering and depicts the human experience of *deus absconditus*.

Had the poets of Lamentations given a speech to God, God's words would silence debate; the struggle with pain would come to closure prematurely. Any

---

4. Elaine Scarry, *The Body in Pain* (New York: Oxford University Press, 1985), 33.

5. Judith Herman, *Trauma and Recovery* (New York: Basic, 1992); and see Wendy Farley, *Tragic Vision and Divine Compassion: A Contemporary Theodicy* (Louisville: Westminster John Knox, 1990).

6. A phrase of Alan Mintz, "The Rhetoric of Lamentations and the Representation of Catastrophe," *Prooftexts* 2 (1982): 1–17.

words from God would trump all speech. Instead, God's silence gives reverence to voices of anger and resistance, of hope and despair. The silence lingers over what we in this culture so thoroughly deny—sorrow, loss, grief, fury and despair. This is why Lamentations can rightly be called "a house for sorrow."

ACROSTICS AND ARRANGEMENTS OF POEMS

Another poetic feature of Lamentations not visible in most English translations, and hard to describe, is the acrostic and alphabetic structures of the poems. An acrostic is a composition written in alphabetical order. Four of the book's five poems are acrostics. The Hebrew alphabet contains twenty-two letters. All the poems contain twenty-two lines or multiples of twenty-two lines. The fifth poem is not acrostic, but because it contains twenty-two lines it is called alphabetic. The intriguing question is, of course, why? Why put poetry of sorrow in alphabetical order? Some say alphabetic order may be a memory aid but I think it is much more. There are lots of complex poems in the Bible that need to be remembered but only a handful of acrostics. The acrostic form is symbolic. It imposes a familiar order on the swirling chaos of the world. It implies that suffering is so enormous, so total, that it spreads from a to z, from א to ת? There are no letters left for more suffering.

Perhaps even more intriguing than the acrostics is the arrangement of the poems. Each of the first three poems contain sixty-six lines but the acrostics in them differ. In the first two poems, the acrostic letter is found only in the first word of a three line verse. But the third poem intensifies the acrostic. There are three "a" lines, three "b" lines, and so forth. Then recall that only chapter three, the intensified acrostic, contains words of hope: God's steadfast love never ceases, God's mercies are new every morning, God is good to those who wait. This acrostic crescendo of hope leads some interpreters to think that confidence in God is the major theme of the book. But the last two poems move back toward numbness and despair. The community prays this way at the end of the book: "Return us to yourself O God … unless you have utterly rejected us and you are angry with us forever" (5:22). The hope in chapter three is but an interlude, a moment of respite in the midst of massive disruption, as if after two chapters of sorrow and fury, readers need a break, some solace, some reason to go forward in the book as well as in life.

If I were composing this book, I would put the words of hope in God at the end. I would make them the grand finale that resolves the pain and sets light against despair. But the poems in Lamentations grow shorter, less energetic, more diminished. It is as if, in the aftermath of tragedy, hope cannot sustain itself. But that may be the way of healing. Hope rises up and then fades, comes and goes, as the survivors slip back into numbed despair. Hope barely survives in Lamentations. It is nearly engulfed yet not utterly silenced by the surrounding chapters.

Interplay of Poetic Voices

Lamentations' first two poems contain voices in conversation, that of a narrator, and that of the city of Jerusalem, personified as a woman. The narrator is at first a distant and chiding commentator on the condition of the "city woman"[7] (1:1–11). Her desperate condition results from her sinfulness. She speaks in the chapter's second half (1:12–22) to lament her circumstances and to appeal for God to see her in her suffering. God does not reply, but the narrator who dominates the second chapter (2:1–19) is an altered person. No longer does he blame the city/woman but, instead, accuses God of deliberate cruelty and mismanagement of the world. She, in turn, pleads again for only one thing, for God to "look and pay attention" to the frightful conditions of her children, the people in the city (2:20–21).

The next chapter contains another voice, of one captured, shamed, and lamenting attack from an unnamed enemy who turns out to be God (Lam 3). But in the midst of his laments, he moves toward hope, only to flip-flop back and forth between dread and the possibility of justice and new life. He, too, desires for God to see his condition and his hope rests upon some confidence that God does see. The second voice in the chapter, that of the community, adds to charges against God (3:40–42) who does not respond to their half-hearted expression of repentance. In the poetically shrinking final chapters, hope disappears nearly completely, yet calls for God to see and pay attention to the community's plight continue (4:16; 5:1–20).

A Theology of Witness

It is this motif of seeing and of the failure to see and pay attention to suffering that forms the center of theological reflections in part 2. I consider Lamentations itself to be a form of literary seeing, a literary mirror, because it honors voices of loss, anger, sorrow, and protest. The poetry achieves this, in part, by excluding the divine voice from the text and leaving the voices of lament alone in the house. A second way Lamentations acts as a forum of seeing suffering occurs in the interchange between the voice of the narrator and voice of the personified city. Imagery that recognizes the massive and indigestible nature of the city's suffering, the narrator's increased compassion to her pleas for a comforter, and the narrator's strong protests against God's contribute to what I call a "theology of witness." By witness, I mean the capacity to take in and see the enormity of suffering for what it is, in all its enormity and overwhelming power, and offer it

---

7. A phrase of Naomi Seidman, "Burning the Book of Lamentations," in *Out of the Garden: Women Writers on the Bible* (ed. Christina Büchmann and Celina Spiegel; New York: Fawcett Columbine, 1992), 285.

back to the sufferer. This is the way the book comforts, a primary first step toward healing. The poetry recognizes the sufferers' true condition and mirrors it back to them. This gives them language to speak about their shared catastrophe, and enables them to take steps out of the isolation that intense suffering produces.

God, of course, appears as an abuser in much of this book. The poetry serves as a raging protest against a God who not only allows disaster and tragedy but who enables and enacts it upon God's own people. *Lamentations and Tears of the World* attempts to come to terms with the book's portrait of God by discussing various theological approaches to biblical texts where God is not only the source of human suffering but who is repetitively so. I consider three approaches and tentatively offer one of my own.

My book closes with an epilogue about the fate of the city woman in Second Isaiah where God finally speaks to her, sees her overwhelming suffering and loss, and attempts to comfort her and make reparation.

The Singers of Lamentations:
(A)Scribing (De)Claiming Poets and Prophets

Nancy C. Lee

My primary work on the book of Lamentations, *The Singers of Lamentations: Cities under Siege, from Ur to Jerusalem to Sarajevo*,[1] began as an exegetical analysis and developed to include some comparative study with laments from other traditional and contemporary contexts of war and suffering, especially literary laments I gathered in the field in the aftermath of the 1990s wars as Yugoslavia unfortunately came apart.[2] *The Singers of Lamentations* represents a small but growing number of scholars who wish to bring biblical and related scholarship into serious dialectic conversation with later historic as well as current cultural contexts of suffering and lament. In the area of lament more generally, I collaborated with Bosnian-Croat poet (and biblical translations scholar) Borislav Arapović and edited the first English book edition of his lament poetry, *Between Despair and Lamentation*; I have written a number of articles on lament, including a new understanding of the acrostics in Lamentations,[3] the Lamentations portion in the new Westminster Study Bible, and a follow-up essay to *The Singers of Lamentations*.[4]

The Singers of Lamentations began taking shape nearly twenty years ago while I was analyzing poetry in Jeremiah for a master's thesis with Walter Brueggemann. After recognizing and arguing for a poetic wordplay alluding to Cain and Abel appearing in both the book of Jeremiah and in Lamentations,[5] I set forth

---

1. BibInt 60; Leiden: Brill, 2002.

2. During a Fulbright doctoral fellowship in Croatia (and also to Bosnia-Herzegovina).

3. "Non Sequiturs in the 'Order' of Retributive Justice ('*ayin* ... *pe* ... *tsaddiq*?): Acrostic Reversals in Lamentations."

4. "Prophet and Singer in the Fray: the Book of Jeremiah," in *Uprooting and Planting: Essays on Jeremiah for Leslie Allen* (ed. John Goldingay; Library of Hebrew Bible/Old Testament Studies 359; London: T&T Clark, 2007)

5. "Exposing a Buried Subtext in Jeremiah and Lamentations: Going After Baal and ... Abel," in *Troubling Jeremiah* (ed. A. R. Pete Diamond, Kathleen O'Connor, and Louis Stulman; JSOTSup 260; Sheffield: Sheffield Academic Press, 1999).

to examine the poetic artistry of Lamentations in depth for my doctoral work with Bill Brown. What emerged for me with careful analysis was not simply the possibility that Jeremiah (or one following in his rhetorical tradition) was a voice in Lamentations but, just as importantly, that a female voice or singer in poetic dialogue with the prophetic voice could also be recognized there and traced in a few texts within the book of Jeremiah. In *The Singers of Lamentations*, I call her "Jerusalem's Poet."[6] Here (below) I will take this suggestion yet a step further. Whether one prefers to see in Lamentations an author's or poet's literary "dramatic dialogue" or a kind of textual crystallization of oral poets that were in dialogical performance, I followed this dance of voices to see where they would lead. Because my focus on the biblical texts was on the interplay of poetic voices, greater attention in the work is given to the first three chapters of Lamentations where this occurs, though Lam 4 and 5 are also analyzed.

What follows is a summary of what I believe are seven contributions to the scholarly conversation from *The Singers of Lamentations*, its title a modest tribute to Albert Lord's seminal work, *The Singer of Tales*, and to his colleagues and successors who have for many years contributed to growing understandings of oral poetry, with gratitude to the inspiring poets themselves.[7] First, a few general observations.

The songs of Lamentations were most likely composed surrounding the events between 597 and 586 B.C.E. in Jerusalem and Judah, including the exile of leadership by the Babylonians, deportations of the population, siege and destruction. The songs reflect a situation of mourning and lament for the Judeans, though the precise time of the poetic compositions are uncertain. I believe it is far more likely that the poems were composed by survivors who actually experienced the tragedy and trauma, than by individuals indirectly affected but who imitated the style.

Lament genres are found performed across cultures worldwide and through history, including the ancient Near East. Anthropological research documents ample evidence of such individuals composing lament songs, performed in ritual settings, but also anywhere an individual in a community might choose. Singers composed by drawing upon and modifying older stock lyrics and genres from a living oral tradition, and in the case of Judah, perhaps from lyrics describing previous destructions and suffering in Israel; singers improvised to create "new" songs addressed to their immediate context. Due to the complexity of voices, interruptions, disagreeing perspectives, and rapid juxtaposition of images one finds in the immediacy of war poetry, in my view, it is more likely that the book of Lamentations is a crystallization of fragments of poetic singers' utterances by

6. Lee, *The Singers of Lamentations*, 46.

7. See especially the work of Susan Niditch, Robert Culley, Michael Fishbane, and Mishael Caspi.

a scribe or redactor, rather than a dialogic literary work by a single "author" or poet. However, it is not necessary to decide finally how the text before us was created in order to gain understanding or be profoundly moved by it. No matter what theoretical approaches one uses to analyze the text, it had to be created and/or performed by "real people" in specific historical context, regardless of how uncertain we are with those details. Thankfully the value and purposes of "texts" are not static or limited, but transcend time, place, and persons to reach us all. As John Miles Foley reminds us, even if "texts are not transcriptions [of oral performance] but lettered works in the traditional idiom, rhetorically the singer persists and the performance goes on."[8]

Poetry Exploding the Senses: Fruit from Methodological Approaches

The first contribution of *The Singers of Lamentations* was an effort to utilize an *oral poetic method* with the work (to my knowledge, rarely utilized with this text), drawing findings from anthropological fieldwork and understandings by scholars of lament genres across many traditional cultures around the world, in addition to the customary ancient Near Eastern works. The approach was not to the exclusion of the findings of other methods, which I respect, draw upon, and cite, including a sociorhetorical approach. I believe textual understanding is most comprehensive when multiple approaches are engaged. An oral poetic one (as scholars in the field know, even when working with written texts) can bring some significant insights by its capability to embrace not only the integrity of the literature and the ways it works, but also traditional processes of composition, performance, and the impact of historical and cultural contexts. Insights from the study of oral tradition in biblical studies have been applied to narrative texts, yet insufficiently tapped for biblical poetry as it stands, not what stands "behind it." The danger to be avoided is claiming that one method is best and all-sufficient, universally trumping others. Instead, in a dialectic of exploration, we should raise interpretive questions, and gain from one another.

In *The Singers* I included specific anthropological research on lament genres from areas of the old Yugoslavia, both on oral performance and literary laments that still retain oral traditional elements, including those I collected from the recent war context. Thus a second contribution of *Singers* was to consider how *features of traditional oral poetry* across this and other cultures are suggestive as a heuristic tool for interpreting ways the poetry of Lamentations worked in its context. What follows are some of those oral poetic features that emerged, beginning first with the *dialogical* element.

---

8. *The Singer of Tales in Performance* (Bloomington: Indiana University Press, 1995), xiv.

In recent years biblical scholars have fruitfully pursued more of the dialogic in narrative and poetry, including differing or dissenting social voices.[9] Complementarily, a recognition of the dialogic in all sorts of genres and performance has long been affirmed in oral poetic approaches[10] of ethnographers, musicologists, and some biblical critics. The dialogic is nothing new, is pervasive of course, in the very structure and flow of Jewish midrashim, the talmud, and so forth.

In the cultures of Croatia, Bosnia, Serbia, and others, in performance of mourning songs, women might sing alone or might participate in a call and response style in which a soloist improvises and is answered by another. Traditionally in other countries, a lead singer and chorus are in dialogue.[11] An important point that seems to repeatedly escape modern literary critics of the Bible is that in their ancient life setting, the "composer" and the performing singer—expressing "voice(s)" that would become textual—were usually *one and the same person,* but the composer/singer often remained anonymous when his or her texts were written down. The overconcern by modern critics with the problem of our too easily identifying a voice in or of the text with a historical author or figure is, on the one hand, far less an issue with an oral-traditional approach for the above reason. On the other hand, an oral traditional approach will rarely attribute an original poem to someone, a historical person, because in traditional oral poetry there is no "original" or first text. Every oral poet or singer comes in a line of tradition in which all have participated in employing the culture's or subculture's previous formulas and language, yet innovating for their context, sometimes in stunning ways; but ironically, the song is new with every performance, and the song really belonged *to the community.* Names seem to be attached when a performer was so good that everyone recognized him or her; nevertheless, the ones who have the power to name, "use" authoritative names, and include singers, in writing of texts and canonizing, is also always a question of power, ideology and politics. With regard to Israelite prophets (regardless of whether some of them wrote as well, reflecting oral style), and Jeremiah in particular, it is appropriate to say that the poetry in that book is associated with the historical prophet (also a composer/singer) who innovated a prophetic message in and for his time; but what we have in the book's poetry may also include innovations of Jeremianic prophets or other singers who came after him, whether they answered his songs *in the next week,* or in the next thirty years, who can say?

---

9. Especially the Bakhtin school; Mikhail M. Bakhtin, *The Dialogic Imagination: Four Essays* (ed. Michael Holquist; trans. Caryl Emerson and Michael Holquist; Austin: University of Texas Press, 1981); for Lamentations, see in this present volume, Carleen Mandolfo's essay; William Lanahan's "The Speaking Voice in the Book of Lamentations" (*JBL* 93 [1974]: 41–49) was an important shift.

10. Albert B. Lord, *The Singer of Tales* (New York: Atheneum, 1968), 13–29.

11. Foley, *Singer of Tales in Performance,* 106; and Ruth Finnegan, *Oral Literature in Africa* (Oxford: Clarendon, 1970), 147–66, cited in Lee, *The Singers of Lamentations,* 21.

In *The Singers of Lamentations* I also noted that in addition to the dialogue of voices typical of mourning contexts, lament performance, and perhaps the prophetic voice acting as comforter in Lamentations, there are *other oral traditional elements* characterizing lament poems, as found in former Yugoslavian cultures. One does find there also a practice of *transforming the dirge genre* (for an individual) to refer to the entire community or nation after a war. Not only that adaptation of genre, but two additional important oral traditional elements can be seen combined in three examples below, in three different cultures, over a very wide historical timeframe: *communal dirge* poetry, the *personification* of a city, village, land, or nation, and the *simile that renders human suffering related to nature's suggestive forms* (like wilting or dying vegetation). The first is from a poem by Dara Sekulić of Sarajevo, "Close Pulse":

> We're like desolate wood
> Tree by tree like dense ribs
> Linked by deep roots.
> When one is felled another's branch snaps.
> Falling it leans against its fellow....[12]

Similarly, about one hundred years earlier, note these same two features within a poem for the Greek island of Khíos, struck by an earthquake in 1881:

> O Khíos, once so highly praised,
>   favored by all the world.
> How you are now so deathly pale,
>   consumed by bitter grief!
> How withered the splendid blossom there;
>   where now is your lasting loveliness?[13]

Finally, about 2,400 years earlier, in Lam 2:8c–9a (see also Lam 1:4), there is the personification of destroyed Jerusalem, also with allusion to nature imagery. The biblical Hebrew root (עמל) can have the nuances to collapse, wilt, languish but usually refers to the wilting or withering of vegetation and is often used in parallel with "mourn" (עבל). In this case, the city rampart and wall no longer stand firm or erect, but surprisingly wilt over like a dying plant:

> He caused rampart and wall to *mourn* [עבל];
> together they *collapse/wilt/languish* [עמל].

---

12. Lee, *The Singers of Lamentations*, 21–29. Cited poem in Mario Suško, ed., *Contemporary Poetry of Bosnia and Hercegovina* (Sarajevo: International Peace Center, 1993), 45.

13. Translated by Nancy C. Lee from Hedwig Jahnow's citation in *Das hebräische Leichenlied im Rahmen der Völkerdichtung* (BZAW 36; Giessen: Töpelmann, 1923), 178.

Her gates have sunk into the ground.[14]

I will come to this comparison of poets again below, but in *Singers of Lamentations* I note that the poet of Lam 2:8–9 must have a very close relationship or be the same poet as the one in Jer 14:2 due to the parallel joining together of precise terms and building of imagery into this shared theme. In Jer 14:2,

Judah mourns [עבל],
           and her gates collapse/wilt/languish [עמל].
They are black upon the ground;
           a cry of Jerusalem goes up.

A number of scholars note that the personification of city structures mourning is also formulaic in ancient Near Eastern lament texts. There is a tendency to cite a feature formulaic for all poetry of a certain genre in a culture (including biblical), yet not enough examination of the more nuanced innovations carried out by individual poets. Nowhere else in the Hebrew Bible to my knowledge (prior to Jeremiah) is there the poetic innovation rendering city structures mourning like wilting vegetation.[15] The above illustrations suggest that traditional cultures obviously did and still try to live close to the land, in organic unity, and this is reflected with beauty and pathos in poetry that retains traditional features. Additional oral poetic features include recurring poetic themes, formulas, fairly consistent metrics (cultural and genre-based), alliteration, assonance, onomatopoeia, and word clusters built around the same root.

It has long been documented by anthropologists that mourning laments are typically sung by *women* (though not solely) in many traditional cultures and through history, and according to biblical texts and archeological findings from ancient Palestine, women were also singers in ancient Israel.[16] However, not only had the woman's voice long been neglected in Lamentations study till very recently, women as poetic singers in ancient Israel have not been considered to have really contributed much at all to the "composition" of biblical texts, because there is almost no evidence. While literal evidence is sparse on the surface, this should not shut the door to more subtle and hidden possibilities. The woman's voice or perspective in Lamentations (and I argue, in Jer 4 and 10) goes well beyond women's traditional mourning practice of the dirge, and beyond the lament genre's usual concerns. This voice helps spark a dialogical debate *in both books* about God's justice in the context and is very striking in terms of *challenging* both traditional theology and implicitly, traditional gender roles in Israel.

---

14. Lee, *The Singers of Lamentations*, 145.

15. Ibid.

16. Carol Meyers, "Miriam the Musician," in *A Feminist Companion to Exodus to Deuteronomy* (ed. Athalya Brenner; Sheffield: Sheffield Academic Press, 1994), 207–30.

In the poetry of the book of Jeremiah I traced a woman's voice or singer *distinct from the voice of the persona Jerusalem or Daughter Zion* (more on this below). Nearly all scholars who identify female voices in prophetic texts collapse them into that of a city persona, since it is a pervasive motif. I would suggest that while very helpful, this is not sufficient, that rhetorical and literary approaches emphasizing voice and dialogue with differing perspectives alone do not go far enough, but an oral poetic approach enlarges the possibilities for a setting in life and context reflected in the text. In Jeremiah, an unidentified woman singer's voice is in dialogue with Jeremiah's voice. In Lamentations, two lead voices or singers (neither named or identified but one clearly female) are in dialogue through the first two chapters; the first voice to speak comforts the second.[17] They are joined by other voices as the book progresses. In essence I closely analyzed the poetry in texts where these voices appear together, but more importantly analyzed the individual artistry (beyond what is formulaic only) of the male voice, and that of the female voice (see below), in both books.

VOICES IN ANGUISH, SINGING IN THE RUINS, (A)SCRIBING THE ACROSTIC

This brings me to what I believe is the third contribution of *The Singers of Lamentations*—a reexamining of a possible role of Jeremiah (or a singer in that prophetic tradition), as one oral poet among others in dialogue in Lamentations. Since the Enlightenment, scholarly treatment of Lamentations had primarily used a modern historical-literary method in questioning the authorship of the book; serious scholarship cannot simply accept a superscription as evidence, of course. The consensus became that Jeremiah could not have been the author of Lamentations, because certain perspectives and terms in the book are too unlike the prophet's for the work to be his. Yet recent proposals that the work contains multiple voices, and therefore perspectives, should allow for a reconsideration of Jeremiah's role as perhaps one of the book's poetic voices or oral poetic influences. In fact, the prior severing of any connection of Jeremiah to Lamentations had also diverted attention away from the book's internal debate about prophetic and divine justice (see below).

In the past, scholars primarily did a comparison simply by listing the terms that Lamentations and Jeremiah held in common, a rather simplistic and reductionistic approach, but did not attend to the real artistry, the nuances and dynamics, the formulae and innovations of the poetry. In analyzing the first voice in Lamentations, compared to Jeremiah's in dialogue with Jerusalem's poet in the book of Jeremiah (in Jer 4, 8, and 10 and elsewhere), I examined not only the *perspectives* of the voices in both texts, but also the following elements: *how* they

---

17. For a chart of speaking voices in these texts in Jeremiah and Lamentations, see Lee, *The Singers of Lamentations*, 55.

used genres, particular nuances of imagery to build themes, favored terms and rhetorical techniques, and emphasis on particular content in response to the context. A few summative examples will suffice here.

First, in Jer 4, 8, and 10, Jeremiah expresses *empathy* toward the other voice/singer and the people, but he also must convey God's anger and judgment. This same perspective is expressed by the first lead singer in parts of Lam 1, 2, 3, and 4. The *communal dirge* is typically uttered by Hebrew prophets as a warning to a community that both idolatry and social injustice shall lead to its social collapse, the "death" of the nation. This genre opening Lam 1 (and 2 and 4) reveals a prophetic point of view describing disaster after the fact and is consistent with Jeremiah's use of the genre.[18] But Lamentations also reveals a movement in this singer's perspective from the justice of prophetic judgment, to compassion for the suffering city, to anger against God for unjust excessive punishment and failure to protect the innocent, to a call for lament prayer. The two lead singers use two genres to express their grief and grapple with what has happened: the communal dirge (parts of Lam 1, 2, and 4) and the lament prayer to God (parts of Lam 1, 2, 3, and all of 5).[19]

The poetic artistry of the first singer of Lamentations,[20] and as this singer continues through the book, includes the following elements that are virtually matched in Jeremiah's poetic artistry in Jeremiah; these are a few highlights from many more examples. First is the *use and innovation of imagery to build themes.*[21] (1) As noted, the destruction of city structures is a formulaic theme, and in the Bible and ancient Near East it is also formulaic that structures are personified as mourning and may even audibly grieve; apparently only Jeremiah in the Bible innovates the above formulaic theme to render destroyed structures mourning *and also* appearing like *wilting vegetation* (Jer 14:2; Lam 2:8–9).

(2) Personification of cities is formulaic, but the specific phrase describing the city that "sits alone" (ישׁב and בדד roots) is very rare in the Hebrew Bible; the term for "alone" appears only eleven times in the Hebrew Bible; the pair combination appears *only five times* in the Bible, and *four* of these are in Jeremiah and Lamentations; apart from the opening phrase in Lam 1 ("How lonely sits the city"), the most compelling parallels of this are Hazor "sitting alone," also under attack (Jer 49:31) by Babylon, and Jeremiah "sitting alone" in Jer 15:17 (in his call, Yhwh made him like a fortified city alone against the leaders and people).

---

18. The opening cry formulaic for a dirge, איכה, appears far more often in the book of Jeremiah than any other prophetic book (eighteen times) and three times to open Lam 1, 2, and 4. Fragments and some sustained sections of communal dirge are in Jer 4, 9, 10, 12, 13, 14, 25.

19. Hermann Gunkel, "Klagelieder Jeremiae," *RGG* 3:1500; Jahnow, *Das hebräische Leichenlied*, 164–74.

20. For charts of the speakers/singers in Lamentations, see Lee, *The Singers of Lamentations*, 77, 132,168, 182.

21. For a full exposition of these and other features, see ibid., 82–191.

(3) The poetic image of shepherds (leaders) who are to care for the flock (people) is very common in the Hebrew Bible and in Jeremiah (where irresponsible shepherds allow the flock to be scattered; Jer 10:21; 25:36–37), but humans specifically compared to a deer or stag (איל) is found in just six places in the Hebrew Bible; in *only two* of these (Jer 14:3–6; Lam 1:6) does the poetic singer render the leaders and nobles of Jerusalem like deer not able to find pasture and weakly staggering before their pursuer.

The poet also uses certain *devices* that contribute to the innovation of formulaic imagery to build themes. One such device, and scholars have noted it is favored by Jeremiah, is the use of *double meaning*.[22] Four examples of double meaning in Lamentations all work toward a fuller poetic rendering of the female persona of Jerusalem and her horrendous destruction and suffering; all are sympathetic in tone, and the last three here explode in just three verses.[23] (1) In Lam 1:1 a double use of the term רבב conveys the city once "full of" people and "great" among the nations; this *same* Hebrew root is used by Jeremiah in 51:13 (also serving a contrast motif of a communal dirge) to refer to Babylon that resides beside "great" waters, "full of" riches; note the order of the pair of meanings is reversed in the two texts. (2) In the description of Jerusalem's downfall, the term עני has double meaning, referring to "suffering" but also "rape" (Lam 1:7). (3) Jerusalem is described as a נידה (metaphorically a "wanderer" or outcast because of her sin), but there is likely another meaning with the like-sounding נדה, "impure one" (related to the above rape); like a woman, her sanctuary is violated (Lam 1:8). (4) A reference to Jerusalem's clothing (referred to by the term שול) in this horrid scene, depending on translation can mean "in her skirts" (noun) or "when they strip/plunder" (participle of שלל).

When the above artistries of the first lead singer, whom I have compared with and suggested is Jeremianic, are then also considered like a jigsaw puzzle of rhetoric in unfolding dialogue with the woman singer, extraordinary oral poetic dynamics emerge. For example above, just as the intensity of description unfolds of her עני, she bursts in for the first time with a lament at 1:9c crying out to YHWH to see her עני. A careful tracking of the call and response of the singers reveals that they actually interrupt one another to complete a word pair or to complete an inclusio begun by the other.

Fourth, then, I proposed for the first time the possibility of a distinctive female oral poet/singer in Lamentations and in Jeremiah, in dialogue with the Jeremianic voice, who makes striking rhetorical and theological impact. While no one will deny that Zion and the city of Jerusalem are construed as a female persona, this aspect of the poetry can and should be treated as a separate matter in analysis from an additional singer in dialogue.

---

22. William Holladay, "Style, Irony, and Authenticity in Jeremiah," *JBL* 81 (1962): 45–47.
23. Lee, *The Singers of Lamentations*, 101–12.

In *The Singers of Lamentations,* I proposed the same female voice or singer in Jer 4, 8, and 10 can be identified in Lam 1, 2, and 3 because of extremely consistent perspective, repeated use of terms, lament genre, and common escalating emphases.[24] In the Jeremiah and Lamentations texts, she expresses first-person lament about her suffering (with repeated reference across these texts to her "heart," her "travail," her "crushing," her "bitterness") in the devastation of the city, referring to the invasion, destruction of her tents, and loss of children. While the poetry of Jeremiah largely paints the *anger* of God as all-consuming and bringing devastation as punishment for the people's wrongdoing, by Jer 10:23–25 this female singer offers a completely different expression on this topic with her singular lament to YHWH. It is not a speech that can be attributed to Jeremiah's voice:

> *Correct* me, YHWH, but with *justice,*
> and *not* with your *anger,* lest you diminish/belittle me. (10:24)

A "confession" with these precise words is unprecedented in the psalms. Moreover, nowhere does the prophet Jeremiah make this particular theological appeal to YHWH in the book of Jeremiah. This is, I propose, one of the most stunning theological challenges to YHWH in the Hebrew Bible.[25] I shall return to this shortly.

The lament and anger of this singer, anguishing as a mother likely in "real life," carries over into the book of Lamentations and intensifies. She continues to lament, and following traditional prophetic theology *up to a point,* she admits the devastation is punishment for sin, but transforms the complaint typical of a lament into an *expanded accusation,* with growing anger, against God for carrying out excessive violent punishment. This accusation emerges after concerted interplay of her voice with Jeremiah's own complaint in Lam 2. The tenor of her lament above is in the spirit of the prophet Moses' complaints and matched in its severity only by the later complaints in Job. One role of a traditional dirge singer in the context of mourning can be to accuse, by name, the perpetrator, the one who killed the victim, as a call for "public justice" in the community.[26] In Lam 1, 2, and 3, the woman lament singer and Jeremiah may draw on this popular prac-

---

24. In the canonical flow of the book of Jeremiah, this female singer's laments precede Jeremiah's laments, whose then begin in Jer 11; in the flow of the book of Lamentations, this female singer's laments precede the Jeremianic voice there, who then beseeches her to lament fully in Lam 2:18; he then weeps in lament in Lam 3:49.

25. The only psalmic confessions that come close to this plea in Jer 10:24 are in Ps 38 ("O YHWH, do not reprove me with your wrath or *correct* me with your *anger*) and similarly Ps 6, but they fall short of asking YHWH to correct instead according to *justice;* see Lee, *The Singers of Lamentations,* 70–71.

26. Ibid., 88.

tice, as well as expand the lament accusation, to complain of Yʜᴡʜ's destructive actions, particularly for allowing the suffering and deaths of innocent children.[27]

A Pʀᴇ-Joʙɪᴀɴ Lʏʀɪᴄᴀʟ Dᴇʙᴀᴛᴇ ᴏɴ Gᴏᴅ's Jᴜsᴛɪᴄᴇ

Thus, while the two lead singers in Lamentations do not deny sin and punishment, they implicitly begin to critique a strict theology of retributive justice, in which the wicked/unrighteous are punished and God hears, rescues, and rewards only the good/righteous. So a fifth contribution *The Singers of Lamentations* makes is to illumine this internal debate. These singers also plant the seeds for questioning and undermining a wider theological claim (also common in the ancient Near East) that the deity may lead a war to defeat a nation. The book's struggle with theodicy foreshadows and likely influences such debate in Job, and is relevant to post-Holocaust discussions of the presence/absence of God in historical human catastrophes.

A sixth contribution of *The Singers of Lamentations* is twofold. First, it is to link the internal debate above to a rhetorical or literary *function of the acrostics* found there and elsewhere in the Hebrew Bible. A careful examination of all the other acrostics in the Bible (Pss 9–10; 25; 33; 34; 37; 38; 94; 111; 112; 119; 145; except Prov 31:10–31) shows that each are heavily invested in the idea of retributive justice and accordingly defend God as "just" or "righteous" (the term צדיק is pervasive in them). These psalmic texts reveal a tradition of singers or writers who composed songs espousing retributive justice, a theological "order" hammered home by every letter (and line) of their acrostic form. (Perhaps these acrostics were written by diligent scribes or redactors during the exilic period, yet I know of no real argument or reasons put forth that the acrostic *must* be a written technique and cannot be oral as well.)[28] As I suggested in *The Singers of Lamentations*, there is a stark divergence by the primary voices of Lamentations from the above acrostic psalms (let's say, צדיק psalms) and their perspective of retributive justice; I propose the lead singers in Lamentations used the acrostic for *a very different purpose.*[29]

---

27. Tod Linafelt has illumined this major concern/motif for the children in the book of Lamentations and in its afterlife in later Jewish readings: *Surviving Lamentations: Catastrophe, Lament, and Protest in the Afterlife of a Biblical Book* (Chicago: University of Chicago Press, 2000).

28. See the recent statistical work with acrostics poetry by Cornelius B. Houk, giving evidence for multiple poets in Lamentations, as well as the plausibility of the acrostics as an oral phenomenon: "Multiple Poets in Lamentations," *JSOT* 30 (2005): 111–25; idem, "Acrostic Psalms and Syllables," in *The Psalms and Other Studies on the Old Testament* (ed. Jack C. Knight and Lawrence A. Sinclair; Nashotah, Wis.: Forward Movement Publications, 1990), 54–60.

29. See Carleen Mandolfo, *God in the Dock: Dialogic Tension in the Psalms of Lament* (JSOTSup 357; London: Sheffield Academic Press, 2002), for a helpful recognition of divergent

Second, in a section of *The Singers of Lamentations* called "Cracking the Acrostic Code?" I proposed a new explanation, a rhetorical/theological reason, for *inverting acrostic letters* in Lam 2, 3, and 4, in light of the psalmic acrostics' interests.[30] There have been helpful suggestions for the purpose of the alphabetical (acrostic) structure, in both giving formfulness to the grief of Lamentations, while expressing its range from A to Z. Rarely has there been an adequate explanation of the inversed letters that appear in some of these acrostics, except to posit from epigraphic evidence that there were merely different versions of the alphabetic order at times. Lamentations, however, presents dissident singers (and perhaps a dissident scribe/redactor) who in their rebelling against a simplistic retributive understanding of events, I propose employ the acrostic structure to *invert* that order of justice, with strategic inverting of the letters ע and פ. It is probably no accident that these letters suggest in their root meaning what someone (or YHWH) "sees" and "speaks," and they precede the צ letter. (Indeed, the female singer in Lam 2:18 admits to "rebelling against YHWH's word or, literally, mouth, פה). The צ word to follow that is most often used or emphasized in the psalmic acrostics, and used for YHWH and his *righteous* followers is צדיק. Yet the acrostic with the first inversion of letters in Lam 2 leads not to the expected צדיק but to Jeremiah's appeal to the female singer to "cry out" (צעק) in lament, a virtual wordplay with צדיק! It is unclear whether the poet's rupturing the order is meant to critique YHWH or the promoters of the ideology, or both, but it is deconstructing retributive צדיק rhetoric (usually heavy on praise of YHWH as "righteous") and replacing it with *lament* rhetoric critiquing YHWH. Importantly, the *only other instance of an acrostic in the Hebrew Bible* with *these inverted* letters is in the *lament* of Pss 9–10, and there the צ line is completely missing (!), replaced with descriptions of the wicked persecuting the poor. Importantly, in his own personal lament (Jer 11:20) Jeremiah uses the צדיק term sarcastically, according to William Holladay, to complain against YHWH, and the female singer of Lam 2:18 may be following suit with the term for her own critique of YHWH.[31]

This rhetorical, theological battle heats up in Lam 3 (every acrostic line is tripled), when the first two dissident singers are engaged by two new singers, one of which sounds much like Job's friends, who defends God's ways and calls upon the lament singer to stop such complaints and confess in silence! (It is interesting that the letter order in this chapter is again inverted, and one can delineate Jeremiah's voice in the interplay (on oral poetic grounds); he renders the enemies opening their mouths against them (פ line), and "my eyes" weeping until YHWH sees (ע

---

voices in dialogue in the Psalms, including a didactic voice similar to the צדיק acrostic psalmists.

30. Lee, *The Singers of Lamentations*, 164–66.
31. Cited in Lee, *The Singers of Lamentations*, 123.

line), followed by the צ line that describes the enemies chasing and persecuting him and throwing him in a pit.[32]

Bringing into Focus the "Daughter of My People"

Finally, the seventh contribution of *The Singers of Lamentations* was to lay the interpretive groundwork for a possibility I briefly alluded to in my article "Prophet and Singer in the Fray," that this female voice in the books of Jeremiah and Lamentations may be even more than *just a singer*.[33] After the rhetoric described above by the female singer, which is clearly more than formulaic, with her sophisticated pushing of theological limits, poetic lyricism, and facility with the subtleties of genre, I want to ask, What kind of gifted singer could possibly go toe to toe with Jeremiah? The rhetorical signal lies in Jeremiah's term of endearment, "Daughter of My People." Most commentators assume the prophet uses this to refer to the female persona of the city (Zion or Jerusalem). However, this is only an assumption, related to the usual practice in the ancient Near East of poetic renderings of cities as daughters (Daughter Zion; Daughter Babylon). However, I know of no critical explanation why this phrase or appellative favored by Jeremiah must self-evidently refer to the city persona. Indeed, one must explain the "my people" element. An article by Nancy Bowen examined the phrase used by the prophet Ezekiel, "daughters of your people" which he uses to refer negatively to *women prophets*.[34] The referent to women prophets in that biblical text is clear. I propose that Jeremiah's phrase, or term of endearment, "Daughter of My People" *likely refers to an unnamed female prophet*, and this is the singer with whom he is in dialogue in these two books.[35] They both suffer the persecutions of the war context. This consideration nuances his associated lamenting and weeping for her, Daughter of My People, at certain places in these very texts under consideration ("For the crushing of the Daughter of My People I am crushed; I mourn; dismay has seized me. Is there no balm in Gilead? Is there no physician there? Why is the wound of the Daughter of My People not healed?" Jer 8:21–22; cf. also 14:17). We are wont to interpret all poetry as "merely" symbolic and never "literal," when, indeed, lament poetry from war contexts is certainly capable of referring to graphic injury and suffering and witnessed death of known individuals. This reading could expand what we know of the world of Jeremiah and Lamentations,

---

32. Lee, *The Singers of Lamentations*, 166–81.

33. "Prophet and Singer in the Fray," 208–11.

34. Nancy R. Bowen, "The Daughters of Your People: Female Prophets in Ezekiel 13:17–23," *JBL* 118 (1999): 417–33.

35. At times he amplifies the appellative to "Young Maiden Daughter of My People" or some translate "Virgin Daughter of My People"; it is suggestive that there are examples of women prophets (not always young) who were unmarried (thus "virgins") and pursued a prophetic calling.

if in the end Jeremiah and another prophetic voice that happens to be female, are singing in dialogue in the ruins of destruction. Other voices wrangle with them about who is to blame, but in the end, the theological, social, and above all, *personal*, devastations are all consuming. They are in the fray in a flurry of voices—then they disappear. The book closes with a communal lament to God that suggests a time after the frenzied catastrophe, when those remaining in the land, utterly spent, attempt to carry on and survive war's deprivations. The text conveys no divine answer to their laments, and no indication of the fate of the two lead singers who have fallen silent, like their city.

TALKING BACK:
THE PERSEVERANCE OF JUSTICE IN LAMENTATION

Carleen Mandolfo

When I wrote my dissertation (revised and published with T&T Clark/Sheffield, 2002), my original goal had been to establish some kind of definitive link between the voicing changes in the psalms of lament and the cultic context in which they were originally performed. I was particularly interested in the shift between first and second person speech (the supplicant) addressed directly to the deity and a third person voice (a didactic voice) that spoke in descriptive terms of —rather than to—the deity, or seemed to offer words of advice or admonition to the supplicant in terms of how they should orient themselves to the divine in light of their anguish. Note how this voicing shift manifests in Ps 9 (didactic voice highlighted).[1]

2   I will praise you, YHWH, with all my heart;
    I will relate all your wonders.
3   I will be glad and rejoice in you;
    I will sing in praise of your name, Elyon,
4   when my enemies retreat,
    stumbling and perishing at your presence.

5   For you have upheld my cause and my case,
    sitting on the throne as a just judge.
6   You have rebuked the nations;
    you have destroyed the wicked;
    their name you have blotted out forever and ever.
7   The enemy is no more,[2] in perpetual ruin;
    you have uprooted cities; their very memory is blotted out.

---

1. For my exegesis of this psalm, see *God in the Dock* (Sheffield: Sheffield Academic Press, 2002), 41–48.
2. Or, "the enemies are no more." The noun (האויב) is singular; the verb (תמו) is plural.

> ⁸   *Yhwh abides forever,*
>   *establishing his throne for judgment.*
> ⁹   *He judges the world in justice;*
>   *he adjudicates between the peoples with fairness.*
> ¹⁰ *Yhwh is a fortress for the oppressed,*
>   *a fortress in times of distress.*

It had been assumed in previous scholarship (with rare exceptions) that the two voices are sourced in the supplicant, but rhetorically this seems problematic since the two voices frequently espouse different and often contrasting views about the situation of suffering posed in the poems. Originally, this phenomenon struck me (and my advisor, John Hayes) as reflecting the intervention of a cultic functionary into the lament of a petitioner.

In other words, I envisioned the ritual process as going something like this: A person finds herself in a situation of disease—either due to illness, or interpersonal or social discord—and brings her case before Yhwh at the temple or a shrine, perhaps. Ideally, bringing her case would involve offering an animal sacrifice and reciting a prayer of supplication/complaint. There may have been a repertoire of previously composed psalms for just such an occasion. The recitation would have been performed antiphonally, with the supplicant laying out her case and a cultic functionary interposing words of confidence in Yhwh's saving intent (for those who deserve it, of course). In fact, although I did offer some tentative conclusions to this end, mustering evidence for such a ritual proved daunting.

In the course of my research, however, I realized there was a worthwhile form-critical and sociorhetorical project to be pursued using the same data. While I was unable to uncover definitively the cultic procedure behind these psalms, I found I could contribute to our understanding of the ideological impulses behind the formal features of these psalms (which I prefer to call "grievance" psalms, rather than "lament"). In a nutshell, my work revealed a background of ideo-logical warfare—the voice of experience (supplicant) colliding with the voice of tradition (didactic voice). Sociorhetorical observations led naturally into theo-logical ones. I argued that the supplicant's theological point of view is based in experiential data that often posed a challenge to the exclusively justice-oriented understanding of God's interaction with his human subjects. The challenge posed by this rendering of Israel's divinity is countered within the psalm by the didactic voice that reasserts the "normative" position that "God is a righteous judge" (Ps 7:11). Once this dialogic dynamic was made patent to me, I noticed similar con-versations taking place throughout the biblical corpus, which led me to wonder why so little attention had been paid in biblical scholarship to the voice(s) that poses a challenge to divine authority. My next few projects—on the books of Job and Lamentations—would address this deficit.

As a follow-up to this brief summary of the foundations and genesis of my overarching project, it seems most useful to try, as systematically as possible, to describe the methodological contributions I hope my work has made/will make to the field of lamentation research, as I see it. I have approached biblical texts from three different, but interrelated ways of reading or interests: Form-criticism, narrative ethics, and dialogic theology. In order to give the most concise summary possible, the first category will be addressed primarily by reference to my book, *God in the Dock*, and the second and third categories will reference *Daughter Zion Talks Back to the Prophets* even though both books share these three interests.

Form Criticism[3]

Form criticism has had a long term and influential impact on biblical criticism, but in the past couple of decades its reputation has suffered as some of its manifestations in biblical scholarship came to appear more and more pedantic. Hermann Gunkel's groundbreaking work in this area has had lasting effects, of course, but his understanding of genres as static social categories has been re-evaluated by those in and out of biblical studies. According to Martin Buss,

> In observing connections between aspects of literary form, biblical scholarship can go further than Gunkel did, for he reflected on their nature only intermittently. One can ask on a more regular basis, "How does this language go with certain thoughts and feelings, and how do these go with a given kind of situation?"[4]

Rather than build on Gunkel's (and Mowinckel's) interest in establishing fixed settings for the diverse psalm genres, in *God in the Dock,* I was interested in making connections between the language of lament psalms and the "thoughts and feelings" of the community that produced them. In other words, I wanted to know what ideological worlds created these texts (as well as the way in which these texts sustained those worlds). To get at this I chose to read lament psalms as a type of socio-ideological dialogue. Psalm 7, for example, might be read in this manner, though not necessarily as an exchange among equals.

SUP: Arise, Yhwh, in your anger;
   lift yourself up against the fury of those vexing me.
   Rouse yourself on my behalf.
   Ordain fairness!
   ...

---

3. Some descriptions in this section are borrowed from my *Daughter Zion Talks Back to the Prophets*, ch. 3.

4. Martin J. Buss, *Form Criticism in Its Context* (JSOTSup 274; Sheffield: Sheffield Academic Press, 1999), 415.

DV:　　*Yhwh arbitrates between the peoples.*
SUP:　Judge me, Yʜwʜ, according to my innocence
　　　　and according to my integrity within me.
　　　　Let the wickedness of the evil ones cease
　　　　and establish the just.
　　　　DV:*The one who tests the thoughts and emotions is a just god.* (7:7–10)

Beyond mere exchange, these two voices interanimate one another, which has to do with the shaping influence utterances have on one another. According to Bakhtin, speakers formulate their speech in terms of the response they expect to receive. In dialogic psalms of lament, the presence of the DV's discourse into what is otherwise address to God can be seen as a way of tempering the supplicant's grievance so as to not anger the deity, thus giving the supplicant's case the best shot at reaching a favorable resolution. Formally, then, the DV's discourse might be understood as a *function of the supplicant's request*, rather than a literally distinct voice. Still, although formally functional, the DV's discourse still inhabits a more powerful position than the supplicant's by dint of the fact that it is positing the normative theological position and stating it in the form of "objective" third-person speech.

When I applied this way of thinking about form to the book of Job,[5] I noticed the manner in which Job pays the price for not integrating what would be the equivalent of the didactic voice into his discourse. Rather, in the book of Job, Job's speech is in an adversarial relationship to the didactic voice of the friends' discourse. He refuses to acquiesce to their point of view (although it's arguable that he does acquiesce to God in the end). In response, the friends—with increasing vitriol—essentially accuse Job of blasphemy. On one level, such an accusation seems overblown given the fact that Job's complaint doesn't differ fundamentally from the laments found in the Psalter. But because the voice of tradition, represented by the friends, is not a function of his personal discourse, his lament poses a serious challenge to the theological status quo. This is illustrative of the idea that genres mutate to fit ongoing contexts, an idea that has been increasingly recognized and is related to my larger dialogic enterprise.

> In considering the rhetorical or communicative aspects of texts, form-critical scholars will no longer presume that genres are static or ideal entities that never change. Rather, they will recognize the inherent fluidity of genres, the fact that they are historically, culturally, and discursively dependent, and they will study

---

5. "A Generic Renegade: A Dialogic Theological Reading of Job and Lament Psalms," in *Diachronic and Synchronic: Reading the Psalms in Real Time, Proceedings of the Baylor Symposium on the Book of Psalms* (ed. Joel S. Burnett, W. Dennis Tucker, and W. H. Bellinger; Library of Hebrew Bible/Old Testament Studies 488; New York: T&T Clark, 2007), 45–66.

the means by which genres are transformed to meet the needs of the particular communicative situation of the text.[6]

It is to the poet's credit that the book more or less champions Job's position over the friends', but even this poet couldn't take the side of Job over God himself. And neither can the poets of the psalms (Ps 88 may be an exception[7]).

Reading dialogically allows us to notice how meaning is created in the interplay of discourses rather than in their singularity. Furthermore, it compels us to listen more attentively to divergent points of view, especially those emanating from the more vulnerable party—in this case the supplicant—who is, hermeneutically speaking, always in danger of being subsumed by the more authoritative voice. So, in form-critical terms, what can we deduce about the ideological context that produced such literature?

There are two basic (to be a bit overly simplistic for heuristic purposes) languages interacting—the hegemonic language of divine justice and the opposing language of experience. The supplicant lives in both worlds simultaneously; and while pain may be her visceral partner, the worldview of the DV is the idiom through which she must—generically speaking—experience her pain. These languages come to "interanimate" one another and the expressions of both experience (subjective) and dogma (objective) are altered in the process.

> To the extent that this happens, it becomes more difficult to take for granted the value system of a given language. Those values may still be felt to be right and the language may still seem adequate to its topic, but not indisputably so, because they have been, however cautiously, disputed.[8]

In this process of interanimation, the hegemony of the DV is not unassailable. In Deuteronomistic texts, the position of the DV might appear impregnable, but juxtaposed to the supplicant's speech, the DV's footing becomes less sure. In a manner similar to Job, these psalms protest against the "theodic settlement" of Deuteronomistic theology.[9]

So, even more specifically, how do dialogic psalms register ancient Israel's religious (and political) institutions?[10] It seems fairly clear that religious figures were responsible for preserving the biblical record that has been handed down

---

6. Ehud Ben Zvi and Marvin A. Sweeney, eds. *The Changing Face of Form Criticism for the Twenty-First Century* (Grand Rapids: Eerdmans, 2003), 9–10.

7. See Carleen Mandolfo, "Psalm 88 and the Holocaust: Lament in Search of a Divine Response," *BibInt* 15 (2007): 151–70.

8. Gary Saul Morson and Caryl Emerson, *Mikhail Bakhtin: Creation of a Prosaics* (Stanford, Calif.: Stanford University Press, 1990), 143.

9. Walter Brueggemann (*Theology of the Old Testament: Testimony, Dispute, Advocacy* [Minneapolis: Fortress, 1997], 386) makes this claim for Job and Proverbs.

10. The following paragraph is quoted from Mandolfo, *God in the Dock*, 180.

to us. Logically then, the record reflects their point of view. This is an oversim-
plification, of course. We have no way of knowing who "they" were with any
precision, and certainly "they" were not a unified force who maintained a precise
ideological solidarity throughout several hundred years. On the one hand, we
can say what often has been said, that the biblical account reflects an official or
religiously elite point of view, a view, for example, that grants no legitimacy to
the practice of syncretism, which we are more and more sure was an integral
part of the lives of much of Israel's population. "Official" in this case would constitute a compromise position between the Priestly and Deuteronomic traditions
as hammered out in the formation of the Hebrew Bible.[11] The Priestly vein was
concerned with the maintenance of cosmic order as conceived in the myth of
creation, and recorded in Genesis (and alluded to in many psalms, particularly
hymns). The Deuteronomic agenda, on the other hand—and its emphasis on
Mosaic covenantal obedience—has left its mark throughout the Bible. The entire
history from Deuteronomy to Kings is a chronicle of disobedience and judgment. (Under this rubric, Brueggemann's observation that one of Israel's favorite
metaphors for Yhwh is judge, makes sense.[12]) The Deuteronomic agenda aligns
with the dominant rhetoric of the DV in a number of dialogic psalms. This is
not to suggest a polar opposition in terms of power between the DV and the
historical personage(s) behind the supplicant's voice (which is indeterminable in
any case). Rather, it is to suggest a rhetorical dichotomy. While, it may be fairly
safe to say that the position espoused by the DV represents an elite point of view,
whether the supplicants were in reality the poor and afflicted (on a social level)
is open to debate.

Narrative Ethics and Dialogic Theology

The form-critical work summarized above sets the foundation for constructing a
dialogic theology in which an ethics of narrative and reading plays a central role.
Using Bakhtin's dialogic linguistics[13]—which have a strong ethical component—I
took steps toward developing a dialogic biblical theology that suggests that biblical authority resides in the book's diverse ideological points of view rather than in
a focus on the here-and-there overlapping of otherwise divergent positions. The
ethical upshot of such a position is an emphasis on giving a hearing to voices that
are usually ignored or given short shrift in most biblical theologies and commen-

---

11. See Brueggemann, *Theology of the Old Testament*, 590; also Rainer Albertz, *A History of
Israelite Religion in the Old Testament Period* (trans. J. Bowden; 2 vols.; Louisville: Westminster
John Knox, 1994), 2:468, 481.

12. Brueggemann, *Theology*, 233.

13. See Barbara Green, *Mikhail Bakhtin and Biblical Scholarship: An Introduction* (SemeiaSt 38; Atlanta: Society of Biblical Literature, 2000), for an introduction to Bakhtin's dialogic
linguistics.

taries. In more concrete and socially applicable terms, it models a way of listening to those voices in our own context that are ridden roughshod by the guardians of traditional values.

Toward such a biblical theology I applied the narrative ethical work of Hilde Nelson,[14] who argues that narratives about certain groups of people can be damaging to their subjectivity. This relates closely to Bakhtin's notion of "authoring." According to Bakhtin, we are all the co-authors of one another's identities. In other words, the whole story about us cannot be told by us alone. As human beings, we are "finished" by the gaze of the other.

> Authoring is the key action of human existence. I author myself; I am co-responsible for the shaping of others with whom I interact; and as an artist, I author a work of art—for present purposes, a literary hero, who will author others, and so forth.… I incline toward another, live into his or her experience. I enter as deeply as I am able the space of the other—their particularity—perceive it to some extent with their eye or ear—and then return to my own space, remembering and marking—integrating—what I have experienced.[15]

Part of the job of authoring others involves listening to them as *responsibly* as we can, listening and responding *fairly*. For Bakhtin, these same relationships pertain in the textual sphere. The interaction between text and reader itself constitutes an act of authoring—a dynamic that flows in both directions.

According to Nelson, the narrative we construct about the other has a bearing not only on our understanding of them, but also—and potentially more significantly—on their understanding of themselves. Narratives have this kind of determining power especially when they are what Nelson calls "master narratives"—that is, culturally authoritative narratives. A culture's foundational myths, for example, have this kind of power.

> [N]arratives figure prominently in the moral life: they cultivate our moral emotions and refine our moral perception; they make intelligible what we do and who we are; they teach us our responsibilities; they motivate, guide, and justify our actions; through them, we redefine ourselves.[16]

So, insofar as members of a society buy into the mythic or "master" stories that crisscross their collective conscious, their agency is largely dictated by the particulars of this narrative. Thus, human beings can be damaged by the narratives told about them or that constitute them in a negative light. But an important com-

---

14. *Damaged Identities, Narrative Repair* (Ithaca, N.Y.: Cornell University Press, 2001).
15. Green, *Mikhail Bakhtin and Biblical Scholarship*, 33–34.
16. Nelson, *Damaged Identities, Narrative Repair*, 70.

ponent of this understanding of the formative power of narrative is its ability to repair "damaged" identities. According to Nelson,

> [B]ecause identities are narratively constituted and narratively damaged, they can be narratively repaired. The morally pernicious stories that construct the identity according to the requirements of an abusive power system can be at least partially dislodged and replaced by identity-constituting stories that portray group members as fully developed moral agents.[17]

In *Daughter Zion Talks Back to the Prophets,* I use Nelson's understanding of the constitutive power of narrative—both in its damaging and its reparative aspects—to speak about the way in which YHWH narratively constructs his "wife," Daughter Zion, as an adulterous woman and "whore" through the discourse of his prophets, as well as the way in which Daughter Zion attempts to reconstitute her identity in Lam 1–2. In the books of Hosea, Jeremiah, and Ezekiel, Israel is figured as a woman and subjected to intense verbal abuse as she is constructed as a whore and gang-raped as punishment for her promiscuous behavior. Throughout these texts, Daughter Zion is additionally deprived of agency by the fact that she is rendered virtually voiceless. When she does speak, it is mediated through YHWH's/the prophet's point of view. The combination of these two forms of hegemony suggest to me that the prophets' narratives are what Nelson describes as "morally compromised or flat-out evil, because they unfairly depict particular social groups as lacking in virtue or as existing merely to serve others' ends."[18]

The Bible is a master narrative of mythic proportions that determines the symbolic and ethical contours of entire societies as well as those who inhabit them. It sets up boundaries and determines according to those lines who is in and who is out. The story of God and Zion as it plays out in the prophets is illustrative of the text's identity-shaping power. These prophetic texts constitute mini master narratives in their own right.[19] They uphold the normative worldview—patriarchal, monotheistic, and so forth—of the Bible that distinguishes men from women and believers from apostates. As such, these prophetic representations do what many master narratives (unfortunately) do: they justify violence against those groups they characterize as somehow morally deficient.

But the Bible contains the seeds of its own atonement in this regard. In Lam 1–2, the poet (and more importantly, perhaps, the community that chose to canonize the book) restores the "wife's" voice to her, and allows her to tell a story

---

17. Ibid., xii. The notion of counterstory connects to some degree with Brueggemann's theology of "countertestimony," except that his is more dialogic and hers more dialectic. In other words, Brueggemann's idea does not necessarily embrace the necessity of resolving anything.

18. Ibid., 152.

19. It should be noted that, when I refer to the prophetic "narrative," I am not alluding to a formal (i.e., generic) but rather a conceptual designation.

that constructs an identity for her from her own point of view—a story that to a large extent tempers Yhwh's construction. Rather than the adulterous wife who is responsible for the slaughter of her own children as narrated in prophetic texts, Daughter Zion tells the story of an abused wife of a deity who in his rage and determination to control her agency summons all the muscle of the enemy against her and her children as punishment for her insolence.

The reading approach outlined above, which takes into account the ethics of narration as applied to biblical texts ultimately results in a dialogic theology that provides humanity an avenue for speaking honestly to God about its experience of him. It's a theology that makes demands on God. In his study of lament psalms, Brueggemann finds biblical precedent for this impulse.

> [T]he lament psalms insist upon Israel's finding voice, a voice that tends to be abrasive and insistent. The lament psalm is a Jewish refusal of silence before God...It is a Jewish understanding that an adequate *relationship with God permits and requires a human voice that will speak out against every wrong perpetrated either on earth or by heaven....* I consider this matter of *voice and violence* not to be a theoretical issue but a concrete, practical, pastoral issue because we live in a violent, abusive society in which there is a terrible conspiracy in violence that can only be broken when the silence is broken by *the lesser party.*[20]

Reading in favor of the "lesser parties" can have encouraging real-life repercussions. A dialogic theology suggests that as surely as God authors us, we author God.[21] Conceptually, this posits a deity who is mutable and in process. There are a number of examples of this in the narrative sections of the Bible, and the psalms imply it, but traditional biblical theology stays focused on static, rather than relational, descriptions of God.[22]

---

20. Brueggemann, *Theology of the Old Testament*, 22, emphasis added.

21. This notion is reminiscent of one of the tenets of Jewish mysticism known as *tikkun olam*, which posits that humans are partners in God's creative intentions that have yet to reach fulfillment. Plaskow points out how empowering this notion can be for women in a story about a women's theological conference in 1972 in which God was ultimately defined as "Being" rather than "a Being" (*Standing Again at Sinai: Judaism from a Feminist Perspective* [San Francisco: Harper & Row, 1991], 143–44).

22. Theologians of a more philosophic, rather than textual, bent are more likely to devise more complex descriptions and some have even pushed for relationality as one of God's primary attributes (e.g., Karl Barth, Martin Buber), but biblical theology has tended to try to cull the adjectives most inclusive of God's attributes. Walter Brueggemann and Terence Fretheim are two exceptions. Of course, even while insisting on a god who interpenetrates human beings without coerciveness and with unconditional love, more relational theologians still privilege God in the hierarchy of the divine-human binary, and for the most part privilege man over woman in a dependent hierarchy.

The notion of a mutable god may be understandably disturbing to many believers, but now more than ever we require a deity who models listening and openness to change. Specifically, we need an image of transcendence that allows human existence multiplex manifestations, who facilitates rather than obstructs our growth. And, perhaps most importantly, we need a god that never allows someone to stake a claim of the sort that God would never do that, or accept that, or love that kind of person.

I might be charged with championing a relativistic, amoral deity or a deity as mere projection. To the contrary, I feel that a fully relational god can resist reductive pressures, while revealing that the construction of a transhistorical moral code is dangerous. At the same time, the notion of a relational deity insists that a moral ground is still important, but that it must be carved out of thoughtful and sometimes painful negotiations between parties. In other words, God may still be the first principle, but no longer of a logocentric system of knowledge.

As a biblical scholar, my job as I see it is to read the text closely, read closely the god of the text and the divine-human relationship in it, and demonstrate how it suggests the kind of theology I am outlining here. We simply need to keep reading the text—all of the texts—and foregrounding the dialogic predicament of divine-human interaction each one represents. And finally, such a reading must have the aim of compelling us to reflect on how those texts reflect human-human interaction.

Surviving Lamentations (One More Time)

Tod Linafelt

1

It was merely one of many brilliant off-hand comments that Walter Brueggemann would toss out during the course of a semester, but it was one that I wrote down and remembered and that eventually became the basis for my doctoral dissertation. I cannot now recall what course it was, but the year must have been about 1989, and I was a master's student at Columbia Theological Seminary, sitting in a classroom with Professor Brueggemann (not "Walter" to me at the time) as he read the final lines of the book of Lamentations:

> Why dost thou forget us for ever,
> why dost thou so long forsake us?
> Restore us to thyself, O Lord, that we may be restored!
> Renew our days as of old!
> Or hast thou utterly rejected us?
> Art thou exceedingly angry with us? (5:20–22, RSV)

I know that it was the Revised Standard Version that we were reading, because the translation ended in a question (as neither the NRSV or the JPS do, the other translations I might have used) and because Brueggemann looked up after reading the final questions and said, "If you want to know where these questions are answered, look in Isa 49." Well, I did want to know, and so after class I looked in Isa 49 and found the verses to which Brueggemann must have been referring:

> But Zion said, "The Lord has forsaken me,
> my Lord has forgotten me." (49:14)

Immediately following this nearly direct quote of Lam 5:20, with the word-pair "forget" (שכח) and "forsake" (עזב) chiastically reversed in the prophetic text (and you can believe that we had talked about chiasmus, given the influence of James Muilenburg on Brueggemann), comes the prophet's representation of God's answer to Zion:

Can a woman forget her suckling child,
that she should have no compassion on the son of her womb?
Even these may forget,
yet I will not forget you. (49:15)

So here indeed seemed to be God's answer to the final unanswered questions of the book of Lamentations. And a striking answer it seemed to me, using the metaphor of a nursing mother to imagine God's inability to forget Israel. The bodily and emotional basis of the metaphor lent the passage, which is after all poetry, a vividness that seemed more convincing than any ontological claim about God's impeccable memory. Yet I also remember Brueggemann saying—whether it was in class or some other occasion when I talked with him about these passages, I cannot recall—that one ought not to move too quickly to that answer in Second Isaiah, that the author(s) of Lamentations had decided to leave those final questions unanswered and that we as readers had to honor the crisis of faith represented by the utter silence of God in the face of those questions and the refusal of the book to move to praise. The refusal to move to praise seemed all the more striking and important given that such a move is so common in the lament psalms.

Of course, it is not at all clear that those final lines of Lamentations ought to be rendered as questions in the first place. Indeed, the RSV is really the only major translation that does so.[1] The lines are a notorious crux in translating Lamentations, and I have elsewhere[2] made a more detailed argument for understanding verse 22 as an incomplete conditional sentence, that is, a protasis without an apodosis, or an "if" without a "then":

כי אם מאס מאסתנו	For if truly you have rejected us,
קצפת עלינו עד־מאד	raging bitterly against us—

The implied, but unstated, "then" clause is surely negative: if God has truly rejected, then there is little hope for restoration or for the renewal of "our days as of old" (5:21). But, to my mind, it is of the utmost importance that this judgment is *left unstated*, and therefore the vision of the future, while hardly bright at this point in the poetry (and probably historically), is nevertheless left open. The effect is not that different from the RSV's final, unanswered questions, which by their very form as unanswered questions, leave the book open-ended.

---

1. Though it should be noted that several eminent scholars take verse 22 to be a question, including Westermann, Lohr, and Kraus. It is also rendered as a question in the current liturgical edition of the five *megilloth* produced by the Central Conference of American Rabbis, which represents the Reform movement.

2. Tod Linafelt, "The Refusal of a Conclusion in the Book of Lamentations," *JBL* 120 (2001): 340–43.

What I took away from my initial encounter with the book of Lamentations, then, was a strong sense of the book's open-endedness, of the demand for a response that was nonetheless not forthcoming, and that, even though one could understand a very positive response to precisely the questions raised by Lamentations as having been provided by Second Isaiah, one must not move too quickly to this hopeful vision of the future, lest one water down the distinctive witness of Lamentations itself.

2

A few years after that initial encounter with Lamentations I found myself, as a doctoral student at Emory University, looking for a topic for an annual paper (a scholarly paper that all graduate students were required to present to the whole Hebrew Bible department), and I came back to Lamentations, thinking that perhaps there was more to say about its unanswered demand for a response and its relationship to Second Isaiah. As I began to read in the commentaries and monographs on Lamentations and on Second Isaiah, I realized that almost none made the connection that Brueggemann had suggested so off-handedly and that there was indeed more work to be done. A brief but important article by Carol Newsom helped me to think more about the social context of both Lamentations and Second Isaiah and the ideological (in addition to literary and theological) implications of Second Isaiah's quoting of Lamentations, and Alan Mintz's very fine book *Hurban: Responses to Catastrophe in Hebrew Literature* helped to contextualize both Lamentations and Isaiah within a much broader history of Hebrew literature.[3] The notion that there was a strong, unmet demand for a response in the book of Lamentations led me to wonder if there might not be other attempts, beside Second Isaiah, to address this lack in the history of interpretation. When I found compelling attempts to represent a divine response in the targum to Lamentations (an early translation of the Hebrew text into Aramaic, with substantial expansions) and in the midrash to Lamentations (a compendium of traditional Jewish interpretation), I decided that I had enough to pursue the topic for my annual paper.

Two other elements went into that first paper on Lamentations. First, I had been reading works in post-Holocaust Jewish thought—that is, literary, ethical, and theological reflection on the implications of the Holocaust—and I had been thinking about how such reflections might be brought to bear on biblical interpretation, which to that point had not been done much.[4] Second, I had been

---

3. Carol Newsom, "Response to Norman K. Gottwald, 'Social Class and Ideology in Isaiah 40–55,'" *Semeia* 58 (1992): 73–78; Alan Mintz, *Hurban: Responses to Catastrophe in Hebrew Literature* (New York: Columbia University Press, 1984).

4. See Emil L. Fackenheim, *The Jewish Bible after the Holocaust* (Bloomington: Indiana University Press, 1990).

reading in literary theory and its implications for biblical studies and around this time came across Robert Detweiler's article "Overliving" in an issue of the journal *Semeia* on "Post-structuralism as Exegesis."[5] I found Detweiler's piece to be brilliant and utterly fascinating and still recommend it heartily. In a response to the other articles in the volume, Detweiler picks up on the term "survival" (literally "over-living") as a way of characterizing poststructuralist literary theory and the contemporary practice of interpretation. Walter Benjamin had used the metaphor of survival to think about translation in his essay from 1923, "The Task of the Translator," which had a great influence on European and North American literary theory after appearing in Benjamin's collected works in German in 1955 and then in English translation in 1968.[6] Jacques Derrida picked the metaphor up from Benjamin and ran with it in one of his most in-depth engagements with the Bible, "Des Tours de Babel," which was reprinted in the *Semeia* issue to which Detweiler responded.[7] Detweiler argues that since, in the second half of the twentieth century, the idea of humans actually destroying more or less the entire world has for the first time become thinkable, the trope of survival has become pervasive, even in literary theory, and that poststructuralist literary theory functions "as an intensified negative capability: keeping on, living on, as if we had a future." Detweiler ruminates on the possible literal renderings of the term: "Survival. Sur-vival. *Überleben*. Overliving. To live above. To live again."[8] Thus my interests in post-Holocaust theology (including the testimony of "survivors"), contemporary literary theory, and the book of Lamentations began to coalesce around the notion of "survival." Adding Derrida's reflections on survival (French *survie*) as "afterlife" or "more life," my fundamental approach to the book of Lamentations began to take shape. To my mind, Lamentations was, at a fundamental level, survivor literature; that is, it was written in the wake of and in response to the catastrophic historical event of the fall of Jerusalem and the destruction of the temple. At the same time, it was a book that the reader had to survive, in the sense of being a fairly relentless presentation of suffering, not at all pleasant to read and barely ever hopeful. Moreover, I began to think of the responses to the book that I had found in Second Isaiah, the targum, and the midrash, as "survivals" of the book, in the sense of part of its cultural and religious "afterlife," but also as later texts that allowed the original to survive by calling attention to it and answering it, but ultimately sending the reader back to the original book itself. The annual

---

5. Robert Detweiler, "Overliving," *Semeia* 54 (1991): 239–55.

6. Walter Benjamin, "The Task of the Translator," in idem, *Illuminations* (trans. Harry Zohn; New York: Schocken, 1968), 70–82.

7. Jacques Derrida, "Des Tours de Babel," *Semeia* 54 (1991): 3–34; repr. from *Difference in Translation* (ed. Joseph F. Graham; Ithaca, N.Y.: Cornell University Press, 1985).

8. Detweiler, "Overliving," 240.

graduate student paper that resulted was called "Surviving Lamentations," and it eventually appeared in article form under the same title.[9]

3

The next step, I suppose, seemed obvious to me: if the book of Lamentations, by its very unfinishedness, had generated responses or "survivals" in Second Isaiah, the targum, and the midrash, might there not be still later examples of this survival? My own reading of Lamentations focused quite closely on the figure of Zion from Lam 1 and 2, since it was her intense concern for the fate of her children (which, in the governing metaphor, represent the population of the city of Jerusalem) that seemed most to affect later readers. Thus, for example, although the verse in Isa 49 that gives God's response quotes from the end of chapter 5, long after Zion's voice has disappeared from the book to be replaced by the communal first person, it nevertheless attributes the words to Zion, and in answering it addresses Zion's central concern for the survival of her children:

> The children of your bereavement
> shall yet say in your hearing,
> "The place is too crowded for me,
> make room for me to settle." (49:20)

Likewise, the targum and midrash focused their exegetical and theological energies on those points in the first two chapters where Zion pleaded with God for the lives of her children. But, as I looked at contemporary treatments of Lamentations by scholars and theologians, it seemed that Zion was largely neglected, that interpreters were anxious to move on to Lam 3, where the voice of personified Zion is replaced by the voice of a suffering man, possibly presented as the voice of a defeated soldier. So, in addition to asking whether there might be a continuing tradition of responses to Lamentations that focus on Zion and attempt to provide a response to her that focuses on her threatened or missing children, I also wanted to explore how and when that tradition began to be replaced by a more narrow focus on the suffering man of Lam 3. I was fortunate to be able to pursue these latter questions during a year spent at the Oxford Centre for Hebrew and Jewish Studies, where under the tutelage of Philip Alexander and, especially, Jeremy Schonfield I was able to continue my research in the history of Jewish interpretation of the book of Lamentations and to produce a draft of what would eventually become my Ph.D. dissertation.

I discovered that the next stage in the "survival" of Lamentations and the children of Zion—after the targum and the midrash—was to be found in the

---

9. Tod Linafelt, "Surviving Lamentations," *HBT* 17 (1995): 45–61.

medieval Hebrew poetry of Eleazar ben Kallir. These elegiac poems (or *kinot*), which had become regular liturgical readings for the fast day of Tisha b'Av (or the ninth of Av, the day of mourning for the destruction of both the First and Second Temples), emphasize the figure of Zion and the children she has lost but are focused more on the act and process of mourning and less on the restoration of the children than are the earlier responses to Lamentations, which strove to imagine a time of restoration. Still, by addressing God directly and advocating on behalf of Zion and her children, the poems clearly continued the interpretive trajectory I had identified. But it seemed that this trajectory—with its focus on personified Zion and its willingness to challenge God on the question of the deaths of her children—died out in the modern period. I ended up arguing that there are three primary reasons for the movement away from Zion and her children: (1) a masculine bias toward the male figure of Lam 3; (2) a Christian bias toward the suffering of this male figure, based on a perceived similarity to the figure of Jesus Christ (passages from Lam 3 are traditionally read on Good Friday); and (3) a broader emphasis in both Christian and Jewish interpretation on reconciliation with God rather than confrontation, and the suffering man of Lam 3 fits this emphasis much more easily than the demanding, challenging voice of Zion in Lam 1 and 2.

One place where Zion seemed to me to have survived, albeit somewhat incognito, was in a contemporary short story by Cynthia Ozick, "The Shawl," where several thematic similarities as well as fairly detailed verbal correspondences suggested that the central character Rosa was a post-Holocaust "survival" of the figure of Zion.[10] Lacking the buoyancy of Second Isaiah, the promised future restoration of the targum and midrash, the advocacy of the liturgical poems, and above all any sense of God as addressee or respondent, Ozick's story represents a post-Holocaust revision of the figure of Zion. As such it reminds us that the book of Lamentations itself may be taken as an ancient example of survivor literature, a literature that is more about the *expression* of suffering than the meaning behind it, more about the contingencies of *survival* than the abstractions of sin and guilt, and more about *protest* as a religious posture than capitulation or confession.

The dissertation, under the invaluable direction of Carol Newsom, took shape, then, around these examples from the history of interpretation of the book of Lamentations, with individual chapters on my reading of the book as survivor literature, Second Isaiah, the targum to Lamentations, the midrash on Lamentations, the liturgical poetry of Kallir, and Ozick's story "The Shawl." The dissertation was accepted in the spring of 1997 and was then revised and pub-

---

10. "The Shawl" was first published in the *New Yorker* magazine in 1980. It was reprinted, along with the novella "Rosa," in Cynthia Ozick, *The Shawl: A Story and Novella* (New York: Knopf, 1989).

lished in book form as *Surviving Lamentations: Catastrophe, Lament, and Protest in the Afterlife of a Biblical Book.*[11]

4

What would I do differently if I were to take on the project now? Certainly one thing that is lacking in the book is any in-depth analysis of the poetics of the biblical book, that is, how it works *as poetry.* My initial draft of the study was completed a decade ago, and at the time I had only a vague sense of the importance of poetic form and technique to interpretation. Like so many biblical scholars trained to take a hermeneutic approach to reading the Bible (in other words, an approach focused on the drawing out of *meaning*), my tendency was to focus on thematic and theological issues. Because Brueggemann had introduced me early on to the "rhetorical criticism" of James Muilenburg, I did not do too badly on structure and genre. And because my focus was on the figure of Zion, who breaks into the speech of the voice that opens the book (often identified as the voice of the poet, although that is clearly too simple a view), I had perforce to treat the issues of voice and tone in the poetry. But even though I knew, of course, the basic consensus of how the biblical poetic line works, as I look back on the published version of the book I am embarrassed to see how little use I made of even that basic knowledge, let alone any sustained analysis of the ways in which the poet or poets of Lamentations were both indebted to and pushed beyond the centuries-long tradition of ancient Hebrew poetry that they had inherited. We are fortunate to have now a very fine treatment of the poetics of the book of Lamentations in F. W. Dobbs-Allsopp's commentary in the Interpretation series.[12] Still, it seems to me that there is much work that remains to be done on the poetry of Lamentations, interpreted precisely *as poetry.*

My sense is that we biblical scholars are just now hitting our stride as literary interpreters, and if one were to bring to bear on the book not only training in biblical studies and ancient Near Eastern texts and religion but also a literary sensibility shaped by wide and deep reading in lyric poetry, I have no doubt that the book of Lamentations would yield even more of its artfulness in shaping of grief. It would be a task well worth undertaking.

---

11. Tod Linafelt, *Surviving Lamentations: Catastrophe, Lament, and Protest in the Afterlife of a Biblical Book* (Chicago: University of Chicago Press, 2000).

12. F. W. Dobbs-Allsopp, *Lamentations* (IBC; Louisville: Westminster John Knox, 2002).

Part 2
Biblical Lament:
Communal, Penitential, Individual ...

Lament and the Arts of Resistance: Public and Hidden Transcripts in Lamentations 5

Robert Williamson Jr.

In Israel's laments before Yhwh, issues of power are always at play. Walter Brueggemann has attuned us to this dynamic:

> [Lament] shifts the calculus and *redresses the distribution of power* between the two parties, so that the petitionary party is taken seriously and the God who is addressed is newly engaged in the crisis in a way that puts God at risk. As the lesser, petitionary party (the psalm speaker) is legitimated, so the unmitigated supremacy of the greater party (God) is questioned, and God is made available to the petitioner.[1]

What Brueggemann notes here is that lament is essentially political discourse, brought to voice within a set of power relations in which Yhwh is the dominant power and Israel the subordinate. Lament functions to redress the balance of power between Yhwh and Israel by allowing Israel to express complaint openly before the deity, who is presumed to respond with appropriate action:

> The basis for the conclusion that the petitioner is taken seriously and legitimately granted power in the relation is that the speech of the petitioner is heard, valued, and transmitted as serious speech.[2]

James C. Scott's studies of discourse within the context of power relations indicate, however, that the dynamics of lament may be somewhat more complicated than Brueggemann suggests.[3] Far from always constituting "serious

---

1. Walter Brueggemann, "The Costly Loss of Lament," in idem, *The Psalms and the Life of Faith* (ed. Patrick D. Miller; Minneapolis: Fortress, 1995), 101.

2. Ibid.

3. James C. Scott, *Domination and the Arts of Resistance: Hidden Transcripts* (New Haven: Yale University Press, 1990), passim.

speech," the discourse of subordinates before their dominant authorities, and thus the discourse of Israel before Yhwh, typically involves elements of ritualized public performance, dissembling, flattery, evasion, and even resistance, so that sincerity of speech and response cannot be presumed, particularly when the dominant wields authority with excessive violence, as is the case in the book of Lamentations.[4]

Employing Scott's categories of "public and hidden transcripts" in the speech of subordinates before the powers who dominate them, I will argue that the communal lament of Lam 5 evinces tactics of evasion and resistance such as those Scott describes. In particular, the communal lament of Lam 5:1–21 presents Israel's "public transcript," while Lam 5:22 breaks the bounds of the communal lament and reveals Israel's "hidden transcript." Finally, I will suggest that even within the communal lament itself there exist subtle instances of resistance, "infrapolitics" in Scott's terms, carefully disguised to avoid detection by the dominant power. Lamentations 5 as a whole thus reveals itself to be an expression of resistance to Yhwh's excessively wrathful exercise of authority following the destruction of Jerusalem.

Public and Hidden Transcripts

In his study *Domination and the Arts of Resistance*, James C. Scott examines the discourse between subordinate groups and their dominant authorities, concluding that such speech almost invariably follows certain polite patterns designed to appeal to the self-interest of the dominant. Scott refers to this pattern of speaking as the subordinate group's "public transcript."[5]

> I mean the public performance required of those subject to elaborate and systematic forms of social subordination: the worker to the boss, the tenant or sharecropper to the landlord, the serf to the lord, the slave to the master, the untouchable to the Brahmin, a member of a subject race to one of the dominant race. With rare, but significant, exceptions the public performance of the subordinate will, out of prudence, fear, and the desire to curry favor, be shaped to appeal to the expectations of the powerful.[6]

Analyzing oral histories from a range of subordinate groups, Scott concludes that all such groups, to one degree or another, employ public transcripts. Further, "the public transcript, when it is not positively misleading, is unlikely to tell the whole story about power relations."[7]

---

4. Ibid., 3.
5. Ibid., 2.
6. Ibid.
7. Ibid.

Behind this mask of the "public transcript" resides a second discourse, which Scott calls the "hidden transcript." It is normally employed when the subordinate is "offstage" and out of earshot of the dominant. "Every subordinate group creates, out of its ordeal, a 'hidden transcript' that represents a critique of power spoken behind the back of the dominant."[8] The hidden transcript contains the subordinate's frustration and anger, which cannot be expressed publicly for fear of reprisal.

> For most bondsmen through history, whether untouchables, slaves, serfs, captives, minorities held in contempt, the trick to survival...has been to swallow one's bile, choke back one's rage, and conquer the impulse to physical violence. It is this systematic *frustration of reciprocal action* in relations of domination which, I believe, helps us understand much of the content of the hidden transcript.[9]

Since the hidden transcript develops in response to domination and contains the feelings attendant to excessive and arbitrary abuse of authority, it tends to be more intense as the conditions become more severe.[10]

Eventually the hidden transcript may overwhelm the ability of the subordinate to contain it and burst into the public sphere. Scott cites an example from an oral history of the antebellum U.S. south in which a normally demure black slave named Aggy witnessed the unjustified beating of her daughter by a white slave owner. Unable or unwilling to withhold her anger any longer, Aggy shouted a stream of vitriolic invectives before her white governess, a representative of the dominant authority: "Oh Lor! Hasten de day when de blows, an de bruises, and de aches an de pains, shall come to de white folks, an de buzzards shall eat dem as dey's dead in de streets."[11] In this speech, Aggy's hidden transcript burst the bounds of her quietly subservient public face and emerged into the public sphere.

Communal Lament as Public Transcript

While Scott's theory of hidden and public transcripts may give us insight into the patterns of speech between Israel and YHWH in Lam 5, it requires some nuancing when transferred into that context. As it stands, Scott's theory pertains to situations of domination in which the legitimate complaint of the subordinate is excluded from the public sphere. In the dynamic between Aggy and the white landowner, for instance, there was no mechanism by which Aggy could forthrightly address

---

8. Ibid., xii.
9. Ibid., 37.
10. Ibid., 27, emphasis original.
11. Ibid., 5.

her grievances to the one who held power over her. As a result, her feelings were suppressed and, over time, generated a powerfully emotive hidden transcript. The same would seem to be the case, to varying degrees, in the other situations Scott addresses: worker and boss, serf and lord, untouchable and Brahmin, and so forth. In these instances, the expected posture of the subordinate to the dominant is one of polite deference with the attendant suppression of complaint, particularly that directed against the dominant.

The relationship between Israel and YHWH presents something of a different case, with a possibility of legitimated complaint, as Brueggemann suggests above.[12] Understood within the context of the Deuteronomic covenant, the relationship between YHWH and Israel takes the form of a covenant between suzerain and vassal or, more generally, between client and patron.[13] While the relationship exhibits a clear power deferential between the two parties, there is also a degree of reciprocity, with the patron providing protection in exchange for the client's obedience. In the case of Deuteronomy, YHWH promises Israel blessings in exchange for covenant fidelity (e.g., Deut 28:1–14). Within this reciprocal arrangement, Israel claims the freedom to declare grievances publicly to YHWH, at least within certain bounds, and seems to expect YHWH to act on its behalf.

It is this relative freedom of expression on the part of the subordinate that is unexpected according to Scott's model, necessitating a reexamination of his category "public transcript" for the case of ancient Israel. In Scott's model, the public transcript of the subordinate consists primarily of deferential praise addressed to the dominant. This type of public transcript does exist in the worship life of Israel in the form of the communal praise hymn, but in Israel's case it is not the only available public transcript. An additional form of the public transcript is the communal lament, which provides a sanctioned structure through which Israel may express complaint in the public sphere.[14] Indeed, communal lament not only permits legitimated complaint but by its very nature requires it. The typical communal lament comprises five elements: address and introductory petition, complaint, turn toward God, petition, and vow of praise.[15] The lament is dominated by the expression of petition and grievance, including complaints directed against the deity.[16] There does not seem to be complete freedom of expression,

12. Brueggemann, "Costly Loss of Lament," 101–2.

13. The political paradigm of the covenant envelope of Deuteronomy is influenced, at least in part, by ancient Near Eastern suzerain-vassal treaties, such as that of Esarhaddon (ANET, 534–41).

14. The individual psalms of thanksgiving and lament, couched in terms of the individual's address to the deity, do not as clearly pertain to a discussion of public discourse.

15. Claus Westermann, Praise and Lament in the Psalms (trans. Keith R. Crim and Richard N. Soulen; Atlanta: Knox, 1981), 170. The corresponding verses in Lam 5 are: (1) 5:1; (2) 5:2–18, 20; (3) 5:19; (4) 5:21; (5) (absent).

16. Ibid., 176–78.

however, as communal laments conform to a fairly stereotypical range of expression in terms of both form and content, including certain prescribed elements of deference as listed above. Thus, the communal lament represents a public transcript that allows for the expression of complaint to the dominant party, within certain bounds and following particular modes of address. This sort of legitimated public complaint may function to eliminate, or at least reduce, the intensity of the hidden transcript by helping to maintain the balance of power between YHWH and Israel.

However, the relative reciprocity of power in the client-patron relationship depends on the continued obedience of the lesser party, as Deut 28 makes clear. The blessings promised to Israel "will come upon you and overtake you *if you will obey* YHWH your God" (Deut 28:2). But should the covenant be violated, YHWH threatens to afflict Israel with "disaster, panic, and reproach ... until you perish quickly on account of your wicked deeds by which you have forsaken me" (28:20). If the covenant is violated, YHWH becomes a violent dominant of the sort Scott describes, wielding power mercilessly against the hapless subordinate in a series of curses detailed in Deut 28:15–68 (cf. Lev 26:22–41). In this circumstance, the people may voice their complaint via the communal lament, but YHWH need not listen, as the covenant relationship has been violated. With reciprocity thus denied, the lament no longer functions to redress the balance of power between YHWH and Israel, and Israel's complaint is no longer legitimated. In such situations, we may expect the formation of a hidden transcript, which may be concealed beneath the public transcript of the communal lament.

PUBLIC AND HIDDEN TRANSCRIPT IN LAMENTATIONS 5

The relationship between YHWH and Israel in the book of Lamentations is of this second type, with YHWH depicted not as benefactor but as a scorned patron enacting covenant curses on the disobedient subordinate.[17] Each of the speakers in the first four chapters names YHWH as the agent of destruction, beginning with Daughter Zion:

> From on high [YHWH] sent fire; it went deep into my bones;
>   he spread a net for my feet; he turned me back;
>   he has left me stunned, faint all day long. (Lam 1:13)

The narrator likewise describes YHWH as a divine avenger. YHWH is an "enemy" who has "bent his bow with his right hand set like a foe" (2:4). YHWH is the one who "has destroyed Israel" (2:5). The speaker of Lam 3 delivers the most searing

---

17. Adele Berlin, *Lamentations: A Commentary* (OTL; Louisville: Westminster John Knox, 2002), 21–22.

description of Yhwh as divine destroyer, the agent of Israel's pain and destruction. He depicts Yhwh as a "bear lying in ambush," as a "lion in hiding" (3:10), and as a divine warrior who has "bent his bow and has made me the target of [his] arrow" (3:12).

At the end of a relentless, four-chapter litany of suffering and destruction in the voices of these three figures, the communal voice finally takes up its lament in Lam 5. In this poem, the model of Yhwh as the scorned suzerain is brought to the fore via a number of intertexts with Deut 28, as Berlin has shown.[18] In particular, the description of the ancestral land (נחלה) turned over to strangers and foreigners (5:2) echoes the warning of Deut 28:30–33. The references to heat and famine (Lam 5:9–10) recall the threats of "heat and drought" in Deut 28:22. The shameful treatment of the young men and elders (Lam 5:12–13) seems to fulfill the curse of Deut 28:50, which describes "a grim-faced nation showing no respect to the old or favor to the young."[19] Accordingly, the violence and disgrace that have befallen the people of Jerusalem are understood as Yhwh's punishments for Judah's breach of the covenant.

Further, Lam 5 depicts Yhwh as inflicting upon Israel not only great suffering but also severe public humiliation. This observation is important because, as Scott suggests, it is ultimately the subordinate's experience of *degradation*, even more than of suffering, that is at the root of the hidden transcript.[20] He argues that "indignities are the seedbed of the anger, indignation, frustration, and swallowed bile that nurture the hidden transcript" and that "the experience of humiliation is nearly always far more injurious when it is inflicted before an audience."[21] Notably, the entire complaint of Lam 5 is constructed to draw attention to the degree of the community's public humiliation (חרפה), beginning with the introductory petition:

> Remember, Yhwh, what has happened to us
> Look and see our disgrace [חרפה]. (Lam 5:1)

The entire complaint is thus framed as a sustained description of Israel's public disgrace, which is described in stark imagery throughout the lament: women and maidens being raped (5:11), young men being forced to do the work of animals (5:13), princes being hanged from trees for all to see (5:12).

When the communal voice takes up its lament in Lam 5, it thus speaks as a punished and degraded subordinate addressing a dominant it perceives as angry and excessively violent. As Scott has shown, in such dynamics of power, we may expect the presence of a hidden transcript being masked by the public transcript,

---

18. Ibid.
19. Ibid., 116–23.
20. Scott, *Domination and the Arts of Resistance*, 111–15.
21. Ibid., 111, 113.

in this case concealed beneath the communal lament. In order to identify this hidden transcript, we may thus proceed by comparing the form of Lam 5 with the expected form of the communal lament, taking note of the ways in which the communal voice's speech before YHWH in this chapter differs from the "officially sanctioned" form of the public script.

In this regard, Lam 5 evinces three notable digressions from the communal lament form. First, the complaint section (5:2–18, 20) is significantly longer than those of other communal laments relative to the length of the poem as a whole. The communal voice's relentless recitation of its public humiliation so dominates the poem that Westermann suggests that "the balance has been so radically disrupted that we really have to speak of a transformation of the form."[22] Second, the turn toward God in verse 19 is notably brief compared to the complaint that precedes, ending abruptly after only one verse.[23] It is immediately followed by a reversion to complaint in verse 20, effectively negating the turn toward God altogether. Finally, the poem completely lacks any vow of praise following the petition. This element is instead replaced by verse 22, which accuses YHWH of excessive anger and abandonment: "You [YHWH] have utterly rejected us and are excessively wrathful against us" (5:22). Together these digressions shift the balance of the poem from praise and trust in YHWH toward the expression of pain, disgrace, and ultimately of divine rejection in 5:22. This pattern is further amplified by comparison with the form of the Mesopotamian city lament.[24] Here again Lam 5 lacks a central element of the genre: a depiction of the return of the gods and the restoration of the city. In its place we again encounter verse 22, which, far from depicting the god's return, instead declares YHWH's angry and willful rejection of the city.

Lamentations 5:22 thus represents the culmination of the poem's digressions from the form of both the communal lament and the city lament. In both cases, it appears as speech "out of bounds," which does not belong to the sanctioned public transcript. Indeed, as Westermann notes, Lam 5:22 "runs contrary to the whole tradition of the concluding verses of the communal lament."[25] Amplifying the contradictory nature of the verse relative to the rest of the poem is the

---

22. Westermann, *Praise and Lament*, 174.

23. Delbert Hillers likewise notes that "Lam 5 is remarkable … for the relatively short appeal for help and the correspondingly long description of the nation's trouble" (*Lamentations* [AB 7A; 2nd ed.; Garden City, N.Y.: Doubleday, 1972], 162).

24. On the Mesopotamian city lament in relation to Lam 5, see F. W. Dobbs-Allsopp, *Weep, O Daughter of Zion: A Study of the City-Lament Genre in the Hebrew Bible* (BibOr 44; Rome: Pontifical Biblical Institute, 1993), 30–156; idem, *Lamentations* (IBC; Louisville: Westminster John Knox, 2002), 6–12. The relevance of the Mesopotamian lament for biblical laments, however, remains a debated point. See, e.g., Berlin, *Lamentations*, 22–25.

25. Claus Westermann, *Lamentations: Issues and Interpretation* (Minneapolis: Fortress, 1994), 217.

introductory particle כִּי אִם, which in this context casts the final verse in contrast to what precedes, making 5:22 an abrupt negation of the plea for restoration in 5:21:[26]

> YHWH, cause us to return to you.
>> Let us return.
> Renew our days like days of old.
> But rather [than restoring us],
> you have utterly rejected us
>> and are excessively wrathful against us. (5:21–22)

For some, this sudden disjunction has seemed too severe. Robert Gordis, for one, argues that "the alleged matter-of-fact statement [of 5:22] contradicts the cry of v. 20 ... and is totally incompatible with the plea of v. 22 [*sic*], 'Turn us unto You, turn us back to You, etc.' "[27]

Scott's theory of public and hidden transcripts, however, suggests that such a sharp disjunction need not be dismissed as an interpretive problem. Indeed, verse 22 *does* contradict verse 21, precisely because it breaks the expected form of the communal lament to reveal the community's hidden transcript in the public sphere. The twenty-one preceding verses are a restrained expression of the anger and resentment arising from the community's public degradation and humiliation at the hands of YHWH, choked back to fit within the publicly acceptable transcript. Finally, however, the communal voice can restrain itself no more. With the abrupt and contradictory statement of verse 22, it breaks the bounds of the expected public transcript and, in utter contradiction to its previous speech, declares its

---

26. The history of scholarship has been reviewed by Robert Gordis, "The Conclusion of the Book of Lamentations (5:22)," *JBL* 93 (1974): 289–93; and, more recently, by Tod Linafelt, "The Refusal of a Conclusion in the Book of Lamentations," *JBL* 120 (2001): 340–43. Of the six proposals reviewed by Linafelt, three are clearly to be rejected: (1) inserting a negative into the verse; (2) interpreting the verse as a question introduced by "or"; and (3) rendering the verbs in the pluperfect. Linafelt also rightly rejects the translation of כִּי אִם as "unless," as all other instances are preceded by a negative clause. Three plausible solutions remain: (1) translating as an asseverative, as do the LXX and Peshitta; this usage is attested both in oath formulas (2 Kgs 5:20) and independently (1 Sam 21:6); (2) Linafelt's own solution, which takes כִּי אִם as introducing a protasis with elliptical apodosis ("For if you have truly rejected us, raging bitterly against us..."); and (3) rendering כִּי אִם in the restrictive sense, connoting a reversal or restriction of what precedes (see Waltke-O'Connor §39.3.5d; Joüon-Muraoka §172c). Linafelt rejects this solution as applicable only when כִּי אִם "preceded by a negative, either explicit or implied." However, כִּי אִם has the restrictive sense without a preceding negative in 1 Kgs 20:6 and, more clearly, in Num 24:22. In my view, all three of these latter positions are tenable grammatically, and the choice among them is a matter of interpretation.

27. Robert Gordis, *The Song of Songs and Lamentations: A Study, Modern Translation and Commentary* (rev. ed.; New York: Ktav, 1974), 197–98. Where Gordis refers to "the plea of v. 22" he intends v. 21, as the quotation makes clear.

private, hidden transcript in the public sphere, "But rather [than restoring us], you have utterly rejected us and are excessively wrathful against us!"

LAMENT AND INFRAPOLITICS

According to Scott, awareness of a subordinate group's *hidden* transcript demands a corresponding reexamination of its *public* transcript. Recalling the story of Aggy, the black cook who spoke her hidden transcript to her white governess, Scott observes:

> Aggy's hidden transcript is at complete odds with her public transcript of quiet obedience.... Whatever such an investigation would tell us, this glimpse itself is sufficient to make any naive interpretation of Aggy's previous and subsequent public acts of deference impossible.[28]

Our access to Israel's hidden transcript in Lam 5:22 likewise suggests that we not accept the public transcript of Lam 5:1–21 at face value.

Scott argues that, upon close scrutiny, a subordinate group's public transcript almost invariably contains covert elements of the hidden transcript that are inserted into the public discourse by the subordinate but disguised so as to avoid detection by the dominant. These insertions serve as acts of resistance by which the subordinate can subtly undermine the public transcript while maintaining the appearance of supporting it. Scott's term for this veiled resistance is "infrapolitics," which he describes as "a partly sanitized, ambiguous, and coded version of the hidden transcript ... always present in the public discourse of subordinate groups."[29] Examples of infrapolitical techniques in Scott's analyses include "rumor, gossip, folktales, jokes, songs, rituals, codes, and euphemisms—a good part of the folk culture of subordinate groups."[30] While the forms of infrapolitics in Lam 5 differ from those Scott adduces, infrapolitical tactics may nonetheless be identified.

1. The first infrapolitical tactic apparent in Lam 5 is the use of *intertextual allusions* to give apparently straightforward laments a subtle edge of critique regarding YHWH's exercise of authority. On the one hand, these allusions serve their surface function of reminding YHWH of promises made but not upheld; on the other hand they betray "a hint of the reproach that he has not kept his word."[31] As an example of this type of intertextual resistance, we might consider 5:2, in which the communal voice laments:

---

28. Scott, *Domination and the Arts of Resistance*, 6.
29. Ibid., 19; see also 183–201.
30. Ibid., 19.
31. Iain W. Provan, *Lamentations* (NCBC; Grand Rapids: Eerdmans, 1991), 127.

Our inheritance has been turned over to strangers [נחלתנו נהפכה לזרים]
[and] our homes to foreigners [בתינו לנכרים].

In light of the hidden transcript's claim that YHWH has rejected Israel (5:22), the term נחלה might be construed as functioning multivalently. It mundanely refers, of course, to the actual property that Israel has lost to foreigners. However, it may also make a more subtle connection with the failure of YHWH's promise to maintain the land as an "inheritance" (נחלה) for Israel (see Deut 4:38, 25:19, 26:1).[32] Other intertextual allusions in Lam 5 may serve a similar function. For example, the statement in 5:5 that "we are given no rest [לא הונח לנו]" is most obviously a complaint about living conditions in Jerusalem. However, it may also establish an intertextual connection with YHWH's promise in Deut 12:10, "[YHWH] will give you rest [הניח לכם]," again calling attention to YHWH's failure to maintain the covenant.[33]

2. A second infrapolitical tactic may be evident in the use of the *apparently contradictory statements* of 5:7 and 5:16 in assessing the community's culpability for violating the covenant. In the first statement, the communal voice seems to place responsibility on the sin of its ancestors:

Our ancestors sinned. They are no longer [אבותינו חטאו אינם].
We bear their iniquities [אנחנו עונתיהם סבלנו]. (5:7)

However, in 5:16 the community seems to accept its own responsibility, exclaiming "Woe to us for we have sinned [אוי נא לנו כי חטאנו]." The resulting presentation of wrongdoing and responsibility is "fundamentally tensive," with the contradictory statements of the two verses defying resolution.[34] From the perspective of infrapolitics, we might suggest that this tensiveness is a tactic. The ambiguity allows the communal voice to protest its own innocence (5:7) while appearing to adhere to the "officially sanctioned" interpretation that its suffering is a legitimate punishment for wrongdoing (5:16).

3. A third possible infrapolitical tactic in Lam 5 is *juxtaposition*, by which the communal voice appears to undermine the turn toward God (5:19) by immediately contradicting it (5:20). As I have noted above, this turn toward God is notably short in comparison with the extended complaint section that precedes it, and it seems to follow a highly stereotyped formula.[35]

---

32. Hillers presses the intertextual allusion somewhat further by noting that the sequence of "land ... houses ... waters" in Lam 5:2–4 mirrors the sequence in Deut 6:10–11 (*Lamentations*, 103).

33. Provan, *Lamentations*, 124. See also Deut 12:10; 25:19; 2 Sam 7:1, 11.

34. Dobbs-Allsopp, *Lamentations*, 145–46.

35. Westermann likewise suggests that in this context the praise is "rather reserved," "not spoken with straightforward jubilation," and betrays "a note of bitterness." (*Lamentations*, 216).

You, O Y<small>HWH</small> , reign forever [אתה יחוח לעולם תשב].
Your throne for generation upon generation [כסאך לדר ודר]. (5:19)

After only this one formulaic verse, the communal voice immediately returns to lament, "Why have you forgotten us continually? Why have you abandoned us for many days?" (5:20). The implication of the two verses taken together is that Y<small>HWH</small> may indeed reign forever, but if so, it will be as a forgetful and forsaking deity. The tactic of juxtaposition may thus allow the communal voice to maintain the expected element of the turn toward God while simultaneously undermining and even critiquing it.

4. Juxtaposition, however, is not the only tactic by which the communal voice seems to undercut the turn toward God. Brent A. Strawn notes that the syntactical construction of Lam 5:19 may reveal a more pronounced instance of resistance through *double entendre*.[36] Strawn suggests that כסאך might be understood as an adverbial accusative describing the manner of Y<small>HWH</small>'s sitting.[37] Interpreting in this manner would yield:

You, O Y<small>HWH</small>, sit forever;
On your throne for generation upon generation.

If we accept Strawn's suggestion, the double entendre of this verse is pronounced indeed. Where it might at first be read as an affirmation of the enduring nature of Y<small>HWH</small>'s reign, under closer scrutiny it also admits of the interpretation that Y<small>HWH</small> is a god who sits, perpetually doing nothing.

This latter sense is further emphasized by an intertextual comparison with the nearly identical formulation of Ps 102:

But you, Y<small>HWH</small>, are enthroned forever [אתה יחוח לעולם תשב];
your name (is) for generation upon generation [זכרך לדר ודר]. (Ps 102:13 [Eng 12])

The second verse of the psalm's turn toward God, absent in Lam 5, then depicts Y<small>HWH</small> as arising to restore Jerusalem:

You will rise up [תקום] and have compassion on Zion,
for it is time to favor it;
the appointed time has come. (Ps 102:14 [13]; N<small>RSV</small>)

---

36. Brent A. Strawn, personal communication.
37. On the use of the adverbial accusative, see Waltke-O'Connor, §10.2.2; Joüon-Muraoka, §126h.

Such a depiction of Yʜwʜ "arising" on Israel's behalf is in fact fairly frequent in communal laments, appearing in Pss 44:27 (26) and 74:22 as the communal voice's final plea for restoration:

> Rise up [קוּמָה]! Support us!
> And redeem us for the sake of your faithfulness. (Ps 44:27 [26])

> Rise up [קוּמָה], O God! Plead your case!
> Remember your disgrace because of fools all day long. (Ps 74:22)

In contrast, the communal voice of Lam 5 betrays no hope that Yʜwʜ will arise from the throne; rather, Yʜwʜ sits unceasingly, failing to act on Israel's behalf. Thus, while Lam 5:19 at first gives the appearance of a turn toward Yʜwʜ, closer analysis may reveal a double entendre disavowing Yʜwʜ's willingness to arise on Zion's behalf.

RESISTANCE AND THE RESTORATION OF DIGNITY

The observation that other communal laments such as Pss 44 and 74 end with a plea for Yʜwʜ to arise and restore Jerusalem draws our attention once again to the distinctiveness of the final verse of Lam 5: "But rather [than restoring us], you have utterly rejected us and are excessively wrathful against us." While similar statements do appear in other communal laments, they occur in significantly different rhetorical positions. For example, in Ps 44 the communal voice opens by recounting the ways that Yʜwʜ has acted on Israel's behalf in the past. Then the communal voice turns to complaint, opening with a statement reminiscent of Lam 5:22, "But you have rejected us and abased us" (Ps 44:9a). The psalm continues with an extended account of Yʜwʜ's rejection of Israel. At the end of the lament, however, this recitation of Yʜwʜ's rejection reveals itself to have been part of a rhetorical strategy intended to move Yʜwʜ to action: "Rouse yourself! … Awake! … Rise up! … Redeem us!" (Ps 44:23–26). A similar strategy is evident in Ps 74.

Lamentations 5:22, however, presents quite a different case, seeming to serve the *opposite* rhetorical purpose of these other statements. Rather than providing a motivation for Yʜwʜ to restore Jerusalem, Lam 5:22 *undermines* the plea for restoration. It is this aspect of the verse that has led Westermann to comment that it is "contrary to the whole tradition of the concluding verses of the communal lament."[38] As I have argued, the poem's final verse serves as a dramatic and dangerously public articulation of the hidden transcript before Yʜwʜ. As such, it does not properly belong to the communal lament, but is instead an utterance after the fact. Indeed, the verse stands outside of the rhetorical frame

---

38. Westermann, *Lamentations*, 217.

of the communal lament, which is introduced by the threefold imperative of 5:1 ("Remember! ... Look! ... See!") and completed by the nearly identical structure of 5:21 ("Return! ... Let us return! ... Renew!"). Verse 22, the public articulation of the hidden transcript, is thus unexpected, erupting after the lament's conclusion, as if the communal voice did not mean to speak it but could not refrain.

I do not mean to suggest, however, that Lam 5:22 is anything less than integral to the poem as a whole. Indeed, the twenty-two-verse structure of the poem, which seems to reflect the acrostic structures of the first four chapters of the book, demands the final verse; the poem could not be complete without it. What I intend, rather, is that the poem as a whole consists of two parts: the communal lament of 5:1–21 and the "hidden transcript" of 5:22. That the twenty-two-verse poetic structure holds these two parts together suggests that the communal lament alone is inadequate to address the extent of the humiliation and indignity that the community has suffered.

Polite speech, acts of deference, and veiled infrapolitics cannot restore the community's dignity. According to Scott, this can only be achieved by a direct challenge to the dominant power responsible for the degradation:

> To speak of a loss of dignity and status is necessarily to speak of a public loss. It follows, I think, that a public humiliation can be fully reciprocated only with a public revenge. To be publicly dishonored may lead to offstage discourses of dignity and secret rites of revenge, but these can hardly compare, in their capacity to restore one's status, to a public assertion of honor or a public turning of the tables, preferably before the same audience.[39]

The poetic structure of Lam 5 embodies this principle. The communal voice cannot fall silent at the end of the lament in verse 21; the twenty-two-part structure demands that it speak its deeper, hidden truth. With this public speaking of the hidden transcript as a challenge to YHWH's excessively wrathful exercise of authority, Israel claims the possibility of a future. Lamentations offers no guarantee that YHWH will relent and restore Jerusalem. Nonetheless, the book ends with an act of dignity on the part of Israel, a public challenge to the one who has caused its degradation.

My own understanding of hope in Lamentations thus stands in stark contrast to that of interpreters such as Norman Gottwald, who concludes that Israel's future rests in the possibility that YHWH "might turn his anger and be gracious" to "the chastised nation" out of "divine love and mercy which can never be calculated but comes only as a gift."[40] Continuing to submit meekly to YHWH's abusive exercise of

---

39. Scott, *Domination and the Arts of Resistance*, 214–15.

40. Norman K. Gottwald, *Studies in the Book of Lamentations* (SBT 14; Chicago: Allenson, 1954), 99. Johan Renkema similarly suggests that "the poets know of only One who has the power to reverse their fortunes: the very one who afflicted them in the first place, YHWH their

authority would only further degrade Israel. Instead, the community's hope lies in its public resistance to YHWH and its refusal to accept further punishment without challenge. This, I believe, comes close to the sort of redress of power Brueggemann envisions when he writes:

> Where the cry is not voiced, heaven is not moved and history is not initiated. The end is hopelessness. Where the cry is seriously voiced, heaven may answer and earth may have a new chance. The new resolve in heaven and the new possibility on earth depend on the initiation of protest.[41]

The protest of Lam 5, however, breaks the bounds even of the sanctioned complaint of the communal lament. Israel does not protest here in order to move YHWH to respond but rather because the extent of its degradation can no longer be contained. By boldly and publicly stating that YHWH has acted against it with excessive violence and anger, Israel asserts its voice, its selfhood, regardless of the consequences. In the daring honesty of unedited speech, Israel reclaims its dignity, making possible a viable future with YHWH.[42]

---

god" (*Lamentations* [trans. Brian Doyle; Historical Commentary on the Old Testament; Leuven: Peeters, 1998], 622).

41. Brueggemann, "Costly Loss of Lament," 111.

42. A version of this paper was presented to the Lament in Sacred Texts and Cultures Group at the Annual Meeting (SBL) in Washington, D.C., 19 November 2006. The comments of those present have been quite generative for the revised argument presented here. The paper had its genesis in a seminar with Kathleen M. O'Connor, who first showed me the beauty of Lamentations. Walter Brueggemann, John H. Hayes, and Carol A. Newsom each offered insightful critiques that sharpened the argument considerably. In particular, Brent A. Strawn has been a valued conversation partner, consistently pressing my thinking to greater depth. Of course, none besides the author should be held responsible for the arguments advanced here.

The Priceless Gain of Penitence: From Communal Lament to Penitential Prayer in the "Exilic" Liturgy of Israel*

Mark J. Boda

In his 1986 article, "The Costly Loss of Lament," Walter Brueggemann mourns the absence of lament in the contemporary "functioning canon."[1] He claims that the loss of this speech form has serious implications for the religious faith and practice of contemporary communities. It indicates, first of all, the loss of "genuine covenant interaction" because one party in the covenant relationship has either been silenced or restricted to expressions of praise, producing what he calls "yes-men and women." Second, it signals the stifling of discussions of theodicy so that questions of justice cannot be asked and soon become "invisible and illegitimate." According to Brueggemann, the stakes are high, for such stifling on the religious plane will carry over onto the social plane:

> A community of faith that negates laments soon concludes that the hard issues of justice are improper questions to pose at the throne, because the throne seems to be only a place of praise. I believe it thus follows that if justice questions are improper questions at the throne (which is a conclusion drawn through liturgical use), they soon appear to be improper questions in public places, in schools, in hospitals, with the government, and eventually even in the courts. Justice questions disappear into civility and docility.[2]

This concern for what Brueggemann calls *"psychological inauthenticity"* and *"social immobility"* leads him to conclude: "If we care about authenticity and justice, the recovery of these texts is urgent."[3]

---

* An earlier version of this essay appeared as "The Priceless Gain of Penitence: From Communal Lament to Penitential Prayer in the 'Exilic' Liturgy of Israel," *HBT* 25 (2003): 51–75. Reprinted by permission.

1. Walter Brueggemann, "The Costly Loss of Lament," *JSOT* 36 (1986): 57–71.
2. Ibid., 107.
3. Ibid., 111.

The prophetic edge of this article is difficult to ignore. How can one reject this call to authenticity and justice? But is Brueggemann's thesis correct? Do psychological inauthenticity and social immobility necessarily follow from the loss of lament? And is lament the appropriate path to psychological authenticity and social mobility? His conclusions are drawn from interaction between the ancient text and modern psychological/sociological theory, but can these conclusions be demonstrated from the life of the ancient Jewish community?

In this essay we will investigate two forms within the "exilic" liturgy of Judah in which we can trace a transformation in the expression of lament. The purpose of this paper is threefold. Primarily, it will identify and explain transformations in the liturgical responses of the Jewish community to the fall of the kingdom of Judah, in particular, the modification from the expressions found in the book of Lamentations to those found in narrative accounts of the Persian period Jewish community. It will also compare Brueggemann's conclusions with the evidence from the "exilic" liturgy and, finally, taking his lead, draw implications for worship in contemporary faith communities.

1. Penitential Prayer

1.1. Characteristics

Prayers in canonical books depicting the Persian period Jewish community reveal the emergence of a new form of expression to God for the community that has experienced or is continuing to experience the discipline of God due to sin (Ezra 9; Neh 1; 9; Dan 9; cf. Ps 106).[4] The purpose of this type of prayer, which will be

---

4. This first section on penitential prayer is a synthesis of my larger work on the genre; see Mark J. Boda, *Praying the Tradition: The Origin and Use of Tradition in Nehemiah 9* (BZAW; Berlin: de Gruyter, 1999), 21–73. See further esp. Rodney A. Werline, *Penitential Prayer in Second Temple Judaism: The Development of a Religious Institution* (SBLEJL 13; Atlanta: Scholars Press, 1998); but also Volker Pröbstl, *Nehemia 9, Psalm 106 und Psalm 136 und die Rezeption des Pentateuchs* (Göttingen: Cuvillier, 1997); Judith H. Newman, "Nehemiah 9 and the Scripturalization of Prayer in the Second Temple Period," in *The Function of Scripture in Early Jewish and Christian Tradition* (ed. Craig A. Evans and James A. Sanders; JSNTSup 154; Sheffield: Sheffield Academic Press, 1998), 112–23; idem, *Praying by the Book: The Scripturalization of Prayer in Second Temple Judaism* (SBLEJL 14; Atlanta: Scholars Press, 1999); Richard J. Bautch, *Developments in Genre between Post-exilic Penitential Prayers and the Psalms of Communal Lament* (SBLAcBib 7; Atlanta: Society of Biblical Literature, 2003); and now the collections of essays on penitential prayer in Mark J. Boda, Daniel K. Falk, and Rodney A. Werline, eds., *Seeking the Favor of God, Volume 1: The Origins of Penitential Prayer in Second Temple Judaism* (SBLEJL 21; Atlanta: Society of Biblical Literature; Leiden: Brill, 2006); idem, *Seeking the Favor of God, Volume 2: The Development of Penitential Prayer in Second Temple Judaism* (SBLEJL 22; Atlanta: Society of Biblical Literature; Leiden: Brill, 2007). Bautch treats penitential prayer as a subcategory of lament (so also Pröbstl), even if it is "a genre in its final stages" (138). Although it

tagged penitential prayer, is "to bring an end to the devastating effects of the fall of the state: either to captivity, oppression, or the sorry condition of Palestine."[5] A key feature, therefore, is the clear expression of the distress of the people in the recent past and present (Ezra 9:7, 9; Neh 9:32, 36–37; Dan 9:7, 8, 12, 13, 14, 16, 18). This depiction of distress is offered with emotional depth, speaking of the difficulty as כל־התלאה ("all the hardship," Neh 9:32), בצרה גדולה ("great distress," Neh 9:37), בשת הפנים ("open shame," Ezra 9:7; Dan 9:7, 8), רעה גדלה ("great calamity," Dan 9:12; cf. 9:13, 14), שמם ("desolations," Dan 9:18), and the status of the people as עבדים ("slaves," Neh 9:36; Ezra 9:9) who endure the חרפה ("reproach," Dan 9:16) of the surrounding people. Because these expressions are prayers to God, they include a request, consistently for divine recognition of distress (Neh 1:5–6, 11; 9:32; Dan 9:17–19), but also for a divine modification in disposition (Dan 9:16), divine recollection of promise (Neh 1:8), and/or divine intervention in human affairs (Neh 1:11; Dan 9:19).[6]

Essential to this type of prayer, however, is the admission of the sins of the community both past and present (Ezra 9:6–7, 10, 13–15; Neh 1:6–8; 9:33–35, 37; Dan 9:5–11, 13–16, 18). Declarations of distress and request are always nuanced in these prayers by the confession that the community has sinned against God, and the full semantic range is employed to communicate this sin (רשע, עון, חטא, מרד, מרה, מעל).[7]

An important feature of this type of prayer is its theological orientation. Israel's character credo provides an anchor for the cry of the prayer (Neh 1:5; 9:32; Dan 9:4).[8] Two key nuances are essential to the credos that appear in these prayers. First, they emphasize the awesome greatness of God: one who is האל

---

is challenging to determine the line between lament and penitential prayer, surely when "the lament proper is indeed jettisoned" (139), as Bautch admits for Neh 9 and Ezra 9, it is difficult to maintain the genre tag "lament." See now his "Lament Regained: Trito-Isaiah's Penitential Prayer," in Boda, Falk, and Werline, *Seeking the Favor of God, Volume 1*, 83–99.

5. Boda, *Praying the Tradition*, 28.

6. Ezra 9 is unique among penitential prayer in that it lacks an explicit request. This probably reflects its didactic role in Ezra 9, a prayer that warns the people and inspires their response; see further ibid., 37.

7. See ibid., 203.

8. While von Rad emphasized the short narrative credos ("das kleine geschichtliche Credo") as central to Old Testament theology (Deut 6; 26; Josh 24), it is important not to miss another credo tradition in the Hebrew Bible, the character credo: Exod 34:6–7; Num 14:18; Neh 9:17; Pss 86:15; 103:8; 145:8; Joel 2:13; Jonah 4:2; Nah 1:3; cf. Ps 111:4; 2 Chr 30:9. Even Wright could not ignore this important creedal tradition, which Sakenfeld calls "the Exodus 34 liturgical formula." See Gerhard von Rad, *Gesammelte Studien zum Alten Testament* (TBü; Munich: Kaiser, 1958), 9–86; idem, *The Problem of the Hexateuch and Other Essays* (London: Oliver & Boyd, 1966), 1–78; G. E. Wright, *God Who Acts* (SBT 8; London: SCM, 1952), 85 n. 2; Katharine Doob Sakenfeld, *Faithfulness in Action: Loyalty in Biblical Perspective* (OBT; Philadelphia: Fortress, 1985), 49; Boda, *Praying the Tradition*, 50–51 and literature cited there.

הגדול והנורא ("the great and awesome God") able to rescue the community from their present predicament. Second, they emphasize even more the faithful grace of God: one who שמר הברית והחסד ("keeps covenant faithfully"). This credo provides the foundation for regular declarations of God's grace using the breadth of the Hebrew semantic range for grace (Ezra 9:8–9, 13, 15; Neh 1:10; 9:33, 35; Dan 9:9, 13, 15, 17–18).[9] Furthermore, God is emphasized as one who is צדיק (Ezra 9:15; Neh 9:8, 33; Dan 9:14) and possesses צדקה (Dan 9:7, 16, 18). These terms are not terms of judgment (i.e., God enacts justice) or of justification (i.e., God is justified in what has been done), but rather terms emphasizing God's faithfulness to covenant.[10] Surprisingly the disciplinary side of God's character falls into the background of the prayers and is communicated implicitly through the depiction of distress and only occasionally explicitly in highlighting God's anger (Ezra 9:14; Dan 9:16). Therefore, the great emphasis in these prayers is on the grace of God, which provides hope that the request will be heard, and on the might of God, which provides hope that the request can be fulfilled.

The use of the character credos highlights a final key aspect of these prayers, that is, the important role that the law plays in penitential prayer. The character credos declare that God שמר הברית וחסד לאהביו ולשמרי מצותיו ("keeps covenant faithfully with those who love him and keep his commandments," Neh 1:5; Dan 9:4). These prayers are established not only on the foundation of God's character but also on the declaration of God's will expressed in the law and communicated through the prophets.

The law is used in both negative and positive ways. On the one side, it provides the standard that classifies the behavior of the people as sin. These prayers define sin consistently as a breakage of the law, using the breadth of lexical stock available to them for law (תורות, מצות, חקים, תורה, משפטים).[11] The punishment under which the people are suffering is defined as the result of the curse of the law (Ezra 9:13–14; Neh 1:8; Dan 9:11). These laws, however, are not seen as cold and abstract but rather as the dynamic expressions of God. This is why they are referred to as תורתך ("your law," Neh 9:34), מצותיך ("your commandments," Neh 9:34; Ezra 9:14; Dan 9:5), משפטיך ("your ordinances," Dan 9:5), or עדותיך אשר העידת בהם ("your warnings, which you warned against them," Neh 9:34). Failure to keep these commandments is to חבל חבלנו לך ("act very corruptly against you" (Neh 1:7), to חטאנו לך ("sin against you," Dan 9:8), and to disobey קלך ("your

---

9. תחנה (Ezra 9:8); חסד (Ezra 9:9); פדה (Neh 1:10); אמה (Neh 9:33); טוב (Neh 9:35); סליחה (Dan 9:7); רחמים (Dan 9:13, 18). See now my "Confession as Theological Expression: Ideological Origins of Penitential Prayer," in Boda, Falk, and Werline, *Seeking the Favor of God, Volume 1*, 21–50.

10. For this see Boda, *Praying the Tradition*, 62–64. This can be displayed by comparing Ezra 9:13 and 15. Of course, the implication is that God is just in his actions, for God is merely being faithful to his covenant.

11. See ibid., 203.

voice," Dan 9:11, 14). These commands, as dynamic expressions of God, endured among the people through the prophetic tradition (Ezra 9:11; Dan 9:6, 10).

This negative use of the law is essential in penitential prayer for the delineation of sin and explanation of discipline. However, it is balanced by a more positive aspect. Through the character credos the people are encouraged by the fact that obedience to the commandments results in the preservation of their covenant relationship with God (Neh 1:5; Dan 9:4). Law as covenant is important for their future hope. It is this positive aspect of the law that offers hope in the prayer of Neh 1, as the word commanded to Moses is highlighted in Nehemiah's prayer (cf. Deut 4:25–31; 30:1–5).[12]

1.2. HISTORY AND TRADITION

These penitential prayers are found in narratives describing the Persian period Jewish community, but the precise original historical context of each of the prayers has been hotly debated and probably eludes precise delineation. Evidence of this tradition of prayer with specific allusions to Neh 9 can be discerned in the speeches in the prose inclusio of Zech 1–8,[13] which would suggest that at the outset of the Persian period and possibly even before penitential prayer had emerged as a liturgical convention in the Jewish community. A traditio-historical investigation of the various penitential prayers reveals an amalgamation of Deuteronomic and Priestly traditions.[14] This synthesis of two major strains of Jewish tradition gave rise to a new form of prayer to God that would leave a lasting legacy, as it shaped the liturgical expression of the Jewish community for the following five centuries and beyond.[15] The orientation of this paper, however, is to the past, to investigate further the origins of this fascinating form. The first step is to take a closer look at the book of Lamentations.

2. LAMENTATIONS

2.1. HISTORY AND TRADITION

The book of Lamentations, tucked inconspicuously among the Ketubim of the Hebrew Bible, offers another perspective on Jewish religious expression to God in the wake of the fall of the state. In spite of Provan's disputation of the ability of

---

12. See ibid., 70 n. 116.

13. See my "Zechariah: Master Mason or Penitential Prophet," in *Yahwism after the Exile: Perspectives on Israelite Religion in the Persian Era* (ed. Bob Becking and Rainer Albertz; Studies in Theology and Religion; Assen: Van Gorcum, 2003), 49–69.

14. Boda, *Praying the Tradition*, 43–73.

15. For detailed work on the development of this prayer genre after the biblical corpus, see especially Werline, *Penitential Prayer*.

modern historians to accurately set Lamentations into a particular historical context,[16] these compositions reflect the circumstances and conditions of the closing years of the Judean kingdom in the Babylonian period, a period that saw the fall and devastation of the city, the destruction of the temple, the exile of the king, and the massacre of many people. Although the intensity of the descriptions of disaster in these poems may reflect the rhetorical genius of a master poet, it is likely that they are also the result of personal experience.[17] Not only historical context, but the ideology of the period is reflected in these poems. Here one finds the cynical approach to the sin of former generations (cf. Lam 5:7 and Jer 31:29; Ezek 18:2)[18] and especially emphasis on Zion theology (cf. Lamentations *passim* and Jer 7).[19] Finally, a liturgical tradition from the last phase of the Judean kingdom can be discerned within the lamentations in this book. In a recent article I have highlighted evidence for penitential-lament liturgies during the reign of Zedekiah in Jer 14–15. Drawing on the Priestly tradition of covenant renewal represented in Lev 26, these liturgies combine lament, admission of sin, and Zion theology, the same combination of elements evident in the book of Lamentations (on this further below).

Although the majority of scholars place most of these compositions in the period after the fall of Jerusalem in 587/6, there is considerable debate over temporal order.[20] Based on the evidence of the poems themselves, it is extremely difficult to resolve this debate.[21] For instance, although Lam 5 has sometimes been

---

16. See Iain W. Provan, "Reading Texts against an Historical Background: The Case of Lamentations 1," *SJOT* 1 (1990): 130–43; idem, *Lamentations* (NCBC; Grand Rapids: Eerdmans, 1991), 11–12.

17. Juxtaposing rhetorical sophistication and oral expression as Claus Westermann (*Lamentations: Issues and Interpretation* [Minneapolis: Fortress, 1993], 100–101) does is inappropriate. There is no reason that trained liturgists could not have composed these as authentic expressions of pain for the community.

18. Moshe Weinfeld, *Deuteronomy and the Deuteronomic School* (Oxford: Clarendon, 1972), 30.

19. This strong Zion strain in Lamentations is documented meticulously in Bertil Albrektson, *Studies in the Text and Theology of the Book of Lamentations* (Studia Theologica Lundensia; Lund: Gleerup, 1963), 219–30, 238. Albrektson does not mention, however, the important rhetorical techniques that accentuate the Zion tradition, in particular the personification of the city and walls of Zion in Lam 1–2 to describe the pain and express the heart cry of the people. In a sense, the composers send out God's "precious" Zion to intercede for them. For the importance of Zion as a "voice" in Lamentations, see further William F. Lanahan, "The Speaking Voice in the Book of Lamentations," *JBL* 93 (1974): 43–45; Knut M. Heim, "The Personification of Jerusalem and the Drama of Her Bereavement in Lamentations," in *Zion, City of Our God* (ed. Richard S. Hess and Gordon J. Wenham; Grand Rapids: Eerdmans, 1999), 129–69.

20. For a review of the history of interpretation, see Westermann, *Lamentations*, 54–55, 104–5.

21. Contra, e.g., Gurewicz, who places the poem in temporal order: Lam 3; 2; 4; 1; 5; Gordis: Lam 2/4; 3; 1/5; Brandscheidt: Lam 2; 1; 5; 4; 3. See S. B. Gurewicz, "The Problem of

branded of later origin because of its use of the terms נצח ("forever") and ימים
לארך ("so long"), such expressions are stereotypical in such compositions,[22] and
conceptions of time are relative to the particular situation. Furthermore, use of
the reference in Lam 5:7 to the sins of "our ancestors" as evidence of a late composition is without foundation, considering that such appeals can be found in the
last decade of the kingdom prior to Jerusalem's fall (Jer 31:29; Ezek 18:2). So also
Lam 3 with its stronger didactic tone and weaker connection to the fall of the
state has been placed in a later period. As will be argued below, it also has strong
links to the waning days of the Judean kingdom.

Even though these compositions could have all arisen in the same period,
they do not appear to be from the same composer because of subtle differences
in rhetorical technique, especially in the use of the acrostic form.[23] However, the
consistency in liturgical form (lament, admission of sin) and ideology (Zion theology) within at least Lam 1, 2, 4, 5 would place the composers in a common

---

Lamentations 3," *ABR* 8 (1960): 19–23; Robert Gordis, *The Song of Songs and Lamentations: A
Study, Modern Translation and Commentary* (rev. ed.; New York: Ktav, 1974), 126–27; Renate
Brandscheidt, *Gotteszorn und Menschenleid: Die Gerichtsklage des leidenden Gerechten in Klgl 3*
(TTS; Trier: Paulinus, 1983).

22. E.g., Pss 9:19; 10:11; 23:6; 44:24; 93:5.

23. For an excellent review of earlier scholarship on the unity/disunity of Lamentations,
see Michael S. Moore, "Human Suffering in Lamentations," *RB* 90 (1983): 534–55. Contra
attempts to forge unity in these compositions based on external parallelisms between corresponding cantos in the poems (Renkema), on an overall schema based on Qinah meter (Shea),
or on elaborate chiastic structures (Dorsey) that appear to be more reader fancy than text intention. See Johan Renkema, "The Literary Structure of Lamentations (I–IV)," in *The Structural
Analysis of Biblical and Canaanite Poetry* (ed. Willem van der Meer and Johannes C. de Moor;
JSOTSup 74; Sheffield: Sheffield Academic Press, 1988), 294–396; idem, *Lamentations* (HCOT;
Leuven: Peeters, 1998); William H. Shea, "The Qinah Structure of the Book of Lamentations,"
Bib 60 (1979): 103–7; David A. Dorsey, "Lamentations: Communicating Meaning Through
Structure," *EJ* 6 (1988): 83–90; see the critique by Charles W. Miller, review of Johan Renkema,
Lamentations, RBL (http://bookreviews.org/pdf/2807_1265.pdf). The approaches of Johnson
and Heater are more acceptable because they promote the center stanzas as turning points in
the compositions. However, Heater's explanation of the reversal of ע and פ in the alphabetic
acrostics (cf. Lam 1 with 2–4) as poetic device is no more convincing than Renkema's assertion
that the reversal was a liturgical device; see Bo Johnson, "Form and Message in Lamentations,"
ZAW 97 (1985): 58–73; Homer Heater, "Structure and Meaning in Lamentations," *BibSac* 149
(1992): 314–15; Renkema, *Lamentations*, 47–48. On the other hand, Westermann's (*Lamentations*, 100–104) insistence that these compositions began in oral form and later were adapted
to the written acrostic style is unnecessary if one accepts the penitential-lament liturgical tradition in Zedekian Jerusalem; see Mark J. Boda, "From Complaint to Contrition: Peering through
the Liturgical Window of Jer 14,1–15,4," *ZAW* 113 (2001): 186–97. Johnson is rightly skeptical
of Bergler's attempt to find an acrostic message in Lam 5, although in sentence rather than
alphabetic form; see Siegfried Bergler, "Threni V—Nur ein alphabetisierendes Lied? Versuch
einer Deutung," *VT* 27 (1977): 304–20; Johnson, "Form and Message," 58–73. Even if this can be
sustained, it shows a difference in acrostic technique.

group responsible for temple liturgy in the final moments and aftermath of the destruction of the city, state, and temple.[24]

2.2. COMPARING LAMENTATIONS AND PENITENTIAL PRAYER

2.2.1. Continuity

There is little question that there are at least some points of connection between the compositions in the book of Lamentations and penitential prayer. Although Lamentations does function therapeutically, providing opportunity for expressing pain and sorrow,[25] the presence of malediction (1:21–22; 3:21–22) and request (1:20; 2:18–20; 5:1, 21) shows that such expressions serve the same purpose as penitential prayer: to ask God to transform the despicable circumstances, "to bring an end to the devastating effects of the fall of the state."[26] In both, the dominant form of request is for divine recognition of distress (Lam 1:20; 2:20; 3:50; 5:1). Although the narrative contexts for the penitential prayers give us a clearer picture of mourning rites that accompanied these compositions (see Ezra 9; Neh 1; 9; Dan 9), there are allusions to such rites in Lamentations (1:2, 16, 17, 19; 2:10, 11; 3:28–29, 48–51).[27] Both forms admit the sin of the people and leadership (1:8,

---

24. Similar to Gottwald's "poet who was both a priest and prophet," Albrektson's Jerusalemite "familiar with its temple traditions," Kraus's priestly/cult-prophet circles, Renkema's temple singers; see Norman K. Gottwald, *Studies in the Book of Lamentations* (rev. ed.; SBT 14; London: SCM, 1962), 117; Albrektson, *Studies in the Text*, 230; Hans-Joachim Kraus, *Klagelieder (Threni)* (2nd ed.; BKAT; Neukirchen: Kreis Moers, 1960), 15; Renkema, *Lamentations*, 44–45; Hillers's "layman … connected with the royal court" and Rudolph's individual in the court or military do not account for the highly developed liturgical style. See Delbert R. Hillers, *Lamentations: A New Translation with Introduction and Commentary* (2nd ed.; New York: Doubleday, 1992), xxiii; Wilhelm Rudolph, *Das Buch Ruth. Das Hohe Lied. Die Klagelieder* (KAT; Gütersloh: Gütersloher, 1962), 196. Brunet goes too far in the assertion that Lam 1–4 were written by a nationalistic priestly representative (possibly the high priest Seraiah) against the treasonous Jeremianic prophetic group, as does Buccellati in positing tension between remnants of the Jewish community in Jerusalem and Mizpah. See Gilbert Brunet, *Les lamentations contre Jérémie: Réinterprétation des quatre premières Lamentations* (Paris: Presses universitaires de France, 1968); Giorgio Buccellati, "Gli Israeliti di Palestina al tempo dell'esilio," *BeO* 2 (1960): 199–209.

25. Westermann rightly notes this but goes too far in his claim that Lamentations "generates no intellectualized theology" (*Lamentations*, 86), as if expressions in pain somehow bypass the intellect.

26. Contra Gordis, who claimed that Lam 5 was "placed at the end in order to make the collection suitable for liturgical use," implying that Lam 1–4 were somehow unsuitable.

27. Gunkel and Begrich identify these rites with communal lament, but they also appear with penitential prayers, revealing the organic connection between the two forms; see Hermann Gunkel and Joachim Begrich, *Einleitung in die Psalmen: Die Gattungen der Religiösen Lyrik Israels* (3rd ed.; Göttingen: Vandenhoeck & Ruprecht, 1975), 117–39; see Renkema, *Lamentations*, 42 n. 30.

9, 14, 18, 20, 22; 2:14; 3:42; 4:6, 13, 22; 5:7, 16) and speak of the intergenerational consequences of sin (5:7).[28] Both identify God as responsible for the present circumstances (1:5, 12–17; 2 passim; 3:42–45; 4:11, 16; 5:20, 22), while declaring the righteousness of God (1:18).[29]

2.2.2. Discontinuity

These continuities between the two forms reveal their similar setting (a community living in the wake of the disaster) and common purpose (to bring an end to these circumstances), but a closer investigation reveals several points of discontinuity in terms of formal elements and thematic emphases.[30] First, although the request for divine recognition of distress dominates in both forms, Lamentations regularly employs malediction against the enemies (1:21–22; 3:64–66; 4:21–22), a technique absent from penitential prayer.[31] In Lamentations the description of distress dominates the compositions and is far more detailed and vivid. This element is not absent in penitential prayer but clearly does not eclipse the other elements as in Lamentations. Instead, penitential prayer devotes far more space and attention to the admission of guilt, which constantly comes to the fore. This link between the distress and sin is clearly present in Lamentations but mentioned only sporadically.[32] Although the reference to the sin of former generations in

---

28. For an excellent review of expressions of sin in Lamentations, see Joze Krašovec, "The Source of Hope in the Book of Lamentations," *VT* 42 (1992): 224–30.

29. See my explanation above of this declaration of righteousness in the context of penitential prayer; contra Krašovec, "Source of Hope," 225.

30. Although the focus of this essay is on the relationship between the book of Lamentations and penitential prayer, it is clear that Lamentations itself with its use of elements from the funeral dirge represents a transformation in terms of genre from some of the laments in the Psalter; see Gottwald, *Studies in the Book of Lamentations*, 112; Westermann, *Lamentations*; Renkema, *Lamentations*, 41, 44–45, 63.

31. The closest penitential prayer comes to this is in Neh 9:36–37, which merely alludes to oppressive foreigners over the supplicants.

32. Provan (*Lamentations*, 23) evaluates these confessions as inauthentic, and Dobbs-Allsopp as relatively infrequent and ambiguous (F. W. Dobbs-Allsopp, "Tragedy, Tradition, and Theology in the Book of Lamentations," *JSOT* 74 [1997]: 36–40); both argue that the confessions are undermined in their contexts. I agree that they are relatively infrequent and ambiguous (so also Gottwald, *Studies in the Book of Lamentations*, 68: "we are surprised that more detail is not given"), disagree strongly that they are undermined in their contexts (see further below), and am agnostic over whether they were authentic or not. Gottwald's view that the lack of specificity of sin indicates the "poet's conviction that the sin of Judah was much more serious and deep-rooted than the combination of many overt acts" is stretching the facts (*Studies in the Book of Lamentations*, 69). Furthermore, the references to "sin" in 4:6, 22 are most likely references to "punishment" for sin; see Gordis, *Song of Songs and Lamentations*, 184. Although this implicitly admits sin, it is not as clear as penitential prayer; furthermore, 4:6 seems to intimate that the punishment was excessive.

Lam 5:7 may appear similar to penitential prayer, it is important to notice that the focus of this particular reference is to lament the foolishness of former generations[33] rather than to accept it as part of a communal guilt, as in penitential prayer. Furthermore, although human responsibility for the disaster is admitted, there are indications in Lamentations that those responsible saw the severity of the punishment out of proportion with the sin (1:12; 2:13, 20; 4:6; 5:20, 22).[34]

In terms of thematic emphases, the mercy of God is nearly absent in Lamentations, only appearing in Lam 3 (see below), while as noted it is a major focus in penitential prayer. In contrast, the anger of God is forefront in Lamentations (1:12; 2:1–6, 21–22; 3:42–43; 4:11; 5:22), along with the absence of God's grace (2:2, 17, 21).[35] Finally, the law of God, so dominant in penitential prayer, is rare in Lamentations, only surfacing in 1:18 and 2:9.

3. From Lamentations to Penitential Prayer

The presentation so far has shown the organic connection between these two forms within the liturgical tradition of Israel, but has also revealed fundamental differences. Of course, one cannot disregard the impact of temporal distance on the style of prayer, but time alone cannot explain the differences. What theological distinctions can be discerned between the two traditions? A clue to the theological influence is found in the minority voice of the book of Lamentations itself, evidence that is confirmed by a minority strain within Penitential Prayer.

3.1. Lamentations 3 in Literary and Historical Context

As already suggested, Lam 3 stands out from the other compositions in the book of Lamentations.[36] In terms of rhetorical artistry, it contains the most intricate design in its patterning, employing the acrostic technique in triplets.[37] This feature shows the literary creativity of the composer and indicates that the poem is to be taken as a unity.[38] In terms of rhetorical style, it is unique in its autobio-

---

33. Weinfeld (*Deuteronomy and the Deuteronomic School*, 30) links this declaration to those who quoted the proverb cited by Jeremiah (31:29) and Ezekiel (18:2).

34. In this I agree with Dobbs-Allsopp, "Tragedy, Tradition, and Theology," 36–37, 45; contra Gottwald, *Studies in the Book of Lamentations*, 68: "the sin is the equal of the suffering."

35. See the list of vocabulary of anger in Gottwald, *Studies in the Book of Lamentations*, 72–73; Krašovec, "Source of Hope," 223 n. 2.

36. Renkema (*Lamentations*, 38) speaks of the third song "with its unique style and content"; see also Gordis, *Song of Songs and Lamentations*, 170; Brevard S. Childs, *Introduction to the Old Testament as Scripture* (Philadelphia: Fortress, 1979), 594; Westermann, *Lamentations*, 88.

37. Notice also how it does not begin with איכה, as does Lam 1, 2, 4.

38. This point is advanced by Robert Gordis, who notes: "the time-honored critical procedure of atomizing the text and separating it into two distinct poems fails us completely here"

graphical portrayal of the גבר and its didactic tone that appeals to the reader as a community with an invitation to reflection, repentance, and confession. These rhetorical features draw great attention to this central poem in the book.[39] However, beneath the rhetoric, there is great debate over the integrity of this chapter on the semantic level.

The poem begins as the expression of a man who has suffered affliction at the hand of God and who leads the reader through his transformation from despair (3:18–20) to hope (3:21–24).[40] This expression is then applied universally to others undergoing similar circumstances (3:25–39) and ultimately leads to an invitation to the community as a whole to examine their ways, to return to God, to express their confession, and to voice their pain (3:40–47).[41] It is only within this communal expression and in the section that follows (3:48–51)—as the main speaker expresses his individual pain to God over the destruction of the city—that one finds connections to the rest of the book of Lamentations. This expression of lament in 3:48–51 acts as a transition to an individual prayer that involves thanksgiving as well as request to God in 3:52–66.[42] The acrostic form forces

---

("Commentary on the Text of Lamentations [Part Two]," *JQR* 58 [1967]: 15). Contra Westermann (*Lamentations*, 169), who sees the alphabetic scheme as an "imposition."

39. See Johnson, "Form and Message," 60, 66–68. This view has come under attack in recent years by a few scholars who have questioned the interpretive privilege afforded Lam 3 throughout the history of the interpretation of the book; see Westermann, *Lamentations*, 81; Provan, *Lamentations*, 22–23, 84; Tod Linafelt, *Surviving Lamentations: Catastrophe, Lament, and Protest in the Afterlife of a Biblical Book* (Chicago: University of Chicago Press, 2000), 1–18. All of these trace such interpretive privilege to a general preference for compliance rather than protest modes of speech directed to God, but Linafelt takes this a step further by noting the male and Christian bias of many interpreters. The argument in this article is based on literary artifice and is not meant to denigrate the powerful voice of Lady Zion in Lam 1–2 any more than it is to ignore the voices of lament in Lam 4–5. See now my "Lamentations, Book of," in *Dictionary of the Old Testament: Wisdom, Poetry and Writings* (ed. Tremper Longman III, Peter Enns, and Daniel G. Reid; Downers Grove, Ill.: InterVarsity Press, 2008).

40. Lanahan ("Speaking Voice," 41–49) links this "man" to "a soldier, a veteran who has endured hard use in the war," but the argument is not sustained by the imagery which is used.

41. So also Dobbs-Allsopp, who notes, "It is only at 3.40 that the poet rhetorically draws his audience to a closer identity with the *geber* by breaking into a communal voice, as if to say, 'My experience is your experience!'" ("Tragedy, Tradition, and Theology," 41). Gottwald (*Studies in the Book of Lamentations*, 103) "assumed that the frequent confession of sin in Lamentations presupposes repentance" based on Lam 3:40–42, but although admission of sin is found elsewhere, this is the only place where it is accompanied by a call to examination and repentance. Some have tried to turn the expression of pain in Lam 3:42b–47 into a bitter complaint against God; see Provan, *Lamentations*; Heater, "Structure and Meaning in Lamentations," 309; Dobbs-Allsopp, "Tragedy, Tradition, and Theology," 29–60.

42. Dobbs-Allsopp ("Tragedy, Tradition, and Theology," 41) notes that after 3:47 "the audience is allowed to retreat to their role as onlookers." My view is that the final sections bring us back into the experience of the prophet struggling for survival in a hostile context, although

the interpreter to treat the text as a unity,[43] but the flow of the text is difficult to explain.[44] Is there a particular historical and/or liturgical context that would account for this fascinating amalgamation of individual and communal forms?

As already mentioned, Jer 14–15 provides a window into a prophetic liturgy of penitence in the final days of the kingdom of Judah.[45] There we find the prophet Jeremiah participating in a communal expression of lament and penitence that is ultimately rejected by God. Following the liturgical sections in which lament and penitence are expressed (Jer 14:1–15:9), we are given one of the "confessions of Jeremiah," in which Jeremiah curses the day of his birth (15:10), asks for God's vengeance on his persecutors (15:15), and yet recognizes the disciplinary hand of God upon him (15:18). God's reply to him in 15:19–21 reveals that the prophet needs to "turn" to God because he had "turned" to the people (15:19). It appears that Jeremiah's involvement with the people in the prophetic liturgy of Jer 14–15 was seen as a compromise.

It is fascinating that these same elements can be discerned in Lam 3: individual expression of affliction caused by enemy and God (Lam 3:1–20, 52–66; cf. Jer 15:10–21), individual expression of pain over the destruction of the people and city (Lam 3:48–51; cf. Jer 14:17), and communal expression of penitence (Lam 3:40–42; cf. Jer 14:7, 20) and pain (Lam 3:42–47; cf. Jer 14:8–9, 18–22). Some of the same vocabulary appears (Lam 3:48–51; cf. Jer 14:17), and the experience of this individual parallels that of Jeremiah (cf. Lam 3:53 and Jer 38:6; Lam 3:14 and Jer 20:7; Lam 3:15, 19 and Jer 9:14; 23:15). Although certainty is beyond our grasp, it is possible that Lam 3 arises from the same historical context as Jer 14–15 and betrays Jeremiah's struggle over the penitential liturgies of his generation[46]

---

some see here a reference to the nations ("enemies"), even though this language is better understood in a more limited level of enemies of the speaker within Judah; contra Ralph W. Klein, *Israel in Exile: A Theological Interpretation* (OBT; Philadelphia: Fortress, 1979), 14. This prayer may represent a combination of thanksgiving and prayer (see Childs, *Introduction to the Old Testament*, 595), unless one accepts the work of Gordis and Provan that the precative perfect has been employed here; see Gordis, "Commentary on the Text of Lamentations," 26–27; Iain W. Provan, "Past, Present and Future in Lamentations III 52–66: The Case for the Precative Perfect Re-examined," *VT* 41 (1991): 164–75.

43. So Gordis, *Song of Songs and Lamentations*, 171.

44. Westermann highlights the difficulty in flow, concluding that this is a "composite work, one constructed out of several different types of psalms or psalm fragments," yet also admits that "our compiler has so carefully woven together the various components which once stood as independent texts that the literary seams can hardly be recognized" (*Lamentations*, 88, 191).

45. See Boda, "From Complaint to Contrition," 186–97.

46. Because it explains the appearance of both singular and plural sections, this evidence should satisfy Gordis's (*Song of Songs and Lamentations*, 170–71) criticism of "individualist interpretation" as well as refute Westermann's (*Lamentations*, 181) atomization of the text and attack of "Attempts to relate the other sections of the this chapter … to the whole of Israel as caught in the crisis of 587 B.C." For the history of debate over the individual in Lam 3 and the

or, at the least, that Lam 3 has been written with Jeremiah's experience in view and if so, most likely by those responsible for the final form of Jer 14–15.[47]

But there is a key point of contrast. Unlike the liturgy in Jer 14–15, which employs the bold questions typical of communal lament (Jer 14:8–9, 19), the communal expression encouraged in Lam 3 notes only the severity of God's attack (3:42–47). If Lam 3 can be linked to Jeremiah, it represents the expression of the prophet after the experience of Jer 14–15. He recognizes God's hand against him due to his sin and calls the community to a depth of repentance that transcends mere words (3:40–41).

---

suggestion of King Zedekiah as the "man," see Magne Sæbø, "Who Is 'the Man' in Lamentation 3? A Fresh Approach," in *Understanding Poets and Prophets: Essays in Honour of George Wishart Anderson* (ed. A. Graeme Auld; Sheffield: Sheffield Academic Press, 1993), 294–306. As far as the connection to Jeremiah is concerned, others have noticed this for Lam 3. Norman C. Habel (*Concordia Commentary: Jeremiah, Lamentations* [St. Louis: Concordia, 1968], 378) notes that the "portrait of a suffering individual of Lam 3 seems to be written with the person of Jeremiah in mind." See also Samuel R. Driver (*An Introduction to the Literature of the Old Testament* [8th ed.; Edinburgh: T&T Clark, 1909], 461, 462, 464), Rudolph (*Klagelieder*, 227–45), Kaiser, and Brandscheidt (*Gotteszorn und Menschenleid*, 347–52, esp. 50), who note connections between Lam 3 and Jeremiah, although not on a historical level. Gurewicz ("Lamentations 3," 20, 23) notes that Lam 3 does not mention the destruction of city or temple; thus, "It is quite conceivable that when this particular lament was composed Jerusalem and the Temple were still intact." His link to Jehoiachin in exile is misled (so also Norman W. Porteous, "Jerusalem-Zion: The Growth of a Symbol," in *Verbannung und Heimkehr [Rudolph Festschrift]* [ed. Arnulf Kuschke; Tübingen: Mohr Siebeck, 1961], 244–45), however, especially in light of his observation of "certain phraseological and linguistic similarities to those of Jeremiah." It is interesting that Kraus (*Klagelieder*, 12, 15) identifies the *Sitz im Leben* of Lamentations among the cult prophets using a lament over the destroyed temple. Gordis helpfully traces the phenomenon of "fluid personality," which probably illuminates the frustration of prophets such as Jeremiah whose calling trapped them in a tragic double fluidity: prophet with God versus prophet with people.

47. Quite clearly the Deuteronomistic tradents of Jeremiah are responsible for the final shaping of Jer 14–15 (see esp. Jer 15:1–4). It is interesting that Westermann (*Lamentations*, 180) observes "chief themes of Deuteronomic parenesis" in Lam 3:39–41. Both Westermann (*Lamentations*, 168–93) and Brandscheidt (*Gotteszorn und Menschenleid*, 222–23) have noted many wisdom connections in Lam 3 that, if Weinfeld is correct, may also betray Deuteronomic tradents (Weinfeld, *Deuteronomy and the Deuteronomic School*, 244–319; idem, "Deuteronomy, Book of," *ABD* 2:181–82; although cf. Steven L. McKenzie, "Deuteronomistic History," *ABD* 2:162. Although some Deuteronomistic influence can be discerned in the remainder of Lamentations, Zion theology is clearly dominant; see especially Albrektson, *Studies in the Text*. Gottwald notes this Deuteronomistic-wisdom connection and wisely assesses its impact on Zion theology but does not see the distinction between Lam 1–2/4–5 and 3: "the writer developed an *amalgam of prophetic, Deuteronomistic, and wisdom notions* that radically *surordinated and neutralized the Zion and royal Davidic promises,* and found a *liturgical-pastoral* way of expressing them in the cult" (Norman K. Gottwald, *The Hebrew Bible: A Socio-literary Introduction* [Philadelphia: Fortress, 1985], 546).

Whether or not this link can be accepted, Lam 3 represents an important theological milestone in Jewish liturgical expressions. In it we discover the theological emphases key to transitioning Judah from the bitterness of its lament to the expression of its penitence, and to these emphases we now turn.

As already noted, the key theological emphases are introduced through the experience of the afflicted man in Lam 3:1–20. That which brings him hope in the midst of his affliction is a consideration of the grace of God (3:21–33).[48] In this section the poet employs the lexical stock of grace in the Hebrew tradition: חסד ("covenant faithfulness," 3:22, 32), רחמים ("compassions," 3:22; see 3:32), אמונה ("faithfulness," 3:23), טוב ("good," 3:25, 26, 27), תשועה ("salvation," 3:26). On the basis of this reflection on the grace of God, the poet reveals the impact on one's approach to God by encouraging the people to קוה ("wait," 3:25), דרש ("seek," 3:25), יחל Hiphil + דומם ("wait silently," 23:6), נשׂא + על ("bear the yoke," 3:27), ישב + בדד ("sit alone," 3:28), דמם ("be silent," 3:28), נתן + בעפר פיהו, ("put the mouth in the dust," 3:29), למכהו לחי + נתן ("give the cheek to the smiter," 3:30), and בחרפה + שׂבע ("be filled with reproach", 3:30), that is, passively to accept the discipline of God.

This consideration of God's grace is the first crucial phase of theological reflection, and on the basis of this reflection the composition proceeds to consider the justice of God (3:33–38). Because God is a God of grace, God לא ענה מלבו ("does not afflict with delight," 3:33), does not approve of injustice (3:34–36), but sovereignly dispenses discipline because of sin (3:37–39). On the basis of this consideration of justice based on grace, the poet returns again to reveal the impact on one's approach to God with the searching question: "Why should any living mortal, or any human, offer complaint in view of sins?"[49] Complaint against God for difficult circumstances is inappropriate when these circumstances are the result of sin.[50] Therefore, the poet encourages the people to examine and probe their ways and to return to God. This repentance is to be an expression of the heart to God and to be accompanied by the admission that they have sinned. This appears to go a step deeper than the passing admissions of sin in the remainder of the book of Lamentations.[51] Such penitential expression does not mean a denial of the pain, however, for the speech continues with an honest description

---

48. Krašovec ("Source of Hope," 230–32) linked hope in Lamentations to "the superiority of God's benevolence and mercy," highlighting the key role played by Lam 3. However, he does not notice the distinction between Lam 3 and the rest of the book on this theme.

49. Gordis translates this as "punishment" (i.e., consequence of sin), which is possible. Taking it as "sins," however, is not "merely irrelevant" or "essentially meaningless," as he claims, for it could mean "on account of the fact that one has sinned." In either case, this verse identifies sin as the reason why complaint is inappropriate;

50. Notice the similar message in Josh 7; see Boda, *Praying the Tradition*, 57–61.

51. For this reason I cannot accept Johnson's conclusion ("Form and Message," 73) that Lam 5 is the communal fulfillment of the call in Lam 3.

of God's discipline (3:42–47), after which the speaker expresses his own grief over the destruction (3:48–51).[52]

The cadence of this passage as it moves from theology to human response in two successive waves shows its intention to shape the exilic liturgy of Judah, encouraging penitential waiting upon God based on God's character of grace and justice.

3.2. LAMENTATIONS 3 AND PENITENTIAL PRAYER

Although as noted above there are some connections between all the compositions in the book of Lamentations and penitential prayer, Lam 3 provides the greatest point of contact with these later expressions.[53] Through its didactic style it questions the dominance of lament over penitence, calling the community to a confessional penitence and providing a liturgical template for their communal response.[54]

These connections on the formal level, however, are based on an important shift in theological perspective that can be discerned both in Lam 3 and penitential prayer. In both, great emphasis is placed on the grace of God as expressed in the character credo tradition of Israel (Exod 34:6; Num 14:18; Ps 86).[55] At the same time, Zion theology, so dominant in the other poems in Lamentations,

---

52. Contra Westermann, *Lamentations*, 180.

53. Contra Westermann, who criticized interpreters who "call vv 42–51 a penitential psalm" because, "[a]s can be seen from Ezra 9 and Neh 9, the penitential prayer has a wholly different structure" (*Lamentations*, 182). The elements here are found in penitential prayer.

54. Provan and Dobbs-Allsopp play down the significance of Lam 3 to the overall thrust of the book, going so far as to relegate 3:19–39 to the rhetorical function of "foil" to be read "ironically." Provan (*Lamentations*, 22–23) argues that the remainder of Lam 3, let alone the rest of the book, undermines the hope of 3:19–39. Dobbs-Allsopp ("Tragedy, Tradition, and Theology," esp. 49–50) calls 3:19–39 the "ethical vision" that is "sandwiched in between passages ... that depict radical suffering," accusing past exegetes of lifting these verses out of their context in order "to read off a straightforwardly hopeful meaning." These exegetes do not consider the *Sitz im Leben* I have suggested above, which intertwines prophetic and communal interests in Lam 3. Furthermore, Dobbs-Allsopp's identification of the Zion tradition as an "ethical vision" like Deuteronomistic, prophetic, and wisdom traditions is completely unfounded. If anything, the Zion tradition had become an excuse for disobedience in late monarchial Judah. Westermann (*Lamentations*, 180–81) also denigrates the role of Lam 3 in the book as a whole by seeing 3:26–41 as a "secondary expansion" that does not provide "the key to the understanding of the other songs." Although he is correct in seeing tension between Lam 3 and the rest of the book, it appears from his theory that 3:26–41 represents a significant shift away from the original focus of the songs in the final revision of the book in its present form, thus revealing the key role it plays in the book as a whole.

55. Noted also by Childs, *Introduction to the Old Testament*, 594; Klein, *Israel in Exile*, 15.

recedes to the background in Lam 3,[56] a trend continued in the penitential prayer tradition (on Dan 9, see further below).

The Zion tradition is a tradition of God's grace and favor, celebrating God's election of Jerusalem and the temple as the unique place of rule and worship and choice of the Davidic line as vice-regent. There are strong indications that in the closing days of the Judean kingdom the Jerusalem community was relying on it for mercy in the midst of discipline (see Jer 7).[57] It is interesting that Lam 3 uses a tradition of grace to forge the way ahead theologically, but this tradition of grace is dissociated from the Zion tradition, focusing on God's character without reference to the city.[58] The Zion tradition was not helpful in light of the capture of Zion, exile of the king, and destruction of the temple. Lamentations 3 forged the way ahead through a focus on grace apart from Zion, setting a trajectory that terminated in penitential prayer.

This link between absence of Zion theology and muting of lament can be demonstrated by returning to penitential prayer and looking more closely at the one penitential prayer in which the Zion tradition does play a role. In Dan 9 mention is made of ירושלם ("Jerusalem," 9:7, 12, 16 [2x]), הר-קדשך ("your holy mountain," 9:16), העיר אשר-נקרא שמך ("the city that is called by your name," 9:18, 19), עירך ("your city," 9:16, 19), and מקדשך ("your desolate sanctuary," 9:17).[59] Although Dan 9 is clearly a penitential prayer with the domination of confession of sin and grace of God, it does stand out among the penitential

---

56. Although one does find some allusions to this theology in the pained speech of 3:48–51 ("daughter of my people," "daughters of my city"), these allusions are insignificant compared to the dominating expressions in the rest of the book, where Zion theology appears to contribute to the bitterness of the lament.

57. Contra Dobbs-Allsopp ("Tragedy, Tradition, and Theology," 29–60), who incorrectly identified the Zion tradition as an "ethical vision." This is not to deny that the Zion tradition was used in compositions responding to the fall, as Klein has noted in tracing the theme of the Kingship of Yahweh in such responses; see Ralph W. Klein, "A Theology for Exiles: The Kingship of Yahweh," *Dialog* 17 (1978): 128–34.

58. This concentration on God's essence is highlighted by Renkema in reference to 3:22–33: "giving account of his renewed faith, the devout one of Lam III puts the elementary confession of Yʜwʜ's essence into words in the very heart of the songs" (Renkema, *Lamentations*, 66; see also Gottwald, *Studies in the Book of Lamentations*, 98–100; Klein, *Israel in Exile*, 15; Krašovec, "Source of Hope," 230–33). Kim Hawtrey ("The Exile as a Crisis for Cultic Religion: Lamentations and Ezekiel," *RTR* 52 [1993]: 74–83) has wisely observed this evidence but uses it unfortunately to argue for a "spiritualization" of priestly and cultic religion, a Western rather than Israelite concept.

59. The perspective of this prayer shows that it arose originally in the context of Jerusalem (see 9:7: "to us … to the men of Judah, the inhabitants of Jerusalem, and all Israel, those who are nearby and those who are far away"; 9:16: "Jerusalem and your people have become a reproach to all those around us"). Its early provenance has been argued by some; see Boda, *Praying the Tradition*, 71 n. 118.

prayers in other respects. Here one finds the boldest request among the penitential prayers with the use of an imperative of action (9:17–19),[60] a clear reference to the anger of God (9:16), a description of Jerusalem and its people becoming a reproach to the surrounding peoples (9:16; cf. Lam 5:1), and an emphasis on the unprecedented calamity of Jerusalem (9:12), all features reminiscent of the book of Lamentations (see above). Daniel 9 reveals the impact of the Zion tradition on the exilic liturgy and showcases the transformation from one form to the other.

The impact of Zion theology on exilic liturgical tradition can also be demonstrated by a closer look at the element of malediction. In penitential prayers there is some focus on enemies of the people, but they are seen as agents of God's wrath and are not cursed. In Lamentations, however, the composers call down curses on these enemies because of what they have done to the community. This can be understood in terms of Zion tradition, for there is a strong international flavor to this tradition in the Hebrew Bible. This emphasis appears regularly throughout the book of Lamentations but is most poignantly displayed on the mouth of foreigners who ask, "Is this the city of which they said, 'The perfection of beauty, a joy to all the earth?'" (2:15), or through the reaction of the nations: "The kings of the earth did not believe, nor did any of the inhabitants of the world, that the adversary and the enemy could enter the gates of Jerusalem" (4:12). The Zion tradition was foundational to Judah's fame and place at the head of the nations. Malediction against enemies who took advantage of Israel is natural in light of the crisis in Zion tradition. By subverting the Zion tradition and emphasizing the responsibility of sinful people, penitential prayer has no room for malediction.

4. Conclusion

4.1. Summary of Results

In the book of Lamentations and in penitential prayer we discover two phases in the "exilic" liturgy of the Jewish community. The initial reaction to the fall, preserved in the book of Lamentations, reflects the shock of the community at the severity of the punishment, in particular, in light of the theology of Zion perpetuated among the royal and priestly leadership in the kingdom. However, in line with the penitential tradition of Lev 26, they admit their sins. Lamentations 3 offers the way forward for the community through an accentuation of a non-Zion grace tradition that lays the foundation for a consideration of the justice of God, seeking to shape the "exilic" liturgy of Judah by questioning the appropriateness

---

60. The prayer goes beyond merely asking for divine recognition of distress, by asking for God to take action (9:19).

of complaint from a sinful community. This sets the trajectory for the emergence of penitential prayer in which pain is still expressed honestly before God by a sinful community but always in balance with confession and repentance.

4.2. IMPLICATIONS

4.2.1. Brueggemann

With these conclusions we return to our initial consideration of Brueggemann's work on lament. He is to be commended for his desire to bridge the scholarly study of the Hebrew Bible with the contemporary needs of religious communities. In his article (and many others) he takes his place legitimately alongside the giants of form-critical study of the Psalter (Gunkel, Mowinckel, Westermann, Johnson, Schmidt, Delekat, Beyerlin, Albertz, and Gerstenberger). His application, however, is misguided, relying more on modern psychological and sociological theory than on ancient evidence.

The transformation observed in the "exilic" liturgy of Israel from the book of Lamentations, with its dominant lament/muted penitence, to penitential prayer, with its dominant penitence/muted lament, does not support Brueggemann's conclusions. Rather than a loss of "genuine covenant interaction" through silence and praise, penitential prayer displays an enduring covenant interaction that encourages passionate expression of the pain while maintaining self-awareness of the sin of humanity. Rather than relying on a Zion theology with its self-interest in the preservation of the kingdom, penitential prayer encourages an honest encounter with the God of grace and justice. If one is looking for psychological authenticity on a communal level, penitential prayer displays a community's mature self-knowledge. Furthermore, rather than encouraging social immobility with protection for the elite, this transformation from lamentation to penitential prayer actually portrays the opposite. In the exilic liturgy of Israel, it is an emphasis on the Zion theology of the elite that encourages the dominance of lament. It is the broken and oppressed of Lam 3 (vv. 52–66) and penitential prayer (Ezra 9:9; Neh 9:36) that encourage repentance.

Brueggemann's fixation with the lament form has raised our awareness of its role within faith communities, but the form cannot sustain the weight of his applications, especially in light of the exilic experience.[61] One cannot make a

---

61. See now Brueggemann's response in "Summons to New Life: A Reflection," in *Repentance in Christian Theology* (ed. Mark J. Boda and Gordon T. Smith; Collegeville, Minn.: Liturgical Press, 2006), 347–69, esp. 361 n. 16. See Harry P. Nasuti's criticism of Brueggemann's fixation with lament (*Defining the Sacred Songs: Genre, Tradition and the Post-critical Interpretation of the Psalms* [JSOTSup 218; Sheffield: Sheffield Academic Press, 1999]) and my reviews of Nasuti's work in *Themelios* 26 (2001): 60–61; *Journal of Hebrew Scriptures* 3 (2001).

direct link between loss of lament and *"psychological inauthenticity"* and *"social immobility."* Lament can be a tool in the hand of the "socially immobile" as much as the "socially underprivileged"; it can become a vehicle of "psychological inauthenticity" as much as "psychological authenticity."[62]

Nevertheless, there is little question that lament is a key component of the liturgical stock of Israel, useful for expressing the hearts of individual and community alike in the midst of disorientation. But one should not ignore an important second stage of disorientation in which supplicants voice their trust in response to God's promised salvation and/or their penitence in response to accusation of sin. Contrast, for instance, the liturgical flow of Josh 7 with that of 2 Kgs 18–19. In the first instance, we see God's rejection of lament as a form in favor of penitence because of sin in the camp. In the second, God responds to lament, promising salvation.[63] In these two examples the "word of God" is the key component that transforms the primary stage of disorientation (lament) to the secondary stage of disorientation (trust, penitence), similar to the prophetic voice that breaks into Lam 3.

With this in mind, we turn finally to some implications for contemporary expression of faith.

4.2.2. Contemporary Expression

Praise, Pain, and Penitence. First, penitential prayer does not represent a "silencing" of pain.[64] Lamentations 3 offers a liturgical response to the exile that balances

---

62. Brueggemann seems to admit this in a later article ("Four Indispensable Conversations among Exiles," *ChrCent* 114 [1997]: 630–32; repr. in Patrick D. Miller, ed., *Deep Memory, Exuberant Hope: Contested Truth in a Post-Christian World* [Minneapolis: Fortress, 2000], 59–68) in which he describes four kinds of speech during the exile (voice of sadness and rage and loss; voice of holiness; voice of imaginative, neighborly transformation; and voice of new social possibility). The first voice is founded on the lament form and is designed for those today who have experienced "the loss of old patterns of hegemony that shakes the privilege of whites and males and their various entourages." Noticeably absent from his list of voices is that of penitence. The difficulty of linking form with social condition also can be seen in the study of apocalyptic literature, which probably has its roots in protest but can be appropriated by power groups as well; see Katrina J. Larkin, *The Eschatology of Second Zechariah: A Study of the Formation of a Mantological Wisdom Anthology* (CBET; Kampen: Kok, 1994); Stephen L. Cook, *Prophecy and Apocalypticism: The Postexilic Social Setting* (Minneapolis: Fortress, 1995).

63. See now Mark J. Boda, "Form Criticism in Transition: Penitential Prayer and Lament, *Sitz im Leben* and Form," in Boda, Falk, and Werline, *Seeking the Favor of God, Volume 1*, 181–92; Brueggemann is more balanced in his earlier work on the Psalms: *The Message of the Psalms: A Theological Commentary* (Augsburg Old Testament Studies; Minneapolis: Augsburg, 1984).

64. Some may accuse me of adopting the traditional hermeneutical mode for "surviving" Lamentations through "passing over or dismissal of the most disturbing or accusatory

authentic confession of penitence with authentic expression of pain, and this same balance is sustained in the penitential prayer tradition. Contemporary faith communities need to afford opportunities for expressing praise, pain, and penitence as essential avenues of communal expression to God. Most contemporary faith communities place the dominant emphasis on praise. Fewer traditions provide avenues for penitence, often for Christian traditions in connection with the celebration of the Lord's Supper. Scarcely, however, does one find opportunities for expressing pain to God in communal contexts.[65] The penitential prayer tradition displays a balance of all three of these modes with its declaration of the character of God, admission of sin, and expression of pain. This same balance can be discerned in the encouragement to the early church in Jas 5:13–16 in which the troubled are encouraged to pray, the happy are encouraged to praise, and the sinful are encouraged to confess.

Grace and Penitence. Second, and finally, what is fascinating and extremely important for worship in contemporary faith communities is that such transformation from lamentation to penitential prayer is prompted not by a consideration of the wrath and discipline of God, as is often the case in Christian revivalistic traditions, but rather by a reconsideration of the grace and salvation of God. The close association of the character credo tradition in the Hebrew Bible with forgiveness and confession of sin confirms this observation (Exod 34:6–7; Num 14:18; Neh 9:17; Pss 86:15; 103:8; 145:8; Joel 2:13; Jonah 4:2; Nah 1:3; cf. Ps 111:4; 2 Chr 30:9). What is interesting in the recitation of the character credo throughout the history of Israel is that the core of the tradition was an emphasis on the gracious character of God, rather than God's disciplinary nature.[66] This same focus on grace as a catalyst for penitence is echoed in the New Testament statement in Rom 2:4, "God's kindness leads you toward repentance,"[67] and the

---

passages in favor of the few passages that seem to evidence hope through penitence and a reconciliation with God"(cf. Linafelt, *Surviving Lamentations*, 2). Rather, this essay challenges recent caricatures of the penitent voice in Lamentations as a voice that silences pain and seeks to legitimate this voice alongside others in the book of Lamentations; see further my "Lamentations, Book of."

65. In this I agree with Westermann who notes: "for many, it is not quite proper to lament; for many it is better to learn to suffer without lamenting," while "[i]n the Bible, however, lamentation has genuine integrity; in the Bible, lamentation reflects the very nature of human existence" (*Lamentations*, 89).

66. Thus the more limited phrase רחום וחנון ארך אפים ורב־חסד, focusing on the mercy of God, is the constant (Exod 34; Pss 86; 103; 145; Joel 2; Jonah 4; Neh 9), and sometimes only a portion of this (Num 14; Ps 111; cf. Nah 1).

67. The Greek word here, χρηστός, is used in the LXX for the word טוב in the phrase הודו ליהוה כי־טוב כי לעולם חסדו (e.g., Ps 107:1 [MT 106:1]).

assurance of 1 John 1:9 that "if we confess our sins, he is faithful and just to forgive us our sins and cleanse us from all unrighteousness."[68]

---

68. The Greek words here are πιστός and δίκαιος. The first is used in the LXX often to translate the Niphal participle of אמן (e.g., Deut 7:9; 1 Sam 3:20). Deut 7:9 is one of the character credos in the Hebrew tradition. The second term is used in the LXX often to translate the term צדיק, in particular in the penitential prayer tradition (Ezra 9:15; Neh 9:8, 33; cf. 1 Sam 24:18; 2 Chr 12:6). For more extensive reflection on the impact of the penitential prayer tradition on early Christianity, see the various contributions to Mark J. Boda, Daniel K. Falk, and Rodney A. Werline, eds., *Seeking the Favor of God, Volume 3: The Impact of Penitential Prayer beyond Second Temple Judaism* (SBLEJL; Atlanta: Society of Biblical Literature; Leiden: Brill, 2008), especially that of Werline.

The Articulate Body:
The Language of Suffering in the
Laments of the Individual

Amy C. Cottrill

At the heart of the laments of the individual lies a suffering body, described extensively in a language of vulnerability and pain. The psalmist uses a specific repertoire of imagery that characterizes the body as weakened, abused, and without an effective mode of moral agency. This language of the afflicted and endangered body is part of the laments' discourse for the individual's expression of powerlessness. Yet language of body powerlessness simultaneously constructs agency for the psalmist, providing an important path to personal and social empowerment. The language of suffering positions the psalmist as both sympathetic and authoritative, and substantiates his desires for the attention of God, the protection and sympathy of witnesses, and destruction of or triumph over his enemy. Finally, then, the language of the body is multivocal; it is simultaneously a language of vulnerability and powerlessness, and also a claim to authority and power.

This essay contains three main sections. First, I provide a typology of imagery that organizes the language of bodily suffering. Second, I read this body language as a discourse of powerlessness *and* agency, relying on the work of medical anthropologist Arthur Kleinman, who has studied language of the body in distress as a culturally valued discourse strategy, a way of self-positioning that is a means to negotiate authority in situations of disempowerment.[1] Third, I discuss the interpretive and ethical implications of reading the language of bodily powerlessness as part of a discourse strategy that simultaneously empowers the psalmist. What does the psalmist want those who witness this language to think, feel, and affirm in response? Without diminishing the experience of pain itself and the need for the expression of pain, the psalmist's self-representation as a sufferer is part of an utterance embedded in which are specific assumptions about

---

1. Arthur Kleinman, *Social Origins of Distress and Disease: Depression, Neurasthenia, and Pain in Modern China* (New Haven: Yale University Press, 1986).

who is responsible for his suffering and what should be done to end that suffering. At least in part, the psalmist seeks empowerment to pursue a particular vision of personal and social restoration that includes the often violent diminishment of his enemy by God and the language of suffering is part of the persuasive intent of these prayers.

I see four main categories of body language in the laments. First is the language of the diminished and overwhelmed body. This portrait is prevalent and inescapable. The psalmist describes his body as weakened (עטף; Pss 61:3; 102:1 [superscription]; 77:4; 142:4; 143:4), languishing (אמלל; 6:3), spent (כלה; 31:11; 39:11; 69:4; 102:4; 71:9; 143:7), tired (יגע; 6:7; 69:4), wasting (עשש; 6:8; 31:10; 31:11), and losing strength (עזב; 38:11; 40:13). The psalmist melts away or, in contrast, becomes desiccated and shrivels (Ps 22). He is overwhelmed by menacing waters that threaten to overpower him (Ps 69). These examples of physical consumption portray a body on the brink of failure. In all of this imagery, the psalmist has an insistent sense of physical powerlessness and lack of agency.

The second category of body language is that of bodily creation and disintegration. The laments' distress discourse conveys the psalmist's affliction by juxtaposing images of the making and unmaking of the psalmist's body.[2] Instances of birth imagery are highly significant in this rhetorical context where embodiment is so fundamentally important. The laments use a dialectic between the creation and destruction of the body that accentuates the body's material vulnerability and extreme physical precariousness (Pss 22; 51; 71; 139).

The "making" of the psalmist is more fully appreciated compared with the more prevalent language of bodily unmaking, described as disintegration, disunity, even utter destruction, far more radical than fading or becoming gradually less powerful. The body here is preyed upon and torn at by wild animals[3] and devoured by enemies (27:2). The psalmist's bones (6:3; 22:15, 18; 31:11; 35:10; 38:4; 42:11; 51:10; 102:4, 6; 109:18; 141:7) are crushed and the heart (51:19; 55:5; 69:21; 109:22) shattered. This is a body made in birth and unmade through pain.

The many images of the psalmist's proximity to death contrast most sharply with the images of the psalmist's birth. The psalmist prays that the light of his eyes be restored, before he "sleeps the sleep of death" (13:4), and says that the "terrors of death" fall upon him (55:4). He describes dwelling in darkness, "like those long dead" (143:3; see also 18:5; 22:16; 28:1; 30:10; 71:20) and being at the brink of Sheol (88:3), cast among those in the pit, who had been slain (חלל) and

---

2. The language of "making" and "unmaking" is indebted to the title of Elaine Scarry's book, *The Body in Pain: The Making and Unmaking of the World* (New York: Oxford University Press, 1985).

3. For instance, in Ps 7:3, threatening lions tear (טרף) and rend (פרק) the body of the psalmist. For other uses of the verb טרף used in reference to the body of the psalmist, see 17:12; 50:22; 22:14.

now lie in a grave (88:3, 5–7). William Brown refers to Sheol as the "anti-womb," aptly communicating the significance of this location as the antithesis of bodily making.[4] The psalmist only marginally exists in the living world.

The third category of bodily distress is the language of wounds and weapons. The wound is a heightened articulation of pain. In contrast to images of the shattered heart or crushed bones, wounds are about public, visible, breached flesh. Representing exterior, visible pain is rhetorically significant because part of the terror of bodily unmaking and death is the threat of social and physical nothingness and invisibility. The somatic idiom of distress in general resists invisibility, yet images of wounds and weapons are especially concrete, palpable, and explicit objectifications of pain. Language of woundedness makes the psalmist's suffering uncomfortably apparent, indicated in depictions of how witnesses recoil in horror (38:12).

Psalm 38 uniquely concentrates these images of breached skin and woundedness in a highly articulate depiction of pain. Representation of the wounded body in this psalm (38:3–12) begins with the image of an arrow piercing the psalmist's skin. As a place "where boundary negotiations take place," the condition of the flesh is an important indicator of bodily representation as weakened and compromised, and this is especially true of Ps 38. Arrows have penetrated into (נחתו בי) and God's hand has settled upon (תנחת עלי) the psalmist.[5] God's arrows and the resulting woundedness represent the body's surface as permeable and harmable. As Elaine Scarry observes, weaponry and woundedness are bound together and intimately connected to the communication of pain.[6] Weapons *mean* pain.

The psalmist proceeds with a lacerating description of an angry wound and an injured body:

My wounds [חבורה] stink [באש] and rot [מקק] because of my foolishness.
    I am twisted [עוה] and bent [שחח] all the time.
All day I walk in gloom.
    For my loins are full of burning [קלה],
there is no soundness in my flesh.
    I am powerless [פוג] and crushed [דכה],
I roar from the groaning of my heart. (Ps 38:6–9)

The psalmist's pain is described here with rare vocabulary that paints an exceedingly precise portrait of an injured, decomposing body. Many of the words

---

4. William P. Brown, "*Creatio Corporis* and the Rhetoric of Defense in Job 10 and Psalm 139," in *God Who Creates: Essays in Honor of W. Sibley Towner* (ed. William P. Brown and S. Dean McBride Jr.; Grand Rapids: Eerdmans, 2000), 116.

5. Claudia Benthien, *Skin: On the Cultural Border Between Self and the World* (trans. Thomas Dunlap; New York: Columbia University Press, 2002), ix.

6. Elaine Scarry, *The Body in Pain*, 16.

in these verses (the noun חבורה and three verbal roots באש, מקק, and קלה, as well as סחרחר in Ps 38:11) occur only in these verses in the Psalms, and two verbal roots (עוה[7] and פוג [38:9; 77:3]) occur only in one other psalm, indicating the precision and meticulousness of the psalmist's language. Psalm 38 clearly strives to overcome the privacy of pain by making it intensely visible, not just by mention of wounds but also by substantial, deliberate, and lengthy depiction.[8]

The following verses further articulate theological and social implications of the psalmist's woundedness. In 38:12, the psalmist represents himself as abandoned by his community, not just by strangers and enemies, but also by loved ones and others who might care for him. The somatic and social significance of the psalmist's wound are interconnected, so that by the end, the wound represents the psalmist's sense of utter abandonment: theological, physical, and social.

In contrast with the heightened articulateness of Ps 38, the fourth category of the psalmist's language of bodily suffering is language of inarticulateness. At various points the psalmist represents himself through audible, but nonverbal, language of agony and desperation. He describes himself as groaning (אנחה; 6:7; 31:11; 38:10; 102:6) and roaring (שאג, שאגה; 38:9; 22:2; 32:3), all descriptions of being overcome by suffering to the point of guttural anguish. Language of inarticulateness contributes to the psalmist's self-portrait of a desperate, incapacitated sufferer.

Elaine Scarry, in *The Body in Pain*, argues that intense, acute pain ultimately triumphs over the body and obliterates language.[9] The destruction of language, for Scarry, is nothing less than the unmaking of the world, the absolute triumph of dominating power over the tortured individual's voice, creative potential,

---

7. See Pss 38:7 and 106:6, not an individual lament. In Ps 106:6, the root refers not to the body but to going astray or doing wrong.

8. The precision of this extensive depiction of pain and woundedness in Ps 38 stands in tension with Elaine Scarry's assertion (*The Body in Pain*, 4) that pain actively resists language and that pain's fundamental unsharability is part of its essential power. Many agree with Scarry. See, e.g., David B. Morris, "The Languages of Pain," in *Exploring the Concept of the Mind* (ed. Richard M. Caplan; Iowa City: University of Iowa Press, 1986), 89–99; Mary-Jo DelVecchio Good et al., eds., *Pain as Human Experience: An Anthropological Perspective* (Berkeley and Los Angeles: University of California Press, 1992). Others challenge Scarry's argument. For instance, Roy Porter argues that Scarry's argument is "surely contradicted by the actual accounts of pain (which, far from being 'inexpressible,' are often expressed with exactitude and eloquence) that ordinary people in the past have left us in great abundance" ("History of the Body," in *New Perspectives on Historical Writing* [ed. Peter Burke; University Park: Pennsylvania State University Press, 1992], 209). For another thorough challenge to Scarry's argument, see also Lucy Bending, *The Representation of Bodily Pain in Late Nineteenth-Century English Culture* (Oxford: Clarendon, 2000), 82–104.

9. Scarry, *The Body in Pain*, 54.

and self.[10] What Scarry fails to observe is the way that pain can both steal and heighten human agency.[11] Without minimizing the kind of destructive power exhibited in torture, extreme pain does not always result in the destruction of identity and worlds. In some cases intense pain may assist or generate the construction of identity. In the laments, the language of pain represents unmaking even as it makes identity for those who suffer.[12]

The work of psychiatrist and medical anthropologist Arthur Kleinman provides an important lens through which to view the psalmist's distress discourse as both one of powerlessness and also one of empowerment. Kleinman discusses the expression of bodily distress and illness as a culturally afforded discursive practice, a cultural language.[13] While all people share certain commonalities because of embodiment, bodies, bodily experiences, and bodily expression happen in different cultural worlds and are attributed vastly different meanings in those worlds.[14] Kleinman understands the expression of physical anguish and

---

10. Ibid., 50–51. See also Peter Singer's excellent review of this book, "Unspeakable Acts" (review of Elaine Scarry, *The Body In Pain: The Making and Unmaking of the World*, and Edward Peters, *Torture*), *New York Review of Books* 33/3, 27 February 1986.

11. Though Scarry conceives of intense pain as always triumphant, dominating the individual and ultimately powerful, other important voices counter with evidence that acute pain in some instances is part of the construction of identity and language. Historian Janel Mueller, for instance, argues that narratives of extreme pain in torture offered a means of articulating and strengthening identity for those who resisted the demands of religious orthodoxy under Mary Tudor. See Janel M. Mueller, "Pain, Persecution, and the Construction of Selfhood in Foxe's *Acts and Monuments*," in *Religion and Culture in Renaissance England* (ed. Claire McEachern and Debora Shuger; Cambridge: Cambridge University Press, 1997), 162.

12. For further discussion of the way expression of pain, especially in incoherent and volatile utterances, can both witness to a sufferer's identity-robbing trauma and offer the means to remember, grieve, and testify, or begin to organize a new identity, see Serene Jones, "'Soul Anatomy': Calvin's Commentary on the Psalms," in *Psalms in Community: Jewish and Christian Textual, Liturgical, and Artistic Traditions* (ed. Harold W. Attridge and Margot E. Fassler; SBLSymS 25; Atlanta: Society of Biblical Literature, 2003), 265–84, esp. 279–81.

13. Kleinman, *Social Origins of Distress*, 17; idem, *The Illness Narratives: Suffering, Healing, and the Human Condition* (New York: Basic Books, 1988), 13. For more on pain as an acculturated, as opposed to natural, experience, see Scott E. Pincikowski, *Bodies of Pain: Suffering in the Works of Hartmann von Aue* (New York: Routledge, 2002).

14. The literature about the relationship between the body, society, and discourse is extensive. The following have been most helpful: Anthony Synnott, *The Body Social: Symbolism, Self and Society* (London: Routledge, 1993); Michel Feher et al., eds., *Fragments for a History of the Human Body* (3 vols.; New York: Zone, 1989); Thomas Csordas, ed., *Embodiment and Experience: The Existential Ground of Culture and Self* (Cambridge: Cambridge University Press, 1994); Mike Featherstone et al., eds., *The Body: Social Process and Cultural Theory* (London: Sage, 1990); Michael O'Donovan-Anderson, ed., *The Incorporated Self: Interdisciplinary Perspectives on Embodiment* (New York: Rowan & Littlefield, 1996); Bryan S. Turner, *The Body and Society* (New York: Basil Blackwell, 1984); Chris Shilling, *The Body and Social Theory* (London: Sage, 1993); Simon J. Williams and Gillian Bendelow, eds., *The Lived Body: Sociological Themes,*

sickness not simply as representative of a physiological experience but as a mode of social interaction embedded in cultural assumptions about the self, body, and larger society.

Kleinman's work in *Social Origins of Distress and Disease* is based primarily on comparative studies between the United States and China. In China, Kleinman argues, emotions and feelings are more likely to be expressed through the body. This process of feeling and expressing distress through the body is called "somatization," in which distress caused by loss, the experience of injustice, stress, despair, or sadness are reflected and expressed in physical, somatic symptoms.[15] The body becomes an "interpretive schema" for life distress.[16] In his research, Kleinman observes that physical symptoms such as headache, dizziness, sleeplessness, anxiety, weakness, and fatigue are frequently diagnosed as neurasthenia in China. This diagnosis is more biological in orientation than depression, which is the diagnosis that similar symptoms frequently earn in the United States. Although neurasthenia originated in the United States as a viable diagnosis and was popular between 1890 and 1930, it is no longer a respected or viable diagnosis and is perceived as outdated by most Western medical professionals. Although the question of the exact relationship between biology, psychology, and social factors in the experience of depression is still a topic of research and discussion, the diagnosis of neurasthenia no longer addresses modern understandings of the self in a satisfactory fashion in the United States.[17] Kleinman traces a series of cultural shifts in the United States that resulted in a transition from the somatic orientation of neurasthenia to one that was increasingly psychological.[18] Kleinman observes that in sociocentric cultures such as China, a focus on the individual's internal, psychological life threatens cultural values of social and political harmony and is consequently not socially valued.[19] Therefore, while the Chinese individual might admit to feelings of sadness, the body provides the most efficacious way of

---

Embodied Issues (London: Routledge, 1998); Roy Porter, "History of the Body," in Burke, *New Perspectives on Historical Writing*, 206–32; Michel Foucault, *Discipline and Punish: The Birth of the Prison* (trans. Alan Sheridan; New York: Vintage, 1979). The increasing literature about how pain is represented and experienced differently in cultural worlds is especially relevant. See especially Lucy Bending, *The Representation of Bodily Pain in Late Nineteenth-Century English Culture* (Oxford: Clarendon, 2000); Steven Bruhm, *Gothic Bodies: The Politics of Pain in Romantic Fiction* (Philadelphia: University of Pennsylvania Press, 1994); Florike Egmond and Robert Zwijnenberg, eds., *Bodily Extremities: Preoccupations with the Human Body in Early Modern European Culture* (Burlington, Vt.: Ashgate, 2003); Pincikowski, *Bodies of Pain*, 2002; Roselyne Rey, *The History of Pain* (Cambridge: Harvard University Press, 1995).

15. Kleinman, *Social Origins of Distress*, 51.

16. Ibid., 173.

17. Kleinman (ibid., 39) observes that depression is only recently viewed as psychological. The first descriptions of depression, originally called melancholia, were somatopsychic.

18. Ibid., 22; idem, *The Illness Narratives*, 102.

19. Kleinman, *The Illness Narratives*, 109.

experiencing and expressing distress. In the cultural world of the laments, which was sociocentric and not prone to psychological ways of constructing the self, the body becomes a way of experiencing and expressing all kinds of distress— social, personal, and physical.

Most important for my purposes is Kleinman's idea that the rhetoric of somatization serves a beneficial function for the sufferer. The "somatic idiom"[20] of distress is not only a language of powerlessness and despair but also a mode of social interaction that offers the individual an advantageous position of power and authority.[21] Kleinman isolates three main benefits to using the culturally valued idiom of distress that relate directly to the psalmist's language of suffering.[22]

First, articulation of pain in a culturally privileged discourse of distress is in itself an act of agency that helps the individual define and characterize suffering.[23] The way one articulates pain and characterizes suffering can contain and provide boundaries for that suffering. In the laments, the language of pain is a language that gives sufferers a means of expression that is emotionally, psychologically, and theologically significant, an aspect of the laments that is receiving increasing attention from scholars.[24]

A second way Kleinman argues that the somatic idiom of distress is a means of empowerment is as a rhetorical device for persuading and exerting social authority. The use of this language sometimes empowers the sufferer by helping him control local relationships and acquire access to resources, such as medical and/or personal attention from friends, neighbors, employers, and family.[25] As Kleinman describes, being sick "may serve to authorize and sanction failure (in work, school, marriage, sexual relations), may marshal social support otherwise unavailable (for example, love and aid from an estranged spouse), may sanction the expression of anger that is otherwise illegitimate, may provide time out and away from terribly difficult circumstances."[26] In some instances, the expression of

---

20. Kleinman, *Social Origins of Distress*, 167.

21. See also David B. Morris, *The Culture of Pain* (Berkeley and Los Angeles: University of California Press, 1991), 193.

22. Kleinman does not enumerate the possible benefits of articulating bodily distress in privileged idioms. I have culled these observations from his work and presented them in this fashion to facilitate intelligibility.

23. Kleinman, *Social Origins of Distress*, 151.

24. See, e.g., Walter Brueggemann, "The Costly Loss of Lament," *JSOT* 36 (1986): 57–71; idem, "The Formfulness of Grief," *Int* 31 (1977): 263–75; Sally A. Brown and Patrick Miller, eds., *Lament: Reclaiming Practices in Pulpit, Pew, and Public Square* (Louisville: Westminster John Knox, 2005); Kristin M. Swenson, *Living through Pain: Psalms and the Search for Wholeness* (Waco, Tex.: Baylor University Press, 2005); David R. Blumenthal, "Liturgies of Anger," *Cross Currents* 52/2 (2002): 178–99; Ee Kon Kim, "'Outcry': Its Context in Biblical Theology," *Int* 42 (July 1988): 229–39; Jones, "Soul Anatomy."

25. Kleinman, *Social Origins of Distress*, 173.

26. Ibid., 146.

illness opens up behavioral options that the sufferer perceives to be limited. This element of moral agency is not always a facet of using the bodily distress idiom, however. Being ill and expressing illness may, of course, lead to increased powerlessness. Kleinman describes a situation in which the meaning of illness, as he says, "oscillates between agency and structure," such that distress can be significant in different ways within the experience of one person.[27] That is, the individual's adoption of a particular idiom of distress can be, at once, a way of communicating powerlessness and despair and a mode of social interaction that affords power and authority to seek beneficial change. Neither aspect negates the other.

An example from the laments exemplifies Kleinman's argument. Above, I described proximity to death as among the most extreme representations of bodily powerlessness. The speaker's physical relegation to the realm of the dead, however, is not without rhetorical power in the psalmist's attempts to change his situation and is, ironically, the basis upon which the psalmist makes his most blatant appeal to empower himself in his negotiation with God for assistance. Especially in Ps 6:6, the psalmist uses his near-death location to socially position God as well, emphasizing their mutual dependence: "For there is no remembrance of you in death. In Sheol who praises you?" Similarly, in Ps 30:10, the psalmist asks "Can dust praise you?" The psalmist reminds God that the psalmist's lack of power means diminishment for God as well. The psalmist employs the rhetoric of bodily powerlessness in a bid for some degree of relational power. In order for God to maintain God's position, praise is required from the embodied living. Physical disempowerment, therefore, is not unambiguously a means of expressing powerlessness. The body's suffering is also the position from which the psalmist articulates his sense of power in relation to God.

Kleinman isolates a third important way the language of bodily distress often functions as a means of empowerment for disenfranchised or isolated individuals. The somatic expression of distress offers others in the social world culturally sanctioned ways of expressing support and caring for the suffering person.[28] In China, for instance, Kleinman observes that expression of distress in psychological terms often results in further alienation for the sufferer; the psychological expression of distress does not offer others a socially legitimate means of responding to the sufferer. When the sufferer adopts a somatic idiom of distress, however, relief for the individual and reintegration into the community is often achieved. The somatic idiom of distress offers others a recognizable role to play that is culturally respected.[29] According to Kleinman, therefore, adopting the somatic idiom of distress organizes one's own experience, but also organizes others' responses, a tremendously powerful rhetorical tool. James Boyd White describes a similar

---

27. Ibid.
28. Ibid., 178.
29. Ibid., 151.

process in the interaction between a reader and an author, in which the author "define[s] an ideal reader, which it asks its audience to become, or to approximate, for the moment at least and perhaps forever."[30] What kind of ideal reader is posited by the psalmist's physical distress discourse? The psalmist's ideal witness or reader is one who is sympathetic, protective, and possibly active on behalf of the psalmist's restoration.

What Kleinman describes in the ability of the somatic idiom of distress to afford others a culturally acceptable and valued way of responding is perhaps part of simply recognizing that the laments are a persuasive discourse. The psalmist attempts to persuade his hearers to feel, think, and respond in beneficial ways. The particular ability of somatic distress to organize the responses of hearers is evident in some modern scholars' interpretation of this language. For instance, Susanne Gillmayr-Bucher argues that the body language of the Psalms not only adds to the passion, intensity of expression, and pathos of the psalmist, but also invites a particular response by allowing the reader to share the experience of the psalmist through body language.[31] She argues that the intensity of body language prohibits a voyeuristic or indifferent response to the suffering the psalmist describes.[32] In Gillmayr-Bucher's view, the reader does not remain only a witness in the context of this bodily encounter with the psalmist; the reader's own physical experiences might be read into the words of the psalmist through the commonly accessible nature of the body language.[33] Through body imagery, the reader is invited to inhabit the perspective of the psalmist.

Gillmayr-Bucher becomes the psalmist's ideal reader, and there is much to recommend that position as a response to this suffering body. Embedded in her analysis is an ethical argument that to remain distant from the psalmist's physical suffering is inappropriate and undesirable.[34] Her implicit commitment to reading the language of bodily suffering as an activity loaded with ethical significance is

---

30. James Boyd White, *When Words Lose Their Meaning: Constitutions and Reconstitutions of Language, Character, and Community* (Chicago: University of Chicago Press, 1984), 15.

31. Susanne Gillmayr-Bucher, "Body Images in the Psalms," *JSOT* 28 (2004): 301–26.

32. In fact, Gillmayr-Bucher frequently describes the intimacy the reader feels with the psalmist through body language as nearly inevitable, as one is "forced" into engagement by the body language (ibid., 310–12, 314, 325.) In Gillmayr-Bucher's view, this language is not just highly persuasive, it constructs a compulsory experience of sympathy. Though no one can be forced to do anything in reading, I believe Gillmayr-Bucher's observation is correct insofar as language of bodily suffering offers a particularly insistent invitation to identify with the suffering of the psalmist.

33. Ibid., 325.

34. Gillmayr-Bucher does not characterize her argument as an ethical one. Moreover, the parameters of her article do not necessarily demand that she elaborate on this idea. Yet she makes suggestive comments about the relationship between the reader and the psalmist in the context of the body language that have important implications for my own interpretation of the laments. Therefore, her work provides a way of exploring this aspect of the empowering poten-

vital. Indeed, to remain distant or unmoved in the presence of this embodied suffering and anguish seems obscene.

There are obvious ethical implications to remaining distant in the presence of suffering, yet there are also ethical implications to not maintaining enough distance. In the psalmist's case, alleviation of pain is frequently portrayed as achieving, through God's help, dominance over the enemy, the one he understands to be the primary cause of his suffering. Repeatedly, the palmist asks that God kill (קטל; 139:19), destroy (אבד; 9:4, 6; 143:12), annihilate (צמת; 54:7; 143:12; 94:23), demolish (הרס; 28:5; 58:7), obliterate (נתץ; 52:7), end (כלה; 71:13), or shame (בוש [e.g., 71:24; 6:11; 25:3; 31:18; 35:4; 35:26; 40:1; 70:3; 71:13; 86:17; 109:28]; כלם [e.g., 35:4; 40:15; 70:3], חפר [e.g., 71:24; 35:4; 35:26; 40:15; 70:3]) the foe. Therefore, while identification with the psalmist's anguish may be a sympathetic position from which to engage and respond to the psalmist's suffering, that same sympathy must be balanced by recognition of the persuasive nature of the prayer. The psalmist's description of his bodily distress is inherently tied to his assumptions about what should be done about the cause of his suffering. When one enters into the psalmist's language of physical distress through sympathy, one enters into a perspective that is, at least in part, defined by absorbing pain and the desire for its alleviation through violence against another. To be clear, I do not recommend suspicion or rejection of the psalmist's pain. Yet another ethical response to the language of bodily distress is to assume some degree of sympathetic distance from the psalmist's rage and pain that allows for scrutiny of his desires and the way his desires potentially shape the reader's desires.

To conclude, disempowerment and empowerment function as a rhetorical complex in the laments' somatic idiom of distress, unmerged, yet not mutually exclusive aspects of the psalmist's self-representation as a sufferer. Kleinman's recognition that the expression of bodily suffering positions the speaker as powerless and also empowers the speaker is crucial to understanding the kind of rhetorical identity afforded the psalmist in the language of the laments. The body language is part of a discourse strategy that is about the expression of pain and also about attaining the required resources (attention from God, authority to make demands, sympathetic concern of the audience) to seek the change necessary to relieve suffering. When read as a discourse of disempowerment and empowerment, the articulate body of the laments emerges as a complex and variegated language that reflects the multiple functions of the laments themselves, both as expressions of pain and as rhetorical tools of persuasion.

---

tial of the laments, although I recognize that I push her investigation into areas that she has not addressed directly.

PART 3
LAMENT ACROSS CULTURES

Praise in the Realm of Death: The Dynamics of Hymn-Singing in Ancient Near Eastern Lament Ceremony

Erhard S. Gerstenberger

1. Introduction

Quite often our approach to complaint and laments in ancient Near Eastern traditions occurs via emotional and/or literary avenues. We sympathize with suffering individuals and communities because anguish and pain are universal phenomena. Or we vibrate with the ancient language of anxiety, grief, anger, contestation, as well as with expressions of trust, hope, and mental strength. Such linguistic articulations are like precious ornaments of psychic realities. Their structured beauty generalizes basic experiences making them accessible to listeners and readers. A third approach to psalmic texts of that kind is less representative in our Old Testament research: the cultic one (to which could be added a social-historical perspective), although there have been very notable efforts made to consequently place complaints and laments into a plausible setting. Sigmund Mowinckel's work is looming large in this field of inquiry. I want to follow his paths again, using as a focusing point the elusive question of the occasional presence of praise elements in between dire outcries of agony. Neither the emotional nor the literary interpretation really can do justice to the phenomenon of "praise in the realm of death."

2. Evidence

To procure some evidence and thus illustrate the problem at hand, we could point to a late biblical text such as Dan 3:1–25: three steadfast Jews resist all orders to adore a Babylonian divine statue and are thrown into the "fire-oven." But the extreme heat kills only the police officers; it cannot harm one hair of Shadrach, Meshach, and Abednego. A fourth, divine figure inside the oven takes care of the victims (3:25). The Greek version elaborates the scene. The three condemned men, in liturgical procession, now sing a hymn to Yahweh, blessing his divine power (Dan LXX 3:24). Further, Azariah, probably identical with Abednego, pronounces a solemn, hymnic prayer with confession of guilt and lament, while still in the oven (Dan LXX 3:26–45), full of momentous eulogies to the saving deity. This is an explicit case of hymnic formulations being used in a complaint and lament situation; we are able to observe its (literary? cultic?) emergence in the Greek tradition. Somewhat similar in biblical contexts is, for example, the prayer of Hezekiah in Isa 38:10–20, showing anticipated, seemingly misplaced thanksgivings (38:17–20; see also Jonah 2). Is an inherent dimension of anticipation of divine intervention a sufficient explanation of this phenomenon?

In the same vein, some complaints of the Psalter do employ praise along with preeminent descriptions of suffering and petitions for help. Thus Pss 44 and 89 open their plea before Yahweh with extensive passages of praise. Psalm 44:2–9 (Eng. 1–8) is retrospective, just as Ps 89:2–38 (1–37) extols past deeds of God in favor of his people. But there are also lines that certainly are meant to express continuing experiences of divine power and loving care: "Righteousness and justice are the foundation of your throne" (Ps 89:13 [14]); "Happy are the people who know the festal shout…; they exult in your name all day long" (89:14–15 [15–16]); "through you we push down our foes…; in God we have boasted continually" (44:6, 9 [5, 8]). To what avail is hymnic discourse used under these circumstances? Are the transmitters of complaints, the experts of concomitant ritual, only referring to Yahweh's power for the sake of reminding him of better times and perhaps trying to entice him to action? The same question can be put to individual complaints. They also employ, here and there, laudatory language over against Yahweh. In fact, eulogies of the deity called upon in despair do constitute a standard form-element of individual complaints.[1]

For example, a little personal hymn, set into the context of complaint, petition, and imprecation of enemies (who are considered to have generated the trouble at hand) frustrates our literary logic but falls in line with the liturgical agenda:

> O how abundant is your goodness that you have laid up for those who fear you,
> and accomplished for those who take refuge in you, in the sight of everyone.
> In the shelter of your presence you hide them from human plots;
> you hold them safe under your shelter from contentious tongues.
> Blessed be the LORD, for he wondrously shows his steadfast love to me, when I
> am beset as a city under siege. (Ps 31:20–22 [19–21])[2]

In a living worship service, praise of God is a necessary part of that essential, enacted dialogue with the protective power at least partly responsible for the

---

1. See Erhard S. Gerstenberger, *Psalms, Part 1* (FOTL 14; Grand Rapids: Eerdmans, 1988), 12–13; idem, *Der bittende Mensch* (WMANT 51; Neukirchen-Vluyn: Neukirchener, 1980), 128–30.

2. The last verse I put into the present tense, in order to avoid the wrong impression, as if salvation had already occurred.

threatening situation of the supplicant. Praise in such a situation may encompass many things: acknowledgment of God's potency, reminder of former gracious help, activation of the deity's will to intervene, and so forth. The praise quoted is in direct-address form but clad in general terms, thus affirming validity for everyone. The culminating point, however, is the exemplification of God's glorious might in regard to the supplicant himself or herself (31:22 [21]): ברוך יהוה, "blessed be YHWH," is a basic shout of exuberant joy, used frequently in liturgical events.

A similar tiny inset hymn is Ps 35:9–10:

> My soul shall rejoice in the LORD, exulting in his deliverance.
> All my bones shall say, "O LORD, who is like you?
> You deliver the weak and needy from those who despoil them."

The last two verses of the same complaint psalm are a standard vow to give thanks and praise after deliverance; they do contain another formulaic liturgical expression of pure eulogy, parallel to the *baruk*-formula: "Great be the Lord, who delights in the welfare of his servant" (35:27b). On the whole, many psalms of individual complaint do employ expressions of praise in the immediate vicinity of complaining passages (see, e.g. Pss 5:5–7 [4–6]; 22:4 [3]; 28:6–7; 36:8 [7]; 40:17 [16]; 59:6 [5]; 92:6 [5]).[3]

Proleptic thanksgiving, on the other hand, with allusions to God's great capacities and enduring benevolence, is a feature of such prayers, too. The best example in question probably is Ps 107, which delineates four life-threatening situations that call for supplication to God. The stereotypical formula, however, does not call the prayer in any way petitionary but simply states, according to most translations: those who prayed in hopeless situations and were saved should give thanks. Apparently a clear time sequence is being envisioned: thanksgiving occurs after salvation. But quite possibly, the psalm is talking about proper supplication in distress that already includes anticipated thanks. The narrational contexts of the Hezekiah and the Jonah psalms do suggest such an interpretation. And some individual complaints such as Ps 22 (see 22:23 [22]; 35:18; 59:10, 18 [9, 17]) talk about anticipated praise and thanksgiving quite explicitly and from various perspectives. Psalm 69:31–32 (30–31) calls it a very opportune gift to the Lord, who is being approached for emergency help: "I will praise the name of

---

3. See the relevant passages in Gerstenberger, *Psalms, Part 1*. My comments on Ps 5 and its hymnic part at that point were the following: "Hymnic elements are by no means foreign to complaint psalms. God claims due reverence even in times of distress, and it is in the supplicant's own interest to acknowledge God's power and care" (58). My references as to earlier statements in the same vein go among others to Claus Westermann, *The Praise of God in the Psalms* (trans. Keith R. Crim; Richmond, Va.: Knox, 1965); and Frank Crüsemann, *Studien zur Formgeschichte von Hymnus und Danklied in Israel* (Neukirchen-Vluyn: Neukirchener, 1969).

God with a song; I will magnify him with thanksgiving. This will please the LORD more than an ox or a bull with horns and hoofs."

Proleptic thanksgiving therefore must be seen as an integral part of complaint rituals in ancient Israel, and this particular kind of affirming gratitude is nothing else than one special form of praise to the deity concerned. At least it does function liturgically just like hymnic eulogies do. The negative statement that the "dead" are no longer able to offer thanks and praise (see 6:6 [5]; 88:11–13 [10–12]) illustrates the same fact: hymnic prayers are essential for the deity, too. They do have an authentic "setting" in lamenting rituals.

3. SUMERIAN ANALOGIES

I now propose to look at a body of ancient Near Eastern literature that encompasses a great amount of hymnic materials of various forms and settings. What I have in mind is the Sumerian hymnic tradition, which originated in the third millennium B.C.E. and continued, even in its native linguistic form, well into the first millennium B.C.E. Some people may object to drawing into our discussion such remote texts as the Sumerian ones. I am fully aware of the risks involved in this enterprise. Therefore, I do not even remotely think of "literary influences" of Sumerian hymns on Old Testament praise. But we certainly can count on some basic patterns of thinking and feasting common to the entire ancient Near East, because there has been a long-standing interchange across different cultures and religions of forms and features especially in the cultic realm. Further, the sociological rule probably also holds true for the area under consideration: similar recurring social or religious events create analogous actions and expressions. Thus, for example, some temple designs (house temples with statues of deities) have spread over practically all the Near, Middle, and Far (partially) East as well as Egypt.[4] If architecture as recovered by long-standing archaeological diggings and research betrays common traits, could not cultic rituals and ceremonial texts do the same?

Sumerian hymns are not uniform; terminology used in colophons as well as extant copies of real literary texts are greatly varied. For the most part, it seems, they were recited aloud, accompanied by musical instruments. Length of the text, literary structures, styles, and contents are highly diversified. Our interest is the use of hymnic affirmations in lament contexts, a wide field of investigation, to be sure. We take out some exemplary examples of lament from different (ceremonial

---

4. See Wolfgang Zwickel, *Der Tempelkult in Kanaan und Israel* (FAT 10; Tübingen: Mohr Siebeck, 1994); idem, "Tempel," in *Neues Bibel-Lexikon* (ed. Manfred Görg and Bernard Lang; Zürich: Benziger, 1988–), 3:799–810; Volkmar Fritz, "Tempel II: Alter Orient und Altes Testament," *TRE* 33:46–54.

or life) settings, knowing quite well that all such distinctions are made from our own, modern perspective; they are not endemic to Sumerian literature.

3.1. City Laments

One group of lament literature, comparable to the Old Testament book of Lamentations, is concerned with catastrophes that overcame cities or regions. Devastation by enemies seems to be the prime background for these laments. Cities and temples have been destroyed and people massacred; the local deities have left in mourning; the people try to intervene with the Sumerian highest divine authority, Enlil; starvation is threatening. While there are drastic depictions of the damage wrought and the sufferings inflicted by intruders, the origin of the genre certainly may be connected with historical events of this kind, such as at the end of the Akkad, Ur-III, and Old Babylonian Empires or similar occasions. But constant copying of the relevant texts over long periods and their use also in other than commemorative contexts (e.g., reconstruction work on decrepit temples) suggest a wider amplitude of meaning for those compositions.[5] What about hymnic components in the pertinent texts?

The picture certainly is not uniform, and the different literary traditions and textual conglomerates make it difficult to achieve a clear vision of the ceremonial implications. But there are sporadic hymnic elements in almost all the compositions, and the life setting at least to some extent is reflected in the writings. Thus the Lamentation over the Destruction of Ur, after ten wailing (liturgical) passages (*kirugus*) ends in a segment of prayer wishes (lines 418–435), the last line calling for praise of the moon-god Nanna/Ašimbabbar, who will restore the destroyed city (*meteš ḫé-i-i*, "may praise go forth").[6] A formally parallel lamentation about the destruction of Sumer and Ur ends in a fifth *kirugu* that notably deviates from the wailing tone of the preceding parts. This last piece is a "discourse … against the agent of destruction," "part incantation, part blessing,"[7] and also shows the form of prayer wish ("storm, retreat to your home!"). One surprising example of how much hymnic components are made part of dire lamentation in the face (or imagination) of calamity is the Nippur composition from the time of Išme Dagan,[8]

---

5. See Samuel N. Kramer, "Lamentation over the Destruction of Nipur," *Acta Sumerologica* 13 (1991): 1–26; Piotr Michalowski, *The Lamentation over the Destruction of Sumer and Ur* (Winona Lake, Ind.: Eisenbrauns, 1989); Willem H. Ph. Römer, *Hymnen und Klagelieder in sumerischer Sprache* (AOAT 276; Münster: Ugarit-Verlag, 2001); idem, *Die Klage über die Zerstörung von Ur* (AOAT 309; Münster: Ugarit Verlag, 2004); Steve Tinney, *The Nippur Lament* (Occasional Publications of the S.N. Kramer Fund 16; Philadelphia: University Museum, 1996).

6. Römer, *Die Klage über die Zerstörung von Ur*, LU line 435.

7. Michalowski, *Lamentation over Sumer and Ur*, 15.

8. See above all Kramer, "Lamentation over the Destruction of Nipur"; Tinney, *The Nippur Lament*.

fourth ruler of Isin (ca. 1953–1935 B.C.E.), long after the downfall of the Ur-III Empire. The lamentation features twelve *kirugu*s with a total of 322 lines. "With its first half rooted in lamentations, and its second half distinctly hymnic in character, NL forges a connection between these literatures."[9] The mighty and benevolent performances of the deity are enumerated in grand style from the sixth to the eleventh *kirugu*. The final line proclaims ongoing eulogies: "They will praise forever!" (*me-teš àm-i-i-ne*).[10] The tradition of city laments has been continued in a generalized way by *balag*-compositions[11] without much reference to historical sites or events. *Balag*s originally are musical instruments, harps or drums, used for the accompaniment of mourning rites. The players usually are *gala*-priests. The texts sung take on the same designation, as the colophons intimate. In addition, *balag*-compositions, in the wake of city laments, sometimes utilize regular praise, in contrast to large sections of wailing. To give but one example, the song *Ana Elume* (The Honored One of Heaven)[12] has wonderful eulogies to the sun-god Utu.

> l. a+93 The hero, the great hero, he who decides the fates!
> a+100 The prince, emanating light! The great hero!
> a+101 From the ends of heaven and earth the great hero!
> a+103 You are the child, the respected one, of the pure heavens,
> a+104 you are the elevated child of Enlil.

Praises of the deities seem often to be connected to petitionary ritual, symbolized by the "journeying of the gods to Enlil to plead that he end the devastation."[13]

3.2. DESCENT INTO THE NETHERWORLD

A second realm in which people encountered death and deemed it necessary here and there to sound praises to the ones on high we may see reflected in that litera-

---

9. Michalowski, *Lamentation over Sumer and Ur*, 24.

10. See Tinney, *The Nippur Lament*, NL lines 157–295. The twelfth *kirugu* is a jubilant celebration of the "beautiful day" Enlil has created, with line 322 and its solicitation of praise from the saved ones.

11. See Konrad Volk, *Die Balag-Komposition Uru Am-ma-ir-ra-bi* (Freiburger altorientalistische Studien 18; Stuttgart: Steiner, 1989); Mark E. Cohen, *The Canonical Lamentations of Ancient Mesopotamia* (2 vols.; Potomac, Md.: Capital Decisions, 1988).

12. Cohen, *Canonical Lamentations*, 208–21.

13. Ibid., 38; see also the numerous invocations with a praising intention, e.g., in the balag *Mutin Numuz Dima* (Fashioning Man and Woman; ibid., 222–52. The final hymn of *Elum Gusum* (Honored One, Wild Ox; ibid., 272–318) shows still another style: (e+281) "You are my lord. Light of the city, you are a warrior. (e+282) My shining one, Umungurusha, you are a warrior.... (e+284) Like the sun you whirl about (in) the clouds. (e+285) Like the moon you spread forth your light."

ture dealing with the descent into the netherworld,[14] usually featuring Inanna as the main protagonist. Behind those mythological dramatizations, the universal experiences of dying and being buried probably loom large. In singling out such a general sphere of human pain and frustration, and thus taking "life settings" or "recurring events met by ritualized responses" as a guiding category, I am fully aware (to emphasize this again) that we are using modern conceptualizations. Yet we are forced to do so, because old Sumerian and Akkadian rubrics, so plentifully preserved in colophons, simply are not too meaningful for us. Modern categorization helps us to understand better what was going on in antiquity; we always have to be on the alert, however, that our categories and concepts are different from the ancient ones.

The Inanna-Dumuzi cycle of texts reflecting ritualized ceremonies certainly is an important area to consider in this context. It may be seen in connection with seasonal feasts of the dying and rebirth of nature. At this point I should like to point to one literary example closer to individual death, although the demarcation line toward seasonal dying may be a little haphazard. The extended dirge for Urnamma, founder of the Ur-III dynasty,[15] after narrating his death and burial, elaborately reports about his journey into the netherworld. Lines 81–131 are dedicated to the sacrifices Urnamma offers down there to nine different deities, apparently to win their support. Right after this performance he is installed as a "judge for those abiding in the depth" (132–144). Then a large section of lament follows (145–196). After an intervention by Inanna herself on behalf of Urnamma (197–216), it is Ningešzida, an underworld deity, earlier having received sacrifices from the descended (and deceased) ruler (114–119), who freshly decrees Urnamma's fate, apparently in order to release him (217–233). Consequently, praise is issued for Ningešzida (234–240) as a kind of thanksgiving. The somewhat broken passage ends in the words ^{d}nin-ĝeš-zi-da zà-mí, "(to) lord Ningešzida be praise!"—a common formula to denote hymnic texts (line 240).[16]

---

14. See William W. Hallo and Johannes J. A. van Dijk, *The Exaltation of Inanna* (YNER 3; New Haven: Yale University Press, 1968); Jeremy A. Black, "A-se-er Gi$_6$-ta, a Balag of Inana," *Acta Sum* 7 (1985): 11–87; Gertrud Farber-Flügge, *Der Mythos Inanna und Enki unter besonderer Berücksichtigung der Liste der me* (Studia Pohl 10; Rome: Biblical Institute Press, 1973); William R. Sladek, *Inanna's Descent to the Netherworld* (Ann Arbor, Mich.: University Microfilms, 1974); Bendt Alster, "Inanna Repenting: The Conclusion of 'Inanna's Descent,'" *Acta Sum* 18 (1996), 1–18; idem, "The Mythology of Mourning," *Acta Sum* 5 (1983) 1–16; idem, "Edin-na ú-sag-gá: Reconstruction, History, and Interpretation of a Sumerian Cultic Lament," in *Keilschriftliche Literaturen: ausgewählte Vorträge der XXXII. Rencontre assyriologique internationale, Münster, 8.–12.7.1985* (ed. Karl Hecker and Walter Sommerfeld; BBVO 6; Berlin: Reimer, 1986), 19–31.

15. Last edition by Esther Flückiger-Hawker, *Urnamma of Ur in Sumerian Literary Tradition* (OBO 166; Fribourg: University Fribourg Switzerland; Göttingen: Vandenhoeck & Ruprecht, 1999), 92–182.

16. In terms of funeral dirges, there has been at least one more specimen published by Samuel N. Kramer, which was in fact found on a tablet together with Urnamma A: see his

3.3. Illness and Other Threats

The third life situations confronting people with death in antiquity, as well as in our own time, are grave illness or other threatening conditions of extreme impact. The texts and concomitant rituals of healing, rescue, or rehabilitation are quite diverse.[17] They usually include descriptions of disease or ill-fate, entreaties, vows. Prominent are, even more so than in Old Testament complaints, expressions of praise, either tied to the invocation of the deities or brought to attention in separate passages of the song or prayer. A good number of Sumerian literary genres belong under the rubric of "healing" or "exorcising" songs, such as the *eršemma* ("wail of the *šem*-drum"), *eršaḫunga* (wail to pacify the heart), *šu-ila* ("lifting up of hands"), and *nam-bur-bi* ("its [ritual] release"). Obviously, hymnic elements in the concert of complaint, reproach, and entreaty make good sense, just as in the Old Testament psalms referred to above. They want to assuage the wrath of God, to say the least. Thus, the *eršemma* number 34.2 opens with a long praise section.[18] Line 17 is typical—"Jubilation! My praising! My praising!"—and lines 20–27 consequently all end in the shout "my praising!" (*el-lu ár-re-mu*). Many *eršaḫungas* amplify their invocation to include hymnic attributes.[19] The same phenomenon occurs in *šu-ilas*[20] and late *nam-bur-bis*.[21]

The really important question after this quick review of three realms of life-threatening experiences is: How does praise function in face of death or in commemoration of such situations? What have been the sentiments and rational arguments of ancient people to place (besides reproachful complaints, etc.) adoring words of praise into their wailing and mournful prayers?

Two Elegies on a Pushkin Museum Tablet: A New Sumerian Literary Genre (Moscow: Izd-vo vostochnoĭ lit-ry, 1960).

17. The list of pertinent publications is very long; see, e.g., Mark E. Cohen, *Sumerian Hymnology: The Eršemma* (HUCASup 2; Cincinnati: Hebrew Union College, 1981); Stefan M. Maul, "Herzberuhigungsklagen," in idem, *Die sumerisch-akkadischen Eršahunga-Gebete* (Wiesbaden: Harrassowitz, 1988); idem, *Zukunftsbewältigung: Eine Untersuchung altorientalischen Denkens anhand der babylonisch-assyrischen Löserituale (Nam-bur-bi)* (BaghF 18; Mainz: Zabern, 1994); Graham Cunningham, *"Deliver Me from Evil": Mesopotamian Incantations 2500–1500 B.C.E.* (Studia Pohl Series maior 17; Rome: Pontifical Biblical Institute, 1997); Annette Zgoll, *Die Kunst Betens* (AOAT 308; Münster: Ugarit-Verlag, 2003).

18. Cohen, *Sumerian Hymnology*, 131–35.

19. Maul, "Herzberuhigungsklagen," 18.

20. Zgoll, *Die Kunst Betens*, passim.

21. Maul, *Zukunftsbewältigung*, 87; see also, e.g., 302, lines 12–18: "Ihr, die großen Götter seid es doch, die / die Entscheidung über Himmel und Erde, über Grundwasser (und) Mee[re] recht leiten! / Euer Wort ist Leben, das, was aus eurem Munde kommt, ist H[ei]l, / euer Ausspruch ist doch Leben! Die das Innere des / fernen Himmels betreten, seid doch ihr, die das Unheil entfernen, / das [G]ute bereit[en], die lösen die unheilvollen ‚Kräfte' (und) Omenanzeiger, / die [schreck]lichen, unguten Träu[me], die den Faden des Unheils durchtrennen."

4. The Power of Praise

Theoretical considerations about what praise can or should do in mourning contexts are hardly to be expected within cultic literature. We therefore quite
often ingeniously presuppose that the parameters of hymnic praise in antiquity
correspond to our own modes of thinking. For us, eulogies belong to a set of
interhuman exchange on a sociopsychological level. They are to flatter authorities,
produce benevolence and assistance, enhance interpersonal and social well-being,
and so forth. All this may be true also for ancient hymn-singing, but there may
be more to those acts of laudation so plentifully expressed and performed in all
kind of cultic poetry. The linguistic expressions used to indicate hymnic praise
through ancient and partly well into modern languages may be suggestive of a
basic intention. Praises to deities across ancient Near Eastern cultures and religions are meant to "exalt," "make great," "lift up," "glorify" the gods addressed.
That means that a real transfer of power, from the hymn-singer to the deity, is
taking place. Or, to put it differently, human adoration, materialized in sacrifices,
accompanying cultic rites and not least in significance, hymnic praise, strength-
ens the deity. It is even essential for the deity himself or herself.[22] There are some
passages within extant hymnic materials of old that seem explicitly to make a case
for this interpretation. If this should be correct, we may find the key to understanding praise passages even in lamentations and complaints, those wailing texts
confronting the threat of death.

The prayer of Enheduana, high priestess of Ur installed by her father Sargon
of Akkad known under the Sumerian title *nin-me-šara*, "lady of thousands of
mes," does offer conspicuous hints as to what praise can do.[23] To begin with, the
closing line declares the whole poem, in spite of its plaintive and perhaps juridi-
cal air, a "hymn of praise": *nin-ĝu$_{10}$ ḫi-li gú è ^{d}Inana zà-mí* ("my mistress, clad
in enchantment, [to you] Inanna, be praise!" line 153).[24] In reciting praises for
Inana, the priestess in fact tells her *mes*, her divine powers (lines 65–67, 123–
132), thus helping to constitute the authority of the goddess. Thus Zgoll translates
line 134: "my mistress, this [recitation] has made you greater, you have become

---

22. This seems to be a rather well-known fact in the science of religion and religious
anthropology but a widely ignored one among theologians and philosophers who defend the
omnipotence and omniscience of the exclusive and unique God.

23. See Annette Zgoll, *Der Rechtsfall der En-ḥedu-Ana im Lied nin-me-šara* (AOAT 246;
Münster: Ugarit-Verlag, 1997). The text of 153 lines is given in transliteration and German
translation on pp. 2–17 and as a text-critical edition with all available variants on pp. 205–94.
The author discusses extensively not only philological and literary aspects but also the cultural
and religious implications; see the chapter on "The Reality Represented by the Mes" (66–75).

24. The philological part notes that in most manuscripts the last words "to Inanna be
praise" are somewhat set apart, but they nevertheless are not a colophon but an intrinsic part of
the text (ibid., 494).

the greatest!" The author's overall comment is: "It is En-ḫe-du-Ana's task now, to make effective, in a maeutic (like a midwife's) way, the real potentiality of her Nin-me-šara, namely to help her goddess to give birth to the divine power, the fullness of her *mes*."[25] One should perhaps modify the metaphor of "midwifing" to "creating" or "constituting" divine powers. In any case, the act of praising and making praise publicly known, often mentioned in Sumerian hymns, is part of the performative processes that are inherent in hymnic praise.

The Old Testament gives a comparable scenario in which the power and authority of Yʜwʜ are strengthened or constituted by lesser divine beings, Ps 29:1–2: "Ascribe to Yʜwʜ, O heavenly beings / ascribe to Yʜwʜ glory and strength. / Ascribe to Yʜwʜ the glory of his name; / worship Yʜwʜ in holy splendor." Ascription is really the act of "bringing to," of "furnishing" or "providing," the potentiality Yʜwʜ needs and, of course, can legitimately ask for from his subordinates or vassals.

If there is some truth to these observations, a number of Old Testament passages could be understood along the line indicated. The thanksgiving of Jonah inside the big fish or that of Hezekiah in Isa 38 would not only be anticipated praises but could signify powerful motions to initiate the process of divine rescue. The same would be true for the late Greek version of Dan 2, when the victims in the fire-oven try to create or induce Yʜwʜ's power so necessary for their salvation. Along the same vein, all other adduced Old Testament passages of praise, found in lamenting or complaining contexts, surely indicate an active participation of the supplicants to strengthen divine potentialities of saving the miserable from death.

---

25. Zgoll, *Der Rechtsfall*, 147, with reference in n. 601 to Adam Falkenstein, *Götterlieder* 1 (1959): 21, a description of Enlil's *mes*.

Engaging Lamentations and *The Lament for the South*: A Cross-Textual Reading*

Archie Chi Chung Lee

1. Cross-Textual Reading in Biblical Interpretation

In approaching Lamentations in context, I am confronted with multiple dimensions of the lived experiences of the Chinese people upon whom contemporary sociopolitical realities have, in recent history, inflicted pain and suffering, beginning with the colonial and empire expansion of the West, the resulting humiliating defeat in war, and the loss of geographical integrity. This history of suffering also includes the imperialistic conquest by Japan in Asia during the First and Second World Wars, including the Japanese invasion of China from 1937 to 1945 and the Nanjing massacre during this war period. There are, in addition, incidents such as the Cultural Revolution (1966–1976), initiated by the Chinese Communist Party under the leadership of Mao, and the student demonstrations at Tiananmen Square that ended in bloodshed on 4 June 1989. Public mourning and remembrance of the dead were denied the people on the first anniversary of the 4 June incident, with the mass student movement of 1989 being condemned as "counter-revolutionary turmoil" and the soldiers who fired at the students and the ordinary citizens honored as heroes.[1] In China and in the whole of Asia in general, it is the people of this "wounded generation"[2] who are

---

* This article is a partial result of the project "Naming God in Chinese" funded by the Earmarked Grant from Research Grants Council of the Hong Kong Special Administrative Region, China (CUHK4115/03H). It was first published in *Distant Voices Drawing Near: Essays in Honor of Antoinette Clark Wire* (ed. Holly E. Hearon; Collegeville, Minn.: Liturgical Press, 2004), 173–88. Reprinted by permission.

1. Vera Schwarcz, " 'Memory and Commemoration': The Chinese Search for a Livable Past," in *Popular Protest and Political Culture in Modern China* (ed. Jeffery N. Wasserstrom and Elisabeth J. Perry; 2nd ed.; Boulder, Colo.: Westview, 1994), 170–71.

2. Vera Schwarcz, "In the Shadows of the Red Sun: A New Generation of Chinese Writers," *Asian Review* 3 (1989): 4–16.

the readers engaging Lamentations with their hurts, pains, and, above all, the unfailing aspiration to pursue life in the midst of death.

In this essay I have chosen to focus on a literary work, *The Lament for the South* (*Ai Jiangnan Fu*), which employs a traditional form of lament dating from the fourth century B.C.E. Methodologically, this paper is an exercise in cross-textual hermeneutics applied to the biblical book of Lamentations and a Chinese poetic book, *The Lament for the South*. In Asia, it is the multitextual reality that constitutes the context for this specific interpretative strategy of reading the Bible. The Bible, which originated in the cultural environment of West Asia, was subsequently interpreted and contextualized in the Greco-Roman as well as the Latin worlds, took a detour via Western Christian civilization, and forced its way back to Asian soil as a stranger in its own home and an imperialist book of the empire.[3] The translation and reception history of the Bible among Asian scriptural traditions is, therefore, a significant project in which we biblical scholars in Asia should engage ourselves, in order to recover and understand the hidden phase of biblical interpretation in different global contexts.

In the case of the Chinese, the past four hundred years of biblical interpretation (from the time when the Jesuit missions arrived in China in the late sixteenth century to the Protestant missionary movements in the early eighteenth century) will be an indispensable area of study if we want to understand the history of Christianity in the Chinese context. It will also shed light on the contemporary scene of biblical interpretation in China. Chinese biblical interpretation has captured the intense attention and passionate interest of Professor Antoinette Clark Wire, to whose fine scholarship this article is humbly dedicated.[4]

The present author proposes adopting the reading strategy of cross-textual hermeneutics to address colonial entanglements and to recontextualize the Bible in the Asian, African, and Latin American cultural milieu.[5] This approach takes

---

3. There are various minor streams of tradition in China and India that are exceptions to the main missionary movements of the eighteenth and nineteenth centuries. The Catholic Jesuit missions also form a separate category. See R. S. Sugirtharajah, *The Bible and the Third World: Pre-colonial, Colonial, and Postcolonial Encounters* (Cambridge: Cambridge University Press, 2001); idem, *Asian Biblical Hermeneutics and Postcolonialism: Contesting the Interpretations* (Maryknoll, N.Y.: Orbis, 1998). For a brief history of the Bible in the British Missionary Movement, see Brian Stanley, *The Bible and the Flag: Protestant Missions and British Imperialism in the Nineteenth and Twentieth Centuries* (Leicester: Apollos, 1990).

4. Antoinette Clark Wire, "Chinese Biblical Interpretation since Mid-century," *BibInt* 4 (1996): 101–23.

5. The method has been expounded with examples in a number of articles written by the present author; see Archie C. C. Lee, "The Chinese Creation Myth of Nu Kua and the Biblical Narrative in Gen 1–11," *BibInt* 2 (1994): 312–24; idem, "Death and the Perception of the Divine in Zhuangzi and Koheleth," *Ching Feng* 38 (1995): 68–81; idem, "Exile and Return in the Perspective of 1997," in *Reading from This Place: Social Location and Biblical Interpretation in Global Perspective* (ed. Fernando F. Segovia and Mary Ann Tolbert; Minneapolis: Fortress,

both the Bible and the native text seriously by engaging the two texts in a creative way, making cross-connections between them. In the process the readers' horizons will be widened and their identities formulated at the point of confluence between the two texts. It is hoped that the tension between the two texts will remain adequately ambiguous.[6]

In this essay biblical Lamentations is read together with the Chinese poem *The Lament for the South,* written by Yu Xin (513–81), who sees himself as continuing the tradition of an ancient literary creation of southern China, *The Songs of the South (Chu Ci),* the Chu poetry of Qu Yuan (343—277 B.C.E.). This latter book, which dates from the fourth century B.C.E., is representative of an ancient Chinese lament tradition. The present form of it is generally attributed to Qu Quan.[7] I will first present a brief introduction to *The Lament for the South* before engaging in the cross-textual reading.

2. Yu Xin's *The Lament for The South*

Yu Xin's *Lament for the South* is composed in a Chu poetic form and consists of two parts: a preface of 72 lines and a body of 520 lines.[8] Many stories and legends have been adopted from the Chinese cultural milieu and refashioned in Yu Xin's own literary style. In expressing his grief, Yu Xin identifies with a number of great historical characters in the past. He shows both his literary skill and encyclopedic knowledge in the lament.

1995), 97–108; idem, "Cross-Textual Hermeneutics on Gospel and Culture," *AJT* 10 (1996): 38–48; idem, "Syncretism from the Perspectives of Chinese Religion and Biblical Tradition," *Ching Feng* 39 (1996): 1–24; idem, "Feminist Critique of the Bible and Female Principle in Culture," *AJT* 10 (1996): 240–52; idem, "The Recitation of the Past: A Cross-Textual Reading of Psalm 78 and the Odes," *Ching Feng* 38 (1996): 173–200.

6. Jeffery Kuan has provided a good assessment of the method of cross-textual interpretation against the landscape of biblical hermeneutics in Asia in his "Asian Biblical Interpretation," in *Dictionary of Biblical Interpretation* (ed. John H. Hayes; 2 vols.; Nashville: Abingdon, 1999), 1:70–77. The article also has a bibliography on the method.

7. For translation and annotation of *The Songs of the South,* see David Hawkes, *The Songs of the South: An Ancient Anthology of Poems by Qu Yuan and Other Poets* (Harmondsworth: Penguin, 1985). Hawkes also provides a very good introduction.

8. The Chinese text does not have any system of numbering the lines. This paper follows William T. Graham's arrangement and his translation into English in *The Lament for the South—Yu Hsin's Ai Chiang-nan Fu* (Cambridge: Cambridge University Press, 1980). There are, however, places where the present author finds modified renderings more appropriate, and retranslations are done accordingly. The transliterations adopted in present-day China will be used in rendering Chinese characters except in quotations and in names where conventional practices are widely accepted. See also commentary on Yu Xin in Ni Fan, *Yu Zishan Ji* (Taipei: Taiwan Commercial Press, 1968).

From the outset of the lament Yu Xin speaks from the perspective of a survivor—the same perspective found in each of the poems of Lamentations, as pointed out by F. W. Dobbs-Allsopp.[9] Lamentations is accordingly a "most profoundly life-embracing work," and the poet "stubbornly holds onto life and manifests a will to life,"[10] although his or her identity remains unknown to us. In contrast to Lamentations, the author of *The Lament for the South* is known, and scholars have no dispute over the authorship of Yu Xin. He was sent, at the age of forty-two, as ambassador from his own country, Liang in the south, to Western Wei in the north when Western Wei attacked Liang and destroyed the capital Jiangling in 554.[11] The enemy, Western Wei, then took him captive. Since Western Wei and the subsequent conquerors and rulers in the north all had great appreciation for his intellectual, literary, and administrative skills, he was forced to serve the enemy rulers in the north till his death at the age of sixty-nine (581 c.e.).

The date of the composition of *Lament* seems, to many, to be relatively easy to fix. Lines 11–12 refer to the stars completing their twelve-year cycle and a new cycle having started again, but the course of human history remains moving linearly forward. Yu Xin also laments that time has gone on without any sign of him ever returning. Furthermore, there is a description of the very harsh reality of life that his friends and fellow country-folks experienced as they were captured, exiled to the north, and died one by one over the course of time. It grieves him deeply when he sees himself getting old and being the sole survivor in exile (lines 506 and 510). Taking these general points together, the date of 578 c.e. has been proposed by Ch'en yin-k'o and endorsed by the authors of most commentaries.[12]

During the twenty-eight years of captivity, Yu Xin had written many poems of lament articulating his grief and sorrow and eventually his desperation. He bewails the disastrous fall of his own country and the great loss of life among his people. The fact that he is forced to serve the very enemies who had brought national calamities and catastrophic sufferings upon his people hurts him tremendously. His own family members also were captives of the enemies in the south. The tragedy becomes unbearable when his fellow country-folk harshly

---

9. F. W. Dobbs-Allsopp takes the biblical Lamentations as written from the perspective of the survivors of the calamity of the fall of Jerusalem in *Lamentations: A Bible Commentary for Teaching and Preaching* (IBC; Louisville: Knox, 2002), 46.

10. Ibid., 2, 3.

11. The Chinese way of counting one's age is different from that in the West. When a baby reaches the first birthday he or she is regarded as two years old. There is, therefore, an additional one year to the age of a person compared to the general practice.

12. Ch'en Yin-k'o, "Reading *The Lament for the South*," *Journal of Ch'ing-hua* 13 (1941): 11–16. See the discussion on dating in Graham, *The Lament for the South*, appendix 4, 173–74; William T. Graham, trans., "Yü Hsin and *The Lament for the South*," *HJAS* 36 (1976): 82–113. There are also others scholars who are in favor of a date close to the fall of Liang in 554; see Lu Tongqun, *A Special Study of Yu Xin* (Tianjin: Tainjin People's Press, 1997).

accuse him of betrayal and loss of integrity. In his poems we hear his agonies of self-pity and shame as well as internal conflicts between dynastic loyalty and moral integrity, added to the feeling of pain at the devastating suffering of his people.

Yu Xin's *The Lament for the South* devotes considerable space to the recollection of the past.[13] It recounts the family history of Yu's ancestors, going back to the past seven generations, with an emphasis on their contributions and the honors ascribed to them. The loyalty of the family to the imperial rule is duly remembered and narrated. In time of crisis the Chinese usually resort to the past for inspiration and courage. The present is perceived afresh in view of the recounting of historical events.[14] To Yu Xin, "remembering the past" (*huai gu*) has the aim not only of showing the contribution of his family to the Liang Dynasty but also of defending his loyalty and integrity even in his submission to the enemies. There is a detailed account of the good old days when the country was in peace and prosperity.

This is in contrast to the biblical lament with its remembering of the mighty deeds of God to underline the element of hope, since "[m]emory and hope are intertwined in prayer and worship in Israel."[15] Brevard Childs concludes in his study that the Hebrew word for "remember" (זכר) is mainly employed in Lamentations according to the genre of complaint psalms, but not necessarily in any cultic setting.[16] In the Chinese lament, exemplified in Yu Xin and Qu Yuan, poetic recitation of the past functions to contrast the royal favor experienced by the lamenter in times of national prosperity with the present misery, and there are no complaints against the deity. On the whole, when compared with the biblical laments, the Chinese do not develop anything like the complaint against God in the face of national calamities. Yu Xin states clearly the aim of composing his lament at the end of the preface:

Homeless at Xiating,
A wanderer at Gaoqiao,
Songs of Chu could not make me happy;
The wine of Lu was useless in dispelling sorrow.

---

13. Remembering the past is usually a theme in lament in the Chinese cultural articulation. Yu Xin himself survived under four different dynasties and nine emperors. He was sent as ambassador to Eastern Wei on cordial relations from 542 to 547. For details of the historical background, see Graham, *The Lament for the South*, ch. 2.

14. There is some truth in Prazniak's idea that "Chinese orthodoxy envisioned an ideal past that it sought to recover" (Roxann Prazniak, *Dialogues across Civilizations: Sketches in World History from the Chinese and European Experiences* [Boulder, Colo.: Westview, 1996], 183).

15. Kathleen D. Billman and Daniel L. Migliore, *Rachel's Cry: Prayer of Lament and Rebirth of Hope* (Cleveland: United Church Press, 1999), 32.

16. Brevard S. Childs, *Memory and Tradition in Israel* (SBT 37; London: SCM, 1962), 64.

So looking back I wrote this song
That it might serve as a record;
Not without words of fear and suffering,
It is still, at the core, a lament.
The sun is setting; my road is far away;
How long have I left in this world? (preface, lines 27–36)[17]

Yu Xin imitates and models Qu Yuan, the ancient sage of Chu in the south, in his composition of *The Lament of the South.* The title bears resemblance to the last line of *The Summons of the Soul,* assumed by tradition to have been written by Qu Yuan when he was banished from his country Chu by his own government and then exiled in a foreign land due to false accusation by other officials. The last line of *The Summons of the Soul* calls upon the soul to return to the south: "O Soul, come back! Alas for the southern land." Almost eight hundred years later, Yu Xin laments for his own exile and the fall of his country at Jiangling, which had been the capital of Chu eight hundred years ago.

Their similar historical fate and bitterness at being exiled from the south give rise to a sense of identification between Yu Xin and Qu Yuan, although in the case of the latter his country was not yet defeated, if not far from destruction. In a sense this is a Chinese example of what Tod Linafelt refers to as the survival of literature.[18] Yu Xin not only stands firmly in the line of thought that the suffering people in their pain must sing of their sorrow (lines 69–70), but he also renews the tradition of crying to the soul to return. This shamanistic feature of the quest for union with the mystery of life and the power of the cosmos in times of bitterness is preserved in the writings of Qu Yuan. It also survives in the literary form of *The Lament for the South.*

Qu Yuan wrote another poem entitled *Mourning for the Lost Capital,* to grieve and bewail the fall of the capital city Ying.[19] The city was the capital of Qu Yuan's Chu in 278 B.C.E. and was renamed Jiangling of Yu Xin's Liang in 554 C.E. The destruction of the same city is the cause of grief and despair in both *Mourning for the Lost Capital* and *The Lament for the South.* The cause of deep sorrow in both cases is, however, the reality of the exile in a foreign land. For Qu Yuan, in *Mourning for the Lost Capital* the exile had lasted nine years and there was no

---

17. Xiating and Gaoqiao are presumably place names, although scholars cannot be certain of their identification. They may be used for contrasting ideas of low and high. The song of the Chu state and the wine of the Lu state are known for dispelling sorrow. These two states may also be chosen for the contrast in the conception of locations in the south and the north respectively. See Graham, *The Lament for the South,* 107, and the translation of these lines on 52–53.

18. Tod Linafelt, *Surviving Lamentations: Catastrophe, Lament, and Protest in the Afterlife of a Biblical Book* (Chicago: University of Chicago Press, 2000).

19. The original title is *The Lament for Ying.* Here I follow the translation of Yang Xian-yi and Dai Nai-die, *The Songs of the South* (Beijing: Foreign Language Publishing, 2001), 147.

sign offering any hope of return. In the case of Yu Xin, it is a much longer period of twenty-eight years and, coupled with the fact that Yu Xin was then an old man, the hope of ever returning home alive was close to an impossibility.

In *The Lament for the South*, a strong wish among the exiles to return home is expressed in lines 449–52. Yu Xin, being a desperate and helpless captive from the south, has been longing for return. His being sixty-five years old when the poem was written explains the urgency, anxiety, and fear in the quest for home.[20] To Yu Xin, the lament is very real when it is understood in this Chinese context of cultural centrism. This mentality refuses to submit the highly civilized Chinese culture to the ruthless and merciless destruction by a less-civilized enemy. This explains the great sense of humiliation when the Mongolians defeated the Chinese people in the Song Dynasty in the twelfth century, the Manchurians the Ming Dynasty in the seventeenth century, and again the Western powers the Qing Dynasty in the nineteenth and twentieth centuries. Yu Xin perceives that the defeat of his country Liang is not only a great shock but a tremendous loss. It grieves his heart to see the empire collapse and the mountains and rivers split asunder by the barbaric enemies from the north:

> And yet they split apart mountains and streams,
> And carved up the empire.
> How could a hundred myriad loyal troops
> All at once discard their armor
> To be moved away and chopped down
> Like grass and trees? (preface, lines 49–51)

Calamity of such an immense magnitude demands a satisfactory explanation. The fall of the capital city of Liang signifies the loss of the ancient center of Chinese civilization to the barbarians. To the cultural centrism of the loyal guardian of Chinese civilization, the impact of the capture of the capital city by foreign armies is comparable to the fall of Jerusalem to the Babylonians. The insult of the exile amounts to death and humiliation, being cut off from the source of life in terms of civilization in the Chinese case and the land for biblical Israel. The personified Zion was concerned with the survival of the people of God, as was Qu Yuan (and like Yu Xin, who assumed the embodiment of a superior culture), also deeply preoccupied with the future of the Chinese civilization and his people.

The destruction of the capital city and prolonged exile prompted the quest for justification of the tragedy. The author of *The Mourning for the Lost Capital* does not take the blame upon himself, but protests against being accused of sin:

---

20. Yu Xin's quest to return to his homeland must be seen in relation to the deep influence of the conception of the centrality and superiority of Chinese culture in sharp distinction to that of the barbarians. Dying in a "barbaric" foreign land is regarded as one of the greatest curses.

The birds fly home to their old nests where they came from,
And the fox when they die turns their heads towards their caves.
That I was cast off and banished was truly for no crime.
By day and night I never can forget.[21]

A large portion of the poem describes the rebellion of the enemies and the cruelty of war. The misery and desolation are lamented in lines 443–448 and 453–460. In the description of the sufferings brought about by battles, there is a clear antiwar sentiment and condemnation of human suffering that permeates the words of *Lament*. The two seemingly unrelated sentences quoted from the *Book of Change* (*The Yi Jing*)--"The greatest gift of heaven and earth is life; the greatest treasure of the sage is the throne"--carry an antiwar ideology. This antiwar sentiment is clearly seen when we consult Yu Xin's citation of the same quotation in another of his poems, "A Song of the Sounding of the Horn" (Jiaodiao Qu). Here he adds two words to the above quotation: "Though the greatest treasure of the sage is the throne, the greatest gift of heaven and earth is surely life." Life must be held above the throne, not the other way round. The lives of the citizens are valuable and must not exist merely to serve the throne.[22] Both *The Lament for the South* and Lamentations share this basic critique of war and violence.[23]

Being uprooted and exiled to a foreign land under a foreign rule is a tragic experience. The degree of lament will certainly be intensified if the exiled person dies in an alien land, away from home and without family to mourn one's dead and to perform the burial rituals. Yu Xin's cry for home in the south in his old age can be seen in this context. But his personal grief is part and parcel of larger national calamities. The sufferer can never overcome the loss of so many numerous lives in his homeland.

---

21. Hawkes, *The Song of the South*, 166. King Huai entrusted Qu Yuan with the great responsibility in running the nation. Unfortunately, after the death of King Huai in the third year of his captivity in Qin (296 B.C.E.), the new king Xiang banished Qu Yuan from Jiangling. In 278 B.C.E. the Qin general Bo Qi sacked the capital and the Chu court was forced to move to a new capital in Chen, which was 250 miles to the northeast; see ibid., 162.

22. Lu Tongqun, *A Special Study of Yu Xin*, 67. In quoting and affirming what *The Book of Changes* proposes (i.e., that life is the greatest gift of heaven and earth and the greatest treasure of the sage is the throne), Yu Xin contrasts the present experience of the agony of the loss of life with the fall of the throne.

23. For the idea of the use of the image of women to depict war's atrocities, see Kathleen M. O'Connor, "Lamentations," in *The Women's Bible Commentary: Expanded Edition with Apocrypha* (ed. Carol A. Newsom and Sharon H. Ringe; Louisville: Westminster John Knox, 1998), 187.

3. THE WILL OF HEAVEN AND/OR HUMAN RESPONSIBILITY

I want to pick up another important issue for discussion: the question of agency in calamities and the ground for human suffering. Yu Xin in his lament tries to unlock the mystery of the downfall of the Liang Dynasty: "Neither simply fate nor mistakes in government could explain the destruction of a mighty empire."[24] It seems that, according to Yu Xin, the fall of his dynasty had been anticipated and portended by natural phenomena.

> Wasn't the royal aura of the south
> To end in three hundred years?
> This would explain why
> Swallowing up the world could not
> Prevent the tragedy at Zhidao,
> And standardizing axles and script
> Could not avert the disaster at Pingyang.[25]
> Alas
> When mountains crumbled
> National calamities seemed inescapable
> As spring and autumn seasons passed
> I grieve for the inevitable destruction
> Heaven's Will—human's doing
> Sorrowful and heart breaking. (preface, lines 59–66)

The assumption that the end of the mandate for the royal court and the succession of dynastic rule had been predicted and was comparable to changes in the natural order and seasonal cycle seems to affirm the dominant view on the heavenly will. Yu Xin laments the fact that in his family history his ancestry was originally from the north. Seven generations ago his great-grandparents settled in the south, but now he is being forced to return to the north. The heavenly will moves in full circle and governs people's lives (lines 495–496). These expressions affirming the heavenly will are significant for understanding *Lament*. In his other writings, however, Yu Xin is skeptical of the heavenly will.[26] Scholars usually agree that there are two contradictory conceptions of "heaven" in Yu Xin's mind: one takes it as the natural order; and the other declares that heaven represents a personal and willful character in charge of human affairs.[27]

---

24. Graham, *The Lament of the South*, 55.

25. On the abdication of the last emperor of Qin at Zhidao and the murder of the two emperors of Jin at Pingyang despite the efforts and policies for unification, see ibid., 110. Graham adds: "The fall of the Southern dynasties had also been predicted. Either fate or mistakes in government could explain the destruction of mighty empire" (ibid., 55).

26. Tongqun, *A Special Study of Yu Xin*, 52–59.

27. Ibid., 56.

Seen from the Chinese perspective, two characteristics of Lamentations stand out in contrast: the confession of sin; and the complaint against God. The expression "we have done wrong" does not appear in *Lament*, and the pouring out of one's heart before God in terms of accusation and complaint is not an essential component. When encountering sorrow and grief, the Chinese lament tends to articulate the mystical dimension of the will of heaven (*tian yi*) in conjunction with the social or political factors of the workings of humans (*ren shi*). The historical reality of the actions of forefathers and foremothers in the immediate past causes the inevitable suffering that befalls the present generation. The blame is primarily on human responsibility, but it is always in the larger context of the response of heaven, which is said to be reacting primarily to human performance. In the Chinese lament, the will of heaven is always assumed and implicitly acknowledged. It is in this sense that the effort to disentangle the tension and dynamics of the will of heaven and human responsibility will never be satisfactorily achieved.

The use of the notion of "heaven" (*tian*) is a more explicit way to articulate this very dimension of the mystery of the divine-human collaboration. In line 494, the exclamation "How could Heaven have been so drunk!" is intended to show that something has gone terribly wrong and is beyond our normal comprehension. The only viable means for making sense of this is to assume that heaven, not being of the natural order but an intelligent rational being, must have been drunk.

A survey of the appearance of the word "heaven" (*tian*) in *The Lament for the South* illustrates Yu Xin's conception of this reality of life. The word is used twenty times in *Lament*. In the body it occurs twice in reference to the emperor as "Son of Heaven" and four times in the phrase "heaven and earth" (*tianxia*). Nine of the remaining fourteen occurrences are in the preface (four times) and in the concluding paragraphs (five times), and all convey an understanding beyond the natural order of the blue sky. On the one hand, the tragedy of the defeat of the country is attributed to the wrong policy of the royal court in appointing worthless officials to key positions and the rebellious factions in the country (lines 487–492). On the other hand, by referring to a popular story in the previous dynasty, Yu Xin raises a significant question suggesting that something must be wrong with the whole course of present events. Yu Xin then takes the peculiar position of not laying any blame on heaven. A few lines after Yu quotes the *Book of Songs* (*Shi Jing*)--"In death and life [we are] separated and far apart"[28]-- he ironically asserts that even in the case of the most miserable and unbearable suffering one may not "question Heaven."[29]

---

28. *Book of Songs* (*Shi Jing*), no. 31; see Bernhard Karlgren, *The Book of Odes* (Stockholm: Museum of Far Eastern Antiquities, 1950), 19.

29. Questioning heaven is clearly an allusion to Chu Ci's "Heavenly Questions" (*Tian Wen*). The classical commentary of Wang Yi on the meaning of *Tian Wen* declares that "Heaven

Though far away in life and death,
One may not question Heaven.[30]
Not even though
The rest have almost all withered and fallen.
And, another Lingguang, I alone remain. (Lines 504 –06)[31]

Yu Xin rejects any basis for questioning heaven even though he is in the midst of national destruction, separated from his family and friends who have died and far away from those who are still alive at home in the south. As time goes by, his quest for home and the depth of his grief intensify. Therefore, at the end of *Lament* he complains about the lack of a person who can comprehend the grief he is trying to articulate.

The sun is entering its last conjunction,
The year is about to begin again.
Constantly driven by fear and anxiety,
Grieving in my twilight years.
Among the commoners of Xianyang,[32]
Not only the prince longs for home? (lines 507–510, 520)

Yu Xin expresses a belief in signs sent by heaven in the form of the natural order or astronomical portents. Omens are regarded as giving warning to evildoers and sociopolitical leaders, who take no notice of the signals and raise no alarm by their doings. In *The Lament for the South* there are eight references to astrological phenomena (preface line 12; lines 27–28, 48, 90, 138, 252, 307–308, 390). These, along with natural features such as rivers running dry (line 20) and mountains being shaken to the foundation, constitute a stock of metaphors used to symbolize the fall of a nation. The whole cosmic order was believed to have reacted to dynastic policies and the way that the emperor reigned. Omens and portents were signs of nature taking part in human affairs. They joined in the grief of the people at the destruction and the tragic exile of the people to the north.

A vengeful frost fell in summer;

---

is august and may not be questioned" and therefore favors "Heavenly Questions" instead of "Questioning Heaven."

30. Qu Yuan in his great despair and pain wrote the *Questioning Heaven* (*Tianwen*), a book of 172 questions addressing a variety of concerns from the creation of heaven and earth to the present-day reality. Hawkes's rendering, "the ultimate Questioning," is another alternative translation (Hawkes, *The Song of the South*, 90).

31. Graham, *Lament for the South*, 101. Yu Xin alludes to the collapse of all palaces and temples during the rebellion in Han's time, except the Lingguang Temple, which alone stands.

32. Yu Xin alludes to the story of the captured Chu Crown Prince being hostage in Qin and denied return to his country; see Graham, *Lament for the South*, 161–62.

Angry springs boiled up in autumn.
Qi's wife brought down a wall by her cries;
The Ladies of the Xiang stained bamboo with their tears
Rivers poisonous as the streams of Qin,
Mountains as high as the range of Xing,
Ten miles, five miles,
Long halts, short halts,
Driven by hunger after hibernating swallows (lines 433–39).[33]

The constellation and the natural order function metaphorically to express
the dimension of the mystery of life and the divine intervention represented by
God in Lamentations. Both the Chinese and Hebrew laments have formulated
an expression of "a cry to the beyond" in times of anguish. In Lamentations, it
is a request to God to look and see the terrible face of human suffering (1:9, 11,
20; 2:20; 3:49–50, 59; 5:1). Here divine violence is the cause of bitter complaint
against God from the depths of the human heart (1:13–15; 2:1–8; 3:1–18). Similarly, *Lament* also issues a complaint that the heaven has no eyes or that heaven
has not had its eyes open wide enough. The theological assertion in Lamentations
is that YHWH has made Lady Jerusalem suffer (1:5) and that, as a result, there is
none to comfort her (1:9). When YHWH is first mentioned in Lamentations in
the context of the harsh treatment of the exiles by the enemy, the emphasis is
on YHWH who effected the destruction of Jerusalem, not the enemy. In fact, it is
YHWH who has bitterly become the enemy of the people (2:4–5).[34]

Jannie Hunter observes that the cause of defeat by the enemy is, however, not
attributed to YHWH; it was the grave sin of the city that brought about the city's
downfall.[35] Here not only are the two agents, YHWH and the enemy, both present,
but a grave sin committed by humans is also said to be responsible for the affliction. In Lam 1:12 reference to the day of the fierce anger of YHWH is intended to
bring out YHWH's role in inflicting suffering on the people. Hunter assumes that
the real cause of it all is definitely the sins of the city (1:14) while YHWH is "the
architect of the consequence of sin."[36]

---

33. These lines depict the plight of the Liang captives who were carried off from their own
country to the foreign land. Their cries of lament were indeed echoed in nature. See Graham,
Lament for the South, 154.

34. The city laments in Western Asia exhibit a similar approach in times of the destruction of cities. Why Enlil destroyed his family and city is the most distressing and searching
question the goddesses ever put forward. For a study of the genre in the Hebrew Bible, see F.
W. Dobbs-Allsopp, *Weep, O Daughter of Zion: A Study of the City-Lament Genre in the Hebrew
Bible* (BibOr 44; Rome: Pontifical Biblical Institute, 1993).

35. Jannie Hunter, *Faces of a Lamenting City: The Development and Coherence of the Book
of Lamentations* (Frankfurt am Main: Lang, 1996), 113.

36. Ibid., 115.

In the Chinese *Lament* the cause of the destruction of the empire is not the sins of the people but the cruelty of the enemies and the mismanagement of the empire by the wrong officials, who are either incapable or wicked. Human disasters and national calamities are attributed to conflict and factionalism. It is the rebellious forces of Hou Jing who severely slaughtered and massacred Liang's generals, officials, and civilians. The destruction was so drastic and alarming that survivors were left terrified. Internal conflicts in the court further intensified the sense of desperation. Metaphorical phases are used in the poem to depict the calamities and the civil wars. Yu Xin makes reference to the four ancient states in conflict to drive home his lament for the internal crisis:

> Turbulent, boiling
> Disordered, chaotic
> Heaven and earth were cut off from us
> Spirits and humanity were in tragic cruelty
> Jin and Zheng refused to help
> Lu and Wei were not in harmony.
> They struggled to move the gate of heaven,
> Fought to turn the axis of the earth. (lines 217–224)

Yu Xin's concept of Hou Jing and his rebellion is framed in terms of "the civilized" and "the uncivilized." In the poem Hou Jing is seen as a barbarian, a wild ox with a nomadic nature (lines 111–116). Although *The Lament for the South* highlights this human dimension of the calamity and the personal experience of pain in face of the national disaster of the fall of the Liang Dynasty (preface, lines 13–14), Yu Xin, in his deep lament over the tragic collapse of his country and his miserable situation in captivity, links the sociopolitical events to a transcendental vision of divine disapproval or heavenly dissent. This is in great contrast to the views of most scholars, who stress the human orientation of Chinese culture, which presumably undermines references to the divine.

4. Conclusion

The aim of Yu Xin's *The Lament for the South* is to express his grief and sorrow over the national disaster of destruction of the royal throne and his painful but desperate desire to return to his home in the south. There is no prayer rendered to the divine that brings about the destruction and, therefore, no hope of divine intervention in terms of redemption or revenge against the enemies, as is the case in Lamentations. The transcendental perception of a personal God who can respond in reward and punishment and listen to human cries is not detected in Yu Xin's *Lament*. There is, nevertheless, an articulation of a dimension of mystery that is exhibited in the workings of the natural order giving signs of disapproval to human endeavors.

As for the discourse explaining the cause of destruction and national calamities, human responsibility in the various failings of the royal court, the corruption of government officials and human agency in the cruelty and ruthlessness of the enemy are indisputably cited. The political explanations are put in concrete and specific terms, in contrast to the general reference to human sins in Lamentations. There is naturally no place for complaint against God in the Chinese *Lament*, where atrocities *are* mostly attributed to human workings.

In contrast to Lamentations, the agency of the enemy is not perceived in terms of a divine being that brings about fulfillment of divine intention. The Chinese *Lament* is very critical of the cruelty of the enemy. The accusation against the destructive rebellious force of the enemy, Hou Jing, in the year 548 comes at the beginning of the preface to the *Lament* (preface, lines 1–4) and forms the context of the laments for the people's severe suffering and Yu Xin's subsequent misfortune as a captive in the north (lines 5–8).

The English rendering of the Chinese phrase in the four characters—"Heaven's will human affair" (line 65)—is usually expressed in an either/or mentality, while the Chinese original does not suggest making a choice.[37] It is both heaven's will and human responsibility that brought about the destruction, and this constitutes the core of the lament. Biblical Lamentations is also unclear as to which holds sway when it comes to the controlling factors in human calamities: God's role in punishing and afflicting pain, human sins and rebellion, or the cruelty and arrogance of the enemies? The ambiguity and the tension are properly maintained. Lamentations and *The Lament for the South* both resist the temptation to view human sufferings one-dimensionally. The reality of a constant negotiation between the theodic and the antitheodic impulses must be kept alive.[38]

Lament is the language of the lamenter who is not seeking explanation but the expression of grief. Both Lamentations and *The Lament for the South* provide the sufferer with the means to relate to the profound unknown and the lamenter with a process to discharge the unbearable emotion. They both give the mourner a voice. This language of the lamenter, which is intrinsically characterized by ambiguities and obscurities, is indispensable to those encountering pain and grief in human situations. It gives them a voice to release their grievous and disturbing emotions. Cries of lament, therefore, do not necessarily address God directly, but they are outpourings that "help people to weep over their tragedy and thus release their pain."[39] These free poetic articulations of the profoundly inarticulable and incomprehensible are a valuable human heritage that will survive this present wounded generation.

---

37. Graham translates as: "Whether it was heaven's will or man's doing" (*The Lament for the South*, 56).

38. Dobbs-Allsopp, *Lamentations*, 30.

39. O'Connor, "Lamentations," 187.

The Revival of Lament in Medieval *Piyyuṭîm*

William Morrow

The purpose of this essay is to integrate a reading of a medieval complaint prayer with the argument of my recent book on the history of lament.[1] First I will describe the poem and point out its relevance to a discussion of the lament tradition. Then I will contextualize it within the history of complaint prayer in earlier Jewish sources. Finally, I will explain how the poem sheds light on the emergence of protest prayer in biblical and postbiblical sources more generally.

A word on terminology seems appropriate before proceeding, however. Along with the term "lament," the biblical texts in question have also been called "prayers of complaint,"[2] forms of the "arguing-with-God" tradition,[3] and "protest prayer."[4] Here I will use the terms "lament," "protest," "complaint," and "argumentative prayer" with some flexibility.

The appendix contains the text of Isaac bar Shalom's poem, "There Is No One Like You among the Dumb." This poem registers the destruction of a Jewish community during the Second Crusade. The events it refers to took place on the twentieth day of the month of Nisan, in the year 4907 of the Jewish calendar, or 1147 C.E. Unfortunately, the particular community the poem envisages cannot be identified. But the events recorded reflect a common pattern of the times. During the Crusades many Jewish communities in France and Germany were destroyed, with German Jews being especially hard hit. Usually the Christian mob offered Jews a choice between conversion and death. Faced with these alternatives, Jews for the most part opted for death, connoted by the term for martyrdom: "sanctification of the name." Jewish men would kill their women and children and then kill themselves, if they did not first fall victim to the mob, which would

---

1. William Morrow, *Protest against God: The Eclipse of a Biblical Tradition* (Hebrew Bible Monographs 4; Sheffield: Sheffield Phoenix Press, 2006), 210.

2. John Day, *Psalms* (OTG; Sheffield: JSOT Press, 1992), 20.

3. Anson Laytner, *Arguing with God: A Jewish Tradition* (Northvale, N.J.: Aronson, 1990), xvii–xviii.

4. Craig C. Broyles, *The Conflict of Faith and Experience in the Psalms: A Form-Critical and Theological Study* (JSOTSup 52; Sheffield: JSOT Press, 1989), 52.

then proceed to destroy copies of the Torah and Talmud. This pattern of events is reflected in "There Is No One Like You among the Dumb."[5]

The poem begins by recounting a confrontation between a Christian mob and a community of Jews leading to the demand for conversion in lines 15–21. The refusal of the Jewish population is followed by the slaughter of women and children at the hands of Jewish men in lines 29–49. Then the mob attacks, destroying the Torah and the surviving males in lines 50–70. The poem ends with a call for salvation and revenge in lines 71–91.

The poem was preserved in Ashkenazi liturgies that commemorated the destruction of Jewish communities in the Rhineland. This commemoration took place in services between Passover and the Festival of Weeks. Technically, a poem such as "There Is No One Like You among the Dumb" is called a *zulat*, a supplementary poem inserted between standard prayers.[6] There are literally thousands of such poems, or *piyyuṭim*, composed from the Byzantine era onward as embellishments to the prayers used in the standard liturgy. But "There Is No One Like You among the Dumb" stands out because of its sharp and visceral criticism of God.

How is one to account for this? In offering an explanation for this poem, it is important to note that there are other examples of Jewish protest prayers from the Middle Ages and later. They comprise, however, only a fraction of the total number of *piyyuṭim*. These argumentative prayers are focused on complaining of the destructions during the Crusades or other forms of extreme persecution such as the Chmielnitski pogroms.[7] I will suggest below that there is a theological principal at work in lamenting the experiences of such complete destruction that generally accounts for the irruption of protest in a tradition whose intercessory prayers are, for the most part, conditioned by praise and penitence.

"There Is No One Like You among the Dumb," as is typical of *piyyuṭim*, manifests a rich matrix of intertextual references. I have highlighted only some of these in the appendix, concentrating on biblical references at the phrase level. However, there are also important connections with the Bible on the level of vocabulary, and I have not gone through the poem documenting its talmudic references. These are obviously important, as can be seen from the opening line of the poem. The statement "There is no one like you among the dumb" is a rabbinic paraphrase of Ps 86:8, "There is no one like you among the gods." The paraphrase occurs in b. Giṭ. 56b.[8] This gemarah is connected to problems involved in buying property confiscated by the Roman authorities after the Jewish Wars. In the course of that

---

5. Jakob J. Petuchowski, *Theology and Poetry: Studies in the Medieval Piyyut* (Littman Library of Jewish Civilization; London: Routledge & Kegan Paul, 1978), 81.

6. Ibid., 80.

7. See Laytner, *Arguing with God*, 129–59.

8. Ibid., 81.

discussion, there is a narrative of the events leading up to the defilement of the Second Temple and its destruction. In that context, rabbinic authorities lament the silence of God at Roman blasphemies. The association of the opening line of the poem with the destruction of the Second Temple is an important datum to which I will return below.

The biblical allusions made by the poem are particularly striking because of the attention given to motifs taken from psalms identified as communal laments. Most clearly, the poem is punctuated by a literal repetition of a petition from Ps 83:2. In addition, the poem is framed by quotes from Ps 44 (lines 6, 90), and there are also citations from the communal laments in Isa 64 (line 52) and Ps 80 (line 74). These citations can be augmented by considering the allusions to poems that are laments of the individual (lines 56, 89). While it would be anachronistic to impute to the poet knowledge of modern genre categories, all of these references belong to a particular rhetorical trope that we may call the arguing-with-God tradition. No other form of rhetoric has the same prominence in the poem. Moreover, as in the case of most complaint psalms in the Bible, there is no confession of sin. This is clearly a poem of communal protest against God complete with an accusatory statement in lines 1–2, an accusatory question drawn from Isa 64, extended descriptions of the suffering of the community, as well as concluding petitions.[9]

For many students of lament literature, "There Is No One Like You among the Dumb" comes as something of a surprise. After all, scholars usually proffer the opinion that liturgical lament died out in the postexilic period.[10] But if so, how do we explain the composition and performance of Isaac bar Shalom's poem in the early Middle Ages?

An answer to this question begins by recognizing that the tradition of protest prayer continued in early Judaism (albeit in a somewhat diminished form). Much of the evidence from the rabbinic period has been presented by Anson Laytner.[11]

---

9. For a survey of form-critical discussions on community lament psalms, see Morrow, *Protest against God*, 76–81.

10. See, e.g., Walter Brueggemann, "The Costly Loss of Lament," *JSOT* 36 (1986): 57; Ottmar Fuchs, *Die Klage als Gebet: Eine theologische Besinnung am Beispiel des Psalms 22* (Munich: Kösel, 1982), 441–45; Hermann Gunkel and Joachim Begrich, *Introduction to the Psalms: The Genres of the Religious Lyric of Israel* (trans. James D. Nogalski; Mercer Library of Biblical Studies; Macon, Ga.: Mercer University Press, 1998), 197–98; David Kraemer, *Responses to Suffering in Classical Rabbinic Literature* (New York: Oxford University Press, 1995), 211–18; Karl-Joseph Kuschel, "Ist Gott verantwortlich für das Übel: Überlegungen zu einer Theologie der Anklagen," in *Angesichts des Leids an Gott Glauben? Zur Theologie der Klage* (ed. Gotthard Fuchs; Frankfurt am Main: Knecht, 1996), 228–31; Meinard Limbeck, "Die Klage—Eine verschwundene Gebetsgattung," *TQ* 157 (1977): 13–16; Claus Westermann, *Praise and Lament in the Psalms* (trans. Keith R. Crim and Richard N. Soulen; Atlanta: Knox, 1981), 195–213.

11. Laytner, *Arguing with God*, 41–126.

Laytner's evidence actually does not overthrow so much as qualify the consensus about the demise of lament in the postexilic and postbiblical period. My own work has also attempted to nuance earlier discussions about the eclipse of protest prayer in the later biblical period and after.

The textual record contained in extrabiblical materials from Second Temple times in the Apocrypha, the Pseudepigrapha, and the Dead Sea Scrolls indicates that poems of argumentative prayer ceased to be composed for liturgical contexts.[12] This observation underscores the contrast between the biblical witness and postbiblical religion. The consensus that new complaint prayers were not being composed for liturgical use in later Second Temple times remains safe. However, it is too much to claim that protest prayer was no longer practiced. In fact, a variety of argumentative tropes are attested in postbiblical Jewish literature. These include negative second-person petitions directed to God, informal argumentative prayers, and the rhetoric of Lamentations.

Christians, of course, will be familiar with the petition "lead us not into temptation." What many will not realize, however, is that this kind of petition is grounded in the rhetoric of lament. In *Protest against God* I documented the fact that second-person negative petitions directed to God are characteristic of the argumentative tradition in the psalms and of no other genre. In extrabiblical Second Temple literature, such petitions become used in various kinds of prayers, including both penitential and apotropaic compositions.[13] Behind them is the fear that God may abandon the community, and behind this fear stands the possibility that such an accusation might be made if the situation warranted it. The potential of protest even in penitential prayers is indicated by the appearance of the occasional question directed to God in the genre called *slihot*.[14]

More weight should be given, however, to the ongoing presence of informal complaint prayer. By informal complaint prayer, I mean argumentative prayer directed spontaneously to God by community representatives. There are a number of examples in biblical narrative (most prominently Moses) and prophetic texts (e.g., Exod 5:22–23; 32:11–13; Jer 4:10; Ezek 9:8; Hab 1:2–4).[15] This trope continues in postbiblical literature. There are good examples associated with the Maccabees and the desecration of the Second Temple by Antiochus Epiphanes (1 Macc 2:7–13; 3:50–53). Informal protest calling God to account for his actions also appears in literature connected with the destruction of the Second Temple, most notably in 2 Esdras (e.g., 3:4–36; 4:22–25; 5:23–30; 6:38–59).

The same kind of rhetoric is also attested in rabbinic literature in the genre that Joseph Heinemann calls "the law-court pattern of prayer." This pattern is

---

12. Morrow, *Protest against God*, 176–77.
13. Ibid., 158–59.
14. Laytner, *Arguing with God*, 154–55.
15. Morrow, *Protest against God*, 23.

found in narratives about rabbinic figures, such as Honi the Circle-Maker, and is also attributed to biblical figures in midrash.[16] Consequently, the arguing-with-God tradition was remembered in rabbinic circles. This will explain, among other things, the rabbinic paraphrase that is the basis of the first line of our poem. "There is no one like you among the dumb" is an accusation against God that reflects a rhetoric of protest preserved in rabbinic exegesis. By the same token, it is not surprising to find complaint against God implicated in the midrashim to Lamentations.[17]

In fact, the book of Lamentations and the long tradition of poetry that it initiated also preserve traits of lament. Lamentations employs a number of rhetorical strategies to elicit a response from God in the face of overwhelming communal tragedy. Its poems express grief and anger as well as guilt and repentance.[18] They also contain pleas for God to witness the devastation of the community and to act on its behalf. Psychologically, there is a close relationship between grief and rage,[19] so it would not be surprising if the tradition of writing poetry in the style of Lamentations sustained not only petition and penitence but also protest. In fact, one can find traces of complaint in the *piyyuṭīm* composed for Tisha b'Av, the day that is given over to mourning the destruction of the First and Second Temples and other significant disasters in Jewish history.[20]

One must explain the composition of "There Is No One Like You among the Dumb," therefore, on the assumption that the rhetoric of protest remained a potential in medieval Judaism. Nevertheless, for the most part complaint against God was muted in Byzantine and medieval Jewish literature, where it was expressed at all. For example, *piyyuṭīm* composed by the famous *payṭān*, Eliezar ben Kallir, couch their criticism of God in a subtle mode that stops short of explicit complaints against God.[21] The same is also true of other well-known poems of implied complaint associated with Simeon bar Isaac and Judah Halevi.[22] But what has happened that protest became explicit and liturgically performed in the case of Isaac bar Shalom?

---

16. Joseph Heinemann, *Prayer in the Talmud: Forms and Patterns* (SJ 9; Berlin: de Gruyter, 1977), 208–17.

17. Kraemer, *Responses to Suffering*, 140–46.

18. Tod Linafelt, *Surviving Lamentations: Catastrophe, Lament, and Protest in the Afterlife of a Biblical Book* (Chicago: University of Chicago Press, 2000), 59.

19. Paul Joyce, "Lamentations and the Grief Process: A Psychological Reading," *BibInt* 1 (1993): 312–13.

20. Laytner, *Arguing with God*, 163–64.

21. See the study in Linafelt, *Surviving Lamentations*, 117–32.

22. The poems referred to are "Hasten, My Beloved" (Simeon bar Isaac) and "The Day the Deep Sea Turned" (Judah Halevi); see the discussion in Petuchowski, *Theology and Poetry*, 56–70.

There appear to be two factors. First, the destruction of the Jewish communities in northern Europe entailed the ruin of populations known for their piety and Torah scholarship. The explanation of this violence as due to divine judgment strained credibility. One consequence of the failure of an appeal to divine judgment was the revival of the image of the Aqedah, the binding of Isaac, as a way of processing the devastation of Jewish communities by the Crusades.[23] But the other association made was with the destruction of the temple itself. This was possible because Torah scholarship is identified in rabbinic Judaism as a practice that corresponds to temple service.[24] Note the combination of sacrificial imagery in "There Is No One Like You among the Dumb" and description of the destruction of the Torah scrolls and scholars. Isaac bar Shalom underscores the association of the destruction of the Jewish community with that of the Second Temple by using the quotation from b. Giṭ. 56b, which complains of God's silence during the desecration of the temple by Titus.

Other poems of the Crusader era also equate the destruction of Jewish community with the ruin of the temple.[25] This association appears, for example, in poetry written by Kalonymous ben Judah that is still read during the services of Tisha b'Av. Significantly, these poems of Kalonymous also contain accusatory questions directed at God. For example, as in "There Is No One Like You among the Dumb," toward the end of the *piyyuṭ*, "Oh that my head were water," Kalonymous alludes to the lament of Isa 64:11: "Will you be quiet and restrain yourself, and not gird yourself in wrath?"[26] And in Kalonymous's *piyyuṭ*, "I said, 'Look away from me,'" we read, "How long will you be like a warrior powerless to save?"[27] Even the Hebrew chroniclers of the time cannot resist breaking out in protest as they recount the massacres of their contemporaries. Shelomoh bar Shimshon expostulates, "Who has seen or heard such a thing? … When on one day … there were killed eleven hundred pure souls, including babes and infants.… Will you remain silent for these, O Lord?"[28]

If there is a conceptual difference between such utterances and biblical models, it rests principally on the fact that the medieval examples I have quoted do not stray far from scriptural rhetoric. Note that Isaac bar Shalom, Kalonymous, and Shelomoh bar Shimshon all echo the plea of Isa 64:11, "Will you remain

23. Yosef H. Yerushalmi, *Zakhor: Jewish History and Jewish Memory* (Seattle: University of Washington Press, 1982), 38–39.

24. Max Kadushin, *The Rabbinic Mind* (3rd ed.; New York: Bloch, 1972), 213–14.

25. Linda Weinhouse, "Faith and Fantasy: The Texts of the Jews," *Medieval Encounters* 5 (1999): 393–94; Joseph B. Soloveitchik, *The Lord Is Righteous in All His Ways: Reflections on the Tish'ah be-Av Kinot* (ed. Jacob J. Schacter; Jersey City, N.J.: Ktav, 2006), 259–60.

26. Abraham Rosenfeld, ed., *The Authorized Kinot for the Ninth of Av* (London: Labworth, 1965), 134.

27. Ibid., 141.

28. Cited in Yerushalmi, *Zakhor*, 38.

silent for these, O Lord?" There is a kind of derivation from biblical authority that stands in contrast with the freedom of the psalmists, who seem more innovative in the way they direct their protests against God than the medieval writers. There is reason to suppose, therefore, that even where explicit complaint against God was considered acceptable to medieval Jews, the arguing-with-God tradition remained more constrained than it had in biblical times. But why it should burst out into liturgical expression at all is a point worth pondering.

The explicit protest of "There Is No One Like You among the Dumb" was enabled by an equation between the destruction of medieval Jewry and the desecration of the temple. In this regard, it is interesting to note the distribution of themes between the community laments and the penitential prayers of the Bible itself. Penitential prayers in their own way protest the exile (see Dan 9:4–19; Ezra 9:6–15; Neh 1:5–11; 9:5–37), but it is community laments that protest the actual destruction of the temple (see Isa 63:7–64:11; Pss 74; 79; 80). By the same token, argumentative prayer became prominent in the Second Temple period in literature aligned with the desecration of Antiochus Epiphanes and the Roman destruction.[29]

Of course, the temple was a powerful symbol of the presence of God in the midst of the people. As noted above, rabbinic Judaism believed that the same presence was guaranteed by the study of Torah and Talmud. For these collective institutions to be violently eliminated was to threaten the very foundation of the God-Israel relationship, for God was thought to have authored Israel's history and created all of its fundamental institutions. It is a contradiction in terms that Israel should disappear or that its institutions should be destroyed. By the very virtue of creating them, of calling Israel into being, Israel's deity had a responsibility to ensure their continuity.[30] Such logic underlies not only the protests of collective complaint in the Bible but also those in extrabiblical times, including Isaac bar Shalom's "There Is No One Like You among the Dumb."

These observations can also be viewed from the perspective of trauma theory. Violence can have a detrimental effect on a person's worldview, or what can also be called "the assumptive world" of the victim: beliefs in the benevolence and meaningfulness of the world can be severely undermined.[31] Through generations of exile, Jews assumed that God remained committed to being present to the world and to Israel.[32] Penitential prayer may mourn the loss of land and temple, but it continues to assume that there is a deity to whom one can pray, a God who some-

---

29. Morrow, *Protest against God,* 177.
30. Ibid., 92–93.
31. I. Lisa McCann and Laurie A. Pearlman, *Psychological Trauma and the Adult Survivor: Theory, Therapy and Transformation* (Brunner/Mazal Psychosocial Stress Series 21; New York: Brunner/Mazal, 1990), 60–61.
32. Kadushin, *Rabbinic Mind,* 223–24.

how remains present to the community. But this assumption is undermined when the very institutions that mediate the divine presence are decisively destroyed. At that point, penitence gives way to protest. This became true for medieval Jews when their communities were decimated during the Crusades. With Torah scrolls and Talmuds destroyed and no learned scholars to expound them, God's presence was not simply attenuated—it was decisively removed. Hence, there was a breakdown in the assumptive world of medieval Judaism as devastating as the loss of the temple. It could be met, however, by reviving symbols in the tradition that responded to such a loss in earlier times: community lament.

APPENDIX

THERE IS NO ONE LIKE YOU AMONG THE DUMB

by Isaac bar Shalom (1147 C.E.)[33]

1–7

There is no one like you among the dumb, [Ps 86:8]	אין כמוך באלמים
silent and passive toward those who create trouble!	דומם ושותק למעגימים
Our many enemies are rising up.	צרינו רבים קמים
When they meet together to revile us,	בהוסדם יחד לגדפנו
"Where is your king?" they insult us.	איה מלככם חרפונו
We have not backslidden nor acted treasonably. [Ps 44:18]	לא שכחנו ולא שקרנו
Do not keep silence! [Ps 83:2]	אל דמי לך

8–14

Those driven out from human society became proud, [Job 30:5]	גרושים מן גו גאו
and they crushed your people with force.	ועמך בפרך דכאו
Your enemies have raised their heads;	משנאיך ראש נשאו
those who inquire of ghosts and idols,	דורשי אובות ואלילים
our enemy judges say,	יאמרו אויבינו פלילים

---

33. The Hebrew text is based on Petuchowski, *Theology and Poetry*, 74–77. The translation is by William Morrow.

"What wretched Jews!"

מה היהודים האמללים

Do not keep silence! [Ps 83:2]

אל דמי לך

15–21

"Take some advice for yourselves,

הבו לכם עצה

lest you become a disgrace

פן תהיו לשמצה

or a cause for contention and strife.

הן לריב ומצה

But if you become like us,

ואם תהיו כמונו

draw near and turn toward us,

לנו תקרבו ותפנו

then we will become one people."

לעם אחד והיינו

Do not keep silence! [Ps 83:2]

אל דמי לך

22–28

The afflicted ones cried out and answered,

זעקו לוקים ויענו

"We shall not turn away, nor shall we worship it.

לא נשוב ולא נעבדנו

'You shall regard it as utterly detestable and abominable.' [Deut 7:26]

שקץ תשקצנו ותעב תתעבנו

Our redeemer lives eternally;

חי וקים גאלנו

him shall we worship and give our devotion.

אותו נעבוד ונחטבנו

In a time of distress will come our salvation."

בעת צרה ישועתנו

Do not keep silence! [Ps 83:2]

אל דמי לך

29–35

They prepared a slaughter of children.

טבוח ילדים הכינו

We directed our mind to the sacrificial blessing,

ברכת הזבח כונו

"Hear, Israel, the Lord our God, [Deut 6:4]

שמע ישראל יי אלהינו

the Lord is one," that we might affirm his unity.

יי אחד וניחדנו

Thus for the sanctification of his name were we killed,

ועל קדוש שמו הרגנו

so our wives and children would fall by the sword.

לנפול בחרב נשינו וטפנו

Do not keep silence! [Ps 83:2]

אל דמי לך

36–42

As priests for their whole burnt sacrifice,

כהנים לזבח עולתם

they bound the children and their mothers

עקדו ילדים ואמותם

and burnt their skins by fire,

ושרפו באש את עורותם

to sprinkle the blood of sisters and brothers

לזרוק דמי אחיות ואחים

and to make smoke sacrificial portions,

ולקטר אמורי ניחוחים

both the head and the pieces.

את הראש ואת הנתחים

Do not keep silence! [Ps 83:2]

אל דמי לך

43–49

It was a crowded, charred pile,

מערכה גדושה שזופה

like an oven neither covered nor swept.

כבירה לא קטומה וגרופה

And the whole house of Israel wept at the burning. [Lev 10:6]

וכל בית ישראל יבכו את השרפה

Those falling into the flaming sparks of the Lord

נופלים לרשפי שלהבת יה

were assigned the place of the exiles,

נועדים למחיצת בני עליה

Hananiah, Mishael, and Azariah.

חנניה מישאל ועזריה

Do not keep silence! [Ps 83:2]

אל דמי לך

50–56

They treated the Torah of Moses as dung,

סחי שמו תורת משה

also the Talmud of Rabina and Rab Ashai.

ותלמוד רבינא ורב אשי

Will you restrain yourself and keep silence at this? [Isa 64:11]	העל אלה תתאפק ותחשה
Pages and parchments went to the swords,	עמודים וגוילים לאבחות
and holy letters went flying—	ואתיות קדושות פורחות
divine writing engraved on the tablets! [Exod 32:16]	מכתב אלהים חרות על הלחות
Do not keep silence! [Ps 83:2]	אל דמי לך

57–63

The enemy marched about armed	פסע אויב בזין
and destroyed my bounty and put it to naught.	ואבד טובי ושם לאין
And he killed everything pleasant to the eye. [Lam 2:4]	ויחרוג כל מחמדי עין
To be precise, in 4907	ציון לפרט וארשת
distress was following distress.	צרה אל אחותה נגשת
They have prepared a net for my steps. [Ps 57:7]	הכינו לפעמי רשת
Do not keep silence! [Ps 83:2]	אל דמי לך

64–70

At the time of Nahshon's act of sanctification,	קץ קדוש נחשון
the foe struck God's eye.	נגע צר באישון
On the twentieth of the first month,	בעשרים לחדש הראשון
torn to pieces were those who studied difficult things,	רטשו דורשי חמורות
light things and syllogisms,	וקלות ושוות גזרות
the laws, statutes, and instructions.	החקים והמשפטים והתורות
Do not keep silence! [Ps 83:2]	אל דמי לך

71–77

Almighty One, be zealous for your Torah.

שדי קנא לתורתך

Put on your vengeance and jealousy

לבש נקמתך וקנאתך

and rouse up your might. [Ps 80:3]

ועוררה את גבורתך

Rebuke the swinish animal

גערת חית נובר

with destruction, devastation, and brokenness—

בכליון שוד ושבר

him and his people with disease.

אותו ואת עמו בדבר

Do not keep silence! [Ps 83:2]

אל דמי לך

78–84

Your right hand hews Rahab in pieces; [Isa 51:9]

ימינך רהב מחצבת

crush the skull with a hammer

הרץ גלגלת במקבת

of her who sits so refined. [Isa 47:8]

זאת עדינה היושבת

O dazzling and ruddy one from Seir, [Song 5:10]

צח ואדום משעיר

bring a destructive storm on the princess.

נסוכה בכליון תסעיר

Awaken zeal like a man of war. [Isa 42:13]

כאיש מלחמות קנאה תעיר

Do not keep silence! [Ps 83:2]

אל דמי לך

85–91

Take ownership again of our remnants. [Exod 15:16]

קנה שנית שרידינו

Let us look publicly on your miracles.

ברבים נסיך תראנו

Ordain peace for us.

שלום תשפות לנו

Our Holy One, show mercy on your scattered ones.

חמול זרוייך קדושנו

May a generous spirit support us. [Ps 51:14]

ורוח נדיבה תסמכנו

Rise up, O our help, and redeem us. [Ps 44:27]

קומה עזרתה לנו ופדנו

Do not keep silence! [Ps 83:2]

אל דמי לך

The Lament Traditions of Enslaved African American Women and the Lament Traditions of the Hebrew Bible

Wilma Ann Bailey

This essay will explore the similarities and differences between the lament traditions of enslaved African American women and those of the ancient Israelites. It assumes that, even though the two communities existed in distinctly different historical time periods, a common history of oppression, slavery, and abuse will yield some similarities in their expressions and traditions of complaint. Approaching the Civil War period, enslaved African Americans were in a broad sense familiar with the historiography of ancient Israel and could and did incorporate some of those traditions into their own expressions of pain. Since the enslaved African Americans also shared with the ancient Israelites a culture that was primarily oral and aural in orientation, they may be able to illuminate expressions and practices of the lament traditions of ancient Israel for communities that are more oriented to the printed page and visual images.

Biblical Laments

The biblical lament tradition has been closely studied for quite some time. Various scholars have identified characteristics found in the genre and studied the life situation of the lament as illustrated in narrative and poetic texts of the Hebrew Bible. No two lists of characteristics are identical. Two samples will suffice to illustrate the differences and similarities. The early form critic Sigmund Mowinckel created two broad categories for biblical laments: national psalms of lamentation; and personal psalms of lamentation.[1] He thought that the life situation for the national laments was a "public fast-day" and understood the lament traditions to be a part of "penitential rites" that were usually designed to prevent

---

1. Sigmund Mowinckel, *The Psalms in Israel's Worship* (trans. D. R. Ap-Thomas; 2 vols.; Nashville: Abingdon, 1962), 1:193; 2:1.

a disaster from occurring.[2] According to Mowinckel, common characteristics of biblical lament poems include: "invocation of Yahweh's name"; attributes of God, praise, "cry of supplication"; a "description of the distress"; "the evil and audacious words of the enemies"; a prayer asking God to notice the situation; "a prayer for revenge"; an "appeal to the honour of Yahweh"; and, finally, a statement of "confidence of being heard."[3] Mowinckel, of course, did not find all these characteristics in every psalm of lament, nor could he be certain of their *Sitz im Leben*. Mowinckel assumed that the laments were part of penitential rites, but many of the poems of lament found in the Hebrew Bible do not have a statement of repentance. Psalms 42 and 43, for example, are generally placed within the genre of lament, although they lack statements of penitence. This is an important factor when we compare biblical laments to the African American lament tradition. The ancient Israelites were often bewildered by their suffering, which they sometimes thought was completely unmerited. When they thought that they had done nothing to deserve their suffering, they felt no need to repent. When an identifiable failure on their part resulted in their suffering, they realized that repentance was appropriate. In either case, they cried out to God with the expectation that God would show divine compassion and bring relief. Toni Craven lists fewer characteristics, and, again, they do not always show up in every poem of lament. They include "address to God, complaint, confession of trust, petition, words of assurance, vow of praise."[4] Common to both lists is the statement of complaint. In the thinking of almost all scholars, this is what determines that a poem is a lament.

Because Mowinckel and Craven are studying written texts, both assume that the complaint must be articulated to define the genre. However, in the writings of ancient Israel, one finds references to moans and groans that do not rise to the level of articulated speech and yet express the pain and suffering that the community endured. This is a characteristic that the ancient Israelite community shares with the enslaved African American community. It is perhaps appropriate to include these in the complaint genre, if the moans and groans are understood to be not just ejaculations but sustained sung utterances.

In the narrative tradition of the biblical laments, the *Sitz im Leben* for lamenting is occasionally written into the text. For example, Rizpah's response to the killing of her two sons by the Gibeonites with the permission of David is described in 2 Sam 21: "Rizpah, the daughter of Ayyah, took the sackcloth and spread it for herself upon the rock. From the beginning of the harvest until water fell upon them from the sky, she did not permit a bird of the sky to rest upon

2. Ibid., 1:193–94.

3. Ibid., 1:193–217.

4. Toni Craven, *The Book of Psalms* (Collegeville, Minn.: Liturgical Press, 1992), 27.

them by day or an animal of the field by night."[5] The voice of Rizpah is not heard in the text. In the poetic tradition, however, the life situation is most typically absent, but the words of lamentation are there to be read. Mowinckel suggested a temple provenance for many of the psalms, including the psalms of lament. Because we have only the final version or versions of most biblical laments, we cannot easily get back to the original compositions or their original life situation. Like the victory poem that appears twice in Exod 15 in a shorter and longer version, some of the psalms of lament may have had shorter, simpler versions whose provenance was an actual event of personal or communal tragedy.

We know a little about the role that music played in the laments of ancient Israel. We assume that the laments, like other psalms, were accompanied by music. Because we have only the words, we may be tempted to accord them undue significance. It may be that in ancient times the music was as important, and perhaps more important, than the words. The so-called *qinah* meter, a long line followed by a shorter line in imitation of the progress of grief, is not consistently found in poems identified as laments in the Hebrew Bible, but it may have been favored in some communities. As noted above, biblical laments are primarily identified by characteristics based on their verbal content. Is it possible that another type of lament existed in ancient Israel, a wordless lament identified by moans and groans?

Enslaved African American Women: The Context

The vast majority of African American women are descendents of enslaved persons who were brought to the Americas from Africa prior to 1860.[6] The conditions under which the enslaved people lived are well known. They were forced to work under inhumane conditions. They were beaten and abused. They had family members sold away. Their names and identities were erased and replaced by names and identities chosen for them by those who also enslaved them. They had no control over their present or their future. The plight of enslaved females was even worse. Sexual abuse and humiliation were rampant both on the ships and on dry land. Enslaved women were sold into prostitution.[7] In what was perhaps the first memoir written by an enslaved African American (Caribbean) female, Mary Prince reports that her "indecent" master "had an ugly fashion of stripping himself quite naked, and ordering me to wash him in a tub of water. This was

---

5. All translations are my own unless otherwise specified.

6. The last known slave ship to arrive on the shores of the United States was named the "Wanderer." It disgorged its human cargo in 1858 off the shores of Georgia.

7. William Thomas's testimony in John W. Blassingame, ed., *Slave Testimony: Two Centuries of Letters, Speeches, Interviews and Autobiographies* (Baton Rouge: Louisiana State University Press, 1977), 228.

worse to me than all the licks."[8] When she refused to come, her master beat her. Women were regularly stripped and hung by their hands to be beaten by a master or overseer.[9] Their husbands were sometimes forced by the master or overseer to publicly whip them even when pregnant, which caused frequent miscarriages. Moreover, women were fully expected to do "traditional women's work," including caring for children, cooking, and so forth, and to engage in normal sexual activity after a brutal day's work in the field or the master's house. The lament traditions of these women provided a coping mechanism, a way of acknowledging that they had suffered a great deal, an expression of hope that their lives would improve, and sometimes a plan for liberation.

Frances Anne Kemble, who visited a plantation that was located on an island off the coast of Georgia during the winter of 1838–1839, conducted an early sociological study of the health of enslaved women and their progeny based upon their success or failure in giving birth and keeping children alive. Her method was to question the women about the number of children that they had given birth to and the number still alive at the point of the interview. She also asked them about miscarriages (that will not be reported here because she is not as consistent in reporting miscarriages). Her findings were the following:

Fanny—six births—one alive
Nanny—three births—one alive
Leah—six births—three alive
Sophy—ten births—five alive
Sally—three births—two alive
Sarah—seven births—two alive
Sukey—eleven births—six alive
Molly—nine births—six alive
Edie—seven births—none alive
Mile—fifteen births—six alive
Die—sixteen births—two alive
Molly—eight children—one alive
Venus—eleven children—six alive
Molly (Mr. King's Molly)—nine births—three alive[10]

Kemble (who herself had given birth to two children, both of whom were alive) does not compare these birth-to-life ratios to those of free women, thereby

---

8. Mary Prince, *The History of Mary Prince, a West Indian Slave* (London: Westley & Davis 1831), repr. in Henry Louis Gates Jr., ed., *The Classic Slave Narratives* (New York: New American Library, 2002), 272.

9. Ibid., 262–63. Lewis Clark's testimony in Blassingame, *Slave Testimony*, 156.

10. Frances Anne Kemble, *Journal of a Residence on a Georgian Plantation in 1838–1839* (1863; repr., Athens: University of Georgia Press, 1984), 215, 229–30, 240, 245–46.

eliminating a critical component of sociological method. A sociologist would ask: How do these ratios compare to those of free women, free African American women, and free lower-income women? Kemble conducted her study before the development of the discipline of sociology and thus did not ask those questions. However, having lived through the period, she recognized that these birth-to-life ratios were not normal.

A major issue for the enslaved women on the islands off the Georgia–South Carolina coast that Mrs. Kemble visited was being permitted to have a month's respite from heavy field labor after giving birth. They appealed to Kemble because she was herself a mother and the wife of their current master. Kemble sympathized and tried to help, but her hands were tied because of her own powerlessness. Her husband owned the slaves; she did not. The constant pregnancies while being subjected to brutal working conditions wore these women down and led to early deaths and severe disabilities. But the most painful experience for enslaved women was having their children taken or sold away. The Freedmen's Bank records, which were finally released in 2000, contain page after page of sorrowful statements of loss of children and other family members.[11]

THE LAMENT TRADITIONS OF AFRICAN AMERICAN WOMEN

What can be known about the lament traditions of these African American women? Did they reflect the particular type of suffering that they, as women, endured because of their sex? The lyrics of the spirituals that those women sang are rarely specific about the type of suffering and injuries experienced. The language tends to be more general, expressed as "Got hard trial"[12] and "Nobody Knows the Trouble I've Had."[13] None of the laments of the enslaved African American women speak specifically of sexual abuse, a topic that is very frequently mentioned in the memoirs written by slaves and ex-slaves, both men and women. Perhaps unmerited feelings of shame kept women from articulating that pain. The memories of those abuses may have been reserved for the moaning and groaning songs that are often referred to in the literature. Biblical lament traditions mention rape and other types of sexual exploitation of women (Lam 5:11), but they primarily examine such events as they affect men and the broader society; the voices of the women themselves are seldom heard.

---

11. The Freedmen's Bank came into existence in 1865 and closed in 1874. Most of the persons who registered with the bank were formerly enslaved. They were asked about family members and their whereabouts. The records are available through the data banks of genealogical libraries.

12. From "Poor Rosy," in *Slave Songs of the United States* (ed. William Francis Allen, Charles Pickard Ware, and Lucy McKim Garrison; Bedford, Mass.: Applewood, 1867), 7.

13. In Allen, Ware, and Garrison, *Slave Songs of the United States*, 55.

Separation from and loss of family members are explicitly stated in the song tradition of African Americans. Lines in "I Can't Stay Behind" include "Oh my mudder is gone! My mudder is gone! My mudder is gone into heaven, my Lord!"[14] One version of "Michael Row the Boat Ashore" includes the line, "I wonder where my mother deh...."[15]

African American women carried on some traditions that are known from African cultures and created some of their own. Those traditions have some things in common with biblical lament traditions, but they also differ in significant ways. Olaudah Equiano, an African who was enslaved and forcibly brought to the Americas as a child,[16] reports that in his homeland his mother made periodic visits to the grave of her mother. He writes:

> I was very fond of my mother, and was almost constantly with her. When she went to make these oblations at her mother's tomb which was a kind of small solitary thatched house, I sometimes attended her. There she made her libations, and spent most of the night in cries and lamentations. I have been often extremely terrified on these occasions. The loneliness of the place, the darkness of the night, and the ceremony of libation, naturally awful and gloomy, were heightened by my mother's lamentations; and these occurring with the doleful cries of birds, by which these places were frequented, gave an inexpressible terror to the scene.[17]

Olaudah describes a lament tradition that requires a particular setting that includes a tomb in an isolated area, a nighttime setting, a ritual of reverence (libation), the voice of his mother in lament, and the cooperation of nature and location, which in his mind contributed to the mood of the occasion and elicited from him a feeling not of sorrow, as one would expect, but terror.[18] Because his mother made repeated visits to her mother's tomb, one would expect that the sorrow and grief that she expressed were not solely for the death of her mother but for other grief-causing events in her life that she poured out in the presence of her deceased mother.

Many of the descendents of Africans brought to the United States during the period of enslavement would have been familiar with the practice described above. Nighttime as a setting for lament rituals would have continued out of

---

14. Ibid., 6.

15. Ibid., 23.

16. He was eleven when he was first taken from his home by other Africans. See *The Interesting Life of Olaudah Equiano, or Gustavus Vassa, The African Written by Himself* (Halifax: Nicholson, 1814), repr. in Gates, *The Classic Slave Narratives*, 47.

17. Ibid., 40.

18. W. H. Russell describes a similar scene during which death songs were sung along by boatmen in a desolate place. Funerals of enslaved persons were held at night on the Sea Islands off the Georgia coast; see Allen, Ware, and Garrison, *Slave Songs of the United States*, 19, 47.

necessity, since enslaved persons rarely had flexible time during the day (although Mary Prince reports that, when the master was away for extended periods of time, enslaved persons took advantage of the opportunity to engage in money-making opportunities for themselves[19]). Restrictions on when enslaved persons could be out and about may have limited nighttime travel to visit relatives or friends, but a nocturnal venture to the nearby woods was possible. Colonel Higginson, a collector of the lyrics of spirituals that he heard sung during the Civil War, recalls:

> Often in the starlit evening I have returned from some lonely ride by the swift river, or on the plover-haunted barrens, and, entering the camp, have silently approached some glimmering fire, round which the dusky figures moved in the rhythmical barbaric dance the negroes call a "shout," chanting, often harshly, but always in the most perfect time, some monotonous refrain.[20]

Biblical scholars tend to distinguish sharply between the lament genre and the dirge genre. However, the distinction is not as clear in cultures that do not understand death to be the end of the existence of a person or that may use funerals to express grief over other losses because it was acceptable to mourn at funerals. Carole Merritt describes nighttime funeral practices in *Homecoming: African American Family History in Georgia*, highlighting an African practice of placing objects on graves to prevent spirits from troubling the living community and to free the spirit of the deceased.[21] Although enslaved Africans were far removed from their own ancestors, the belief that ancestors could affect the life of the living community because they continued to be a part of that community did not disappear. New ancestors, of course, came into being as enslaved Africans died in the new world.

The lament traditions, however, were not restricted to the night or specific places. Lucy McKim Garrison recalled that the songs of lament were sung both at work and at home. The tempo of the same song could vary from quick to slow depending upon the context in which it was sung.[22]

Allen, Ware, and Garrison note that:

> the negroes keep exquisite time in singing, and do not suffer themselves to be daunted by any obstacle in the words. The most obstinate Scripture phrases or snatches from hymns they will force to do duty with any tune they please, and

---

19. Prince, *The History of Mary Prince*.

20. Thomas Wentworth Higginson, "Negro Spirituals." Online: http://afroamhistory.about.com/library/blthomas_higginson_spirituals.htm.

21. Carole Merritt, *Homecoming: African-American Family History in Georgia* (Atlanta: African American Family History Association, 1982), 85–86.

22. Allen, Ware, and Garrison, *Slave Songs of the United States*, xxii–xxiii.

will dash heroically through a trochaic tune at the head of a column of iambs with wonderful skill.[23]

Allen, Ware and Garrison also notice that words are used in the laments that they, European Americans, did not at first understand, such as "oona."[24]

The African American song laments are not complex in their verbalized sentiments or structure. Most typically, there is a simple line or two followed by a refrain. The laments were very often personalized. For example, a song might have a name such as Mary that in each round of singing is changed to the name of a person in the community. Gender was not a barrier to being named in the songs. The rhythms and tempos were quite complex. Recorders of the songs were often frustrated by their lack of ability to write down all of the elements of the songs.

Some of the songs of lament seem to have been sung most often by men as they rowed boats from island to island or the mainland. The boat shanties and spirituals such as "Michael Row Your Boat Ashore" were among them. Were there spirituals that were most often sung by women or favored by them? Allen, Ware, and Garrison and the other contributors to *Slave Songs of the United States* connected certain laments and lament practices to women. Garrison reports the words of an enslaved woman who had given birth twenty-two times and had only one child with her. She said of her favorite spiritual, "Poor Rosy," that "It can't be sung [correctly] widout a *full heart and a troubled sperrit*."[25] This is instructive. Certain songs can only be properly sung by people who have experienced great suffering. Young people, no matter the quality of their voices, could not sing the song as it was meant to be sung. The words might emerge, but the feeling was not there. Garrison also notes that "the rests ... do not indicate a cessation in the music, but only on the part of the singers. They overlap in singing ... in such a degree that at no time is there any complete pause."[26] This overlapping model suggests that, when one cannot go on, another picks up the tune. It is a communal effort at mutual comfort. Were biblical laments also sung in an overlapping manner? Given our current state of knowledge about the musical tradition of ancient Israel, it is not possible to know.

Another song that is associated with ritual practices by women is "The Lonesome Valley." Young girls were expected to wear a handkerchief on their heads that were knotted in a particular way. They were not to change their clothes during a period of liminality that ended when they were baptized. This symbolized a girl's time of being in the "lonesome valley."[27] A comparable ritual is not mentioned for boys.

---

23. Ibid., iv.
24. Ibid., xxv.
25. Ibid., xxiii.
26. Ibid.
27. Ibid., 5.

Allen, Ware, and Garrison also report a story associated with a version of "Nobody Knows the Trouble I've Seen." A General Howard was assigned the unhappy duty of informing African American inhabitants of one of the Sea Islands that their lives were about to become significantly more difficult. He could barely talk and asked that they sing while he composed himself. "Immediately an old woman … began 'Nobody Knows the Trouble I've Had,' and the whole audience joined in."[28] A woman took charge of the occasion by leading a song. Ancient Israelite women are known to have been song leaders (Exod 15:20–21) and leaders of ritual mourning practices (Jer 9:17). Once again, there is a connection.

James Weldon Johnson reports a childhood memory of his own that is instructive about a particular role that women played in worship services in African American churches. Johnson was born just after the slave period, but the traditions of the church that he attended as a child emerged during it. Johnson recalls an African American woman in the congregation whose day job was laundress. She was also the lead singer in his church. If a sermon or prayer went on too long, she would "sing down" the speaker with a spiritual.[29] The spirituals were songs of lament, but the African American community had fun with them, too. It should also be noted that, at a time when preachers were invariably male, a woman controlled the length of the sermon. The role that this woman played was not unique to that congregation. Another function of the spirituals during the slave period was to communicate instruction during an impending escape attempt. Harriet Tubman, who made multiple trips to the south to free family members and friends, regularly sang spirituals to signal her arrival and the time of departure for enslaved persons who wished to escape.

The enslaved Africans were obsessed with improving their lives. Because many of the lament songs refer to "heaven," readers often assumed this meant an obsession with the next life. However, Frederick Douglass, who had been a slave, and Colonel Higginson, who transcribed slave songs, thought that the focus of the slave was on a different life on earth. Higginson recalled that the Bible of the slave consisted of only the Apocalypse and the Exodus. He wrote, "Apocalypse is brought to bear. This book, with the books of Moses, constituted their Bible; all that lay between, even the narratives of the life of Jesus, they hardly cared to read or to hear."[30]

---

28. Ibid., 55.

29. James Weldon Johnson and J. Rosamond Johnson, *The Books of American Negro Spirituals* (New York: Viking, 1925; repr., New York: Da Capo, 1969), 22.

30. Higginson, "Negro Spirituals," on the lyrics to "O the Dying Lamb."

The Moaning Tradition

The moaning and groaning traditions of the enslaved Africans were often mentioned by those who heard them. Moaning is also mentioned in the Bible as an expression of the ancient Israelites when they experienced pain and injustice. The moaning tradition of enslaved African American women and men may help to elucidate the moaning tradition of ancient Israel.

References to "moans" or "moaning" have been preserved in a number of biblical texts. Isaiah 59:11 reads: "All of us growl like bears; like doves, we surely moan. We wait for justice, but there is none, for deliverance, but it is far from us." In Isa 38:14 in the context of a poem attributed to King Hezekiah when he was ill, the following statement appears, "I moan like a dove, my eyes fill with water." In the preceding texts, the Hebrew root הגה is used. Isaiah 29:2, using the root אנה, describes a time of great distress when "moaning and lamentation will happen." In Ps 6:7 (6:6 in some English translations), a psalmist writes from a context of personal distress: "I have become weary with my moaning [אנחה]." In a context of enemies and betrayal by a friend, an ancient poet exclaims in Ps 55:18, "Let me complain and let me moan [המה], evening, morning and noon." Another cries out, "Let me remember; O God, let me moan" (Ps 77:4 [77:3]). The Hebrew roots in the above translations could just as easily be translated "groan" in some contexts. It is not always easy to determine which meaning is intended. The dove references, however, would suggest that moaning rather than groaning is the appropriate translation in those texts. A dictionary definition of a moan is "a low, mournful sound of sorrow or pain."[31] This definition, however, may be too limited.

The moans of the African American tradition were not like sighs. They were prolonged sounds shaped to a melodic line, a tune that was composed as needed. Sometimes they had words attached, sometimes not. It can be very difficult to articulate great pain. Any attempt to explain how one feels opens one to being misunderstood and even criticized, which is why many victims and witnesses to great suffering are often silent. The wordless song of lament, the moan, is a way of expressing that pain to the one who needs no explanation while maintaining one's privacy and dignity, particularly in a context of vulnerability and hostility.

The technology for audio recording was not yet invented during the slave period, so recordings of slaves singing do not exist. Those who heard them noted that it was impossible to transcribe their singing because it did not fit neatly into the notes of the European scale. The singing tradition, however, continues in some African American communities. The inhabitants of one such community, Gee's Bend in Boykin, Alabama, continue the moaning tradition. They are descendents of enslaved persons who were brought to that area of the country.

---

31. *Webster's New World College Dictionary* (4th ed.; Foster City, Calif.: IDG Books, 1999).

They have preserved an oral/aural heritage of singing laments into the twenty-first century. One of their songs, as recorded on the CD *How We Got Over: Sacred Songs of Gee's Bend*, is a contemporary representation of a moaning song. It is sung by Mary Lee Bendolph and given the title "Oh, Please (Lord Have Mercy)."[32] It was recorded while she was sitting in a friend's house. The first two words of the song are drawn out, reflecting the feelings of the singer. At the end of the song, the singer interjects the spoken words "I am going home to rest."[33] Those words are not part of the song; they represent her own spontaneously expressed desire.

Is it possible that the references to moaning and groaning in the Hebrew Bible meant wordless or sparsely worded sung laments? If so, the definition of the lament would have to be adjusted to allow for unspoken complaints.

Because "Poor Rosy" is specifically associated with a woman in the context in which the lament was transcribed, a closer look at it is in order. Here are the lyrics as recorded in *Slave Songs of the United States*:

> Poor Rosy, poor gal;
> Poor Rosy, poor gal;
> Rosy break my poor heart,
> Heav'n shall-a be my home.
> I cannot stay in hell one day,
> Heav'n shall-a be my home;
> I'll sing and pray my soul away,
> Heav'n shall-a be my home.
>
> Got hard trial in my way,
> Heav'n shall-a be my home.
> O when I talk, I talk wid God,
> Heav'n shall-a be my home.
>
> I dunno what de people want of me,
> Heav'n shall-a be my home[34]

This lament has a complaint: "hard trial." The nature of the hard trial, however, is not described, as is typical of the African American laments of the period of slavery. It is known, however, that the enslaved woman who loved this song had

---

32. "Oh, Please (Lord Have Mercy)," in *How We Got Over: Sacred Songs of Gee's Bend* (Atlanta: Tinwood Media, 2002). See also Paul Arnett, Joanne Cubbs, and Eugene W. Metcalf Jr., eds., *Gee's Bend: The Architecture of the Quilt* (Atlanta: Tinwood Books, 2006).

33. "Home" is a reference to death.

34. Allen, Ware, Garrison, *Slave Songs of the United States*, 7. Also see a discussion of the psalm in my earlier paper, "The Sorrow Songs: Laments from Ancient Israel and the African American Diaspora," in *Yet with a Steady Beat: Contemporary U.S. Afrocentric Biblical Interpretation* (ed. Randall C. Bailey; SemeiaSt 42; Atlanta: Society of Biblical Literature, 2003).

lost twenty-one of her children. That and being enslaved certainly explains some of the hard trial that she endured. Because she was enslaved at the time the song was transcribed, she may not have been at liberty to be more specific in the song itself. When the woman needs to talk, she talks with God. Talking with God does not require that one speak or sing in ways that other humans understand. God knows her suffering. The listener does not know what she says to God. That is between her and God. The repeated reference to heaven as home is a common theme in the slave songs. We know that heaven was sometimes used as code language to refer to being free. But many enslaved persons also longed for death as a means of escaping their life situation. The line that expresses confusion about what people want is not unique to this spiritual. Narratives of the lives of enslaved people describe brutal beatings and mistreatment for minor mistakes or accidents or normal "life happens" events. Even when enslaved persons worked hard to please a master or overseer, hoping that it would make their life easier, they were not necessarily rewarded for their efforts.

Conclusion

The lament tradition of enslaved African American women raises questions that may be further explored by students of the laments of the Hebrew Bible. Do references to moaning in the Bible reflect a tradition of wordless or sparsely worded sung laments? Were the evening hours a particular time setting for songs of lament? Did people seek out isolated areas or tombs as a mood setting and private space for expressing pain, grief, and loss? Were the sung expressions of lament picked up by others in the community in overlapping rounds as a way of expressing support? What were the original forms of the laments before they became a part of a written text? Oral cultural traditions can be lost in a single generation. Humans being humans, however, share much in common across cultural boundaries. Study of contemporary and near contemporary oral/aural cultures, such as the African American lament tradition, may assist in understanding traditions of communities that are no longer extant, in this case, ancient Israel.

Selections from *Between Despair and Lamentation**

Borislav Arapović

The first section of poems below were written by the poet Borislav Arapović, a
Bosnia-Herzegovinian Croat, in the years just prior to the outbreak of war in
Croatia in 1991 and war in Bosnia-Herzegovina in 1992.

in the days of may

we were ten years old
the world looked at us from pictures on the wall
and from rostra and they gave us maps
to be paid for in installments
in the first days of may we climbed up
past the hanged sailor and sailed away
with crossed masts we nailed down the rudder
turned on the engines
the current bore us towards the end of horizon
centuries away from the source
between bottom and abyss
even the water flees from beneath us
in a world which is no more
pieces of a soaked map float around

silence

darkness everywhere
soundless quiet gloomy silent

---

* The poems included here are by permission and from the first English volume of the
poet's works, *Between Despair and Lamentation* (ed. Nancy C. Lee; trans. Ivana Pozajić Jerić;
Elmhurst, Ill.: Elmhurst College, 2002). Some of these poems appeared in Croatian in earlier
volumes of poetry by Borislav Arapović: *Iz noćnog dnevnika* (From the Diary of the Night,
1989), *Tamnionik* (Darkhouse, 1992) and *Kamenopis* (Stonescript, 1993).

plugged up openings
capped sources
cobwebs across lips
mildew on paper
I pricked up my ears
in the quiet night
in the silence of the grave
all is dead
for thousands of kilometers around
I stammer to myself
I padlocked my throat
I shut my eyes
I pricked up my ears
in the soundless night
in the dull silence
all is dead
I only hear the wheel
the wheel of time
creaking as it
turns backwards

over the sands of the desert

millions of steps millions of kilometers
steadily slowly monotonously
over the sands of the desert
for forty years israel
out of egypt we out of canaan
with no burning bush
with no cloud
with no promise
with no God
no tablets of stone
and by the law of the high priest
slain victims are sacrificed
to the star of apis
and we turn in a frenzied dance
around the golden calf and march
without stopping day and
night
we mill around the desert
in a vicious
circle

our trace disappearing
in the quicksand
and the calf is sublimely silent
dumbly staring
upon screams blindly upon
the victims
we are treading from age
to age
under the heat of
the eternal circle
we do not understand one
another
though all of us together
were suckled on words along with milk
smacking our tongues
from the same mother's breasts
under the curse of the tower
of babel
farther and farther from canaan
all in different directions
and they wonder at us and point at us
marching
into the red sea

                    in a foreign land

I carry my homeland
across the border
in a bundle
in my empty stomach
and my empty heart
and I am ashamed before God and before her
searching
I ask myself
and I do not know
whether to sell her
or to build her a temple

                    where to?

all is waste around me today
I lost yesterday
and there is no tomorrow

and with crushed eyes I wander
through burnt air
painfully plucking my feet from the mud
all is black around me today
yesterday trampled down
and no tomorrow

croatian psalm 137

while still trembling on the edge of time
and in the depth of space
we heard the throb of our name
and the flow of the atoms
of our genes—gehennas

already on euphrates
at the tower of babel
you lined us up
into first ranks

we planted a tree amid cindered rafters
and on its top we stuck
glagolitic writing
and we have been waiting with no response
for eons on end

are we really the ones you will use
to put out the flame of the bush?

where is your abode
why are you not among us too
since you are everywhere
and if you are also with us
why do we not see that we are not alone?

angels of peace

at the gala banquet
where of course
there were to be found
founding fathers
and sovereign
liberators

commanders
marshals
and generals
and other knights of the 20th century
and also those cheaper ones
elected presidents
and statesmen
and others that I pass over
that wear suits off the rack
eating drinking
dancing
taking photographs
speaking
speechifying
shouting
belching
toasting
the peace
and a guest of honor
and all this
each in his own
language
no way they could agree
especially about
the means to be used
words or bullets
but why waste any more time
on this
summa summarum
they again carried
the angel of peace
on a stretcher
into a red cross car
his head bandaged
his wings plucked

The following poems were written by Borislav Arapović in the years 1991 to 1995;
he was an eyewitness of the wars in Croatia and Bosnia-Herzegovina

along the lines blackened by smoke

stars did not always shine on our path
our hordes traveled most of their miles by night

darkness was writing all our pages
illustrated
illuminated
by miniatures of gallows and skeletons
along the lines blackened by smoke
in place of each full stop a gaping abyss
exclamation points replaced by
question marks sticking up in the air
while owls hoot from consonants
and owlets sit among vowels
hanging from trees in some forest
where also for every one of us
there grows the wood for a cross [8 July 1991]

telefax from croatia

in memory of those who fell in the attack on osijek
by tanks by cannon by airplanes
while I was there september 14–17 1991

night midnight fire slaughter hell

....
94471/8 .... 9931 .... 99468.
993580 .... 991202 991212
dialing.............. dialing .... dialing
london .... paris .... stockholm.
helsinki .... washington .... new york

....
—lines dead—no connection—

but I would like to transmit to them by fax
the zig-zag flight of the frightened starlings
disoriented by bullets from planes
and the city pigeons' hoarse cooing
between thundering explosions
and the nightly crashing of growling mortar shells
through the roofs into bloodstreams
and the flight of rats from fleeing feet
through moldy cellars
—once the sky was our ally
—now it's the nether world
then the bloodied kitten's meows
sniffing along a glass-strewn street

and the screeching "goody-goody"
of an escaped parrot
perched on a tree trunk felled by a bomb
across the streetcar rails

and I would like to fax them the pictures
of crosses and tombstones
that the death-hungry bandit monsters
vomit upon us from the stolen sky
of the satanic chuckle of their machine guns
as they sweep over silenced belfries
and of Christ on His cross pierced by a gun burst
and of the smell of corpses left in the wake
of the demonic dance
of the werewolves in their tanks rolling
over the sacred soil of croatia
and the colors of frescoes and mosaics of fruit
strewn over concrete of the market's remnants
I would transmit
and birds feasting on half a dog
next to a white white church
and the calm silence of gaping shop windows
and the ghostly rows of houses
along empty sidewalks
and sketches of unexploded bombs
and the labor of a birthing mother
by a hospital on fire
and holes in the children's clinic's walls
and voices never born
and other wisdom of insanity in uniform
and a head without eyes
and legs without arms
and arms without legs
99301 .... 993531 ....9945 993511
993541 ...... 993592 .... 99482/22
athens .... dublin .... copenhagen ... lisbon
reykjavik ..... sofia .... warsaw
....
—no connection—

and I would like to transmit to them
the prolonged roar of howitzer maws
out of the woods around the city

and the geysers of flaming earth
that crashing and blazing
join hell and heaven
and the gushing of smoke columns
around quenched factory stacks
and the trembling of the secondhand
on my wristwatch
and barking of angry dogs
from deserted squares of osijek
dogs that wonder if the roles are reversed
and now men have turned rabid

and why not also human words—children's voices?
ah yes—
no children's voices are to be heard around osijek
they've been swallowed by the city cellars
I can only transmit their silence
from the school named "the brothers ribar"
hit by a MIG
where the homework title "one summer day"
and faded formulae of physics
still stick out from the blackboard

hurriedly frenetically leafing searching turning
99472 .... 99396 .... 993170 99422
99361 .... 99400 .... 99322 ...... 99431/222
994131 .... 994930 .... 9949228 ....
....dialing.oslo .rome .... the hague ...... prague ..
budapest ...... bucharest .... brussels .... vienna
bern .... berlin .... bonn ....
and all the baals.and.gods of this world ....
....
not a sound—no connection—

oh God in Heaven
is there a fax anywhere
from madrid to moscow
that is not blocked by traders' quotes
assailed by the lies of our killers
that could receive the message
from a shelter full of dread
from a deathly silent classroom [Osijek, 17 September 1991]

                    poppies in dalj town

red poppies
white acacia
blue sky

and then *they* came
and did their deed

so that at dawn
there was no difference
between the squashed petals of poppies
and the splashed petals of blood [7 March 1993]

                    88 of them

            missing, then accidentally discovered
        and on august 27 1992 dug up from the mass grave
            at the municipal garbage dump in mostar
        and lined up on their backs for identification purposes

they stare out of maggoty hollows
with eyes from the underground
with skies in their eyes
and their eyes in the skies [19 April 1993]

                    CODEX CRIMINALIS (I)

                from the letter of a madman—
                    found in mostar in 1993

through the cracks—the incense of darkness seeps
fuming its fumes
unto the grave and the gravedigger
from the damned house of pest's pestilence
outside the circle of panic-stricken emptiness
along with the faith in eternal peace
even without eternal existence
our hopes are burning like extinguished bulbs
while from battlefields and hospitals
and onto diskettes of computer mortuaries
black legions of names are marching
escorted by convoys of evil and
from the chasm across the harbor without a sea

the leap year of 1992 is smoking
from the barrels of darkness
caterpillars rolling
look how within them roulettes are spinning
look how they stop
at the number beyond the sacred number
and
a minute of landmine silence for a friend

Lord—You said: "Let there be light!"
but who was it who said "Let there be darkness"?
and forgive them for they know (not)
what they are doing
black souls in white bodies
new york geneva aids whisky
and ministers of death
werewolves howling with wolves
in the city only cemeteries are asleep

hark
in the night to the last chord
of the city symphony
smothered by the olive colored organ
through the roof and through vanished windows
into the canyon of the wounded river—
a grave—without gravestone
our depths and our towers
sacred and wretched
just like the picture
from the threefold celebration of mind ecology
when the rumpled star donned a beak and claws
and the pewter moon wandered away
and some celestial mechanism started its motion
of demoniac angels
thunderbolts crests graves

you too will march along with us
we'll enclose your ribs in barbed wire
dress up your skeletons in uniforms
put helmets on your skulls
hang medals on your vertebrae
you will march with us up front
right by the flags

in the parade under the arch of triumph
antemurale christianitatis

crazy—who's crazy?
there are bars between us
but who is the one behind them?

our butcher shops are empty
our morgues are full
at the global media auctions
croatian meat is the cheapest
with or without inner organs,
upper, lower, middle,
mummified with preservatives
cooked in blue cauldrons
with the sleepwear of the prostitute
of the setting sun
where by the snoring of the senile lion
and simpering of powdered poodles
it is served with champagne

the fratroutrage
of the fairy dance of the western
and eastern crosses
in the shadow of the crescent
to the strains of the waltz of demonocracy
controlled by saintly blind men
while madmen teach the crazy to obey the maniacs
and gangsters litigate with mafia about rights

but between the shivering barefooted bosnian woman
or the vukovar madonna with her headless child
and the palace of justice there lie
a million miles a million millionnaires
and a billion paragraphs of toothless resolutions

our beautiful homeland is furrowed with graves
where the living sing to the dead
and the dead laugh at the living
where the dead listen and the living do not hear

and bonebreaking prayers
from each side

are faxed into celestial databases
to the tricolor Christ and the other one
for peace on earth
for us to be on it for them to be under it
when offered bread they offer cannonballs

dry rain bursting from the sky brings
the morphine and heroin
of the fifth season of the five-point year
to them the monopoly of slaughter
to us of wailing

no! hey!? from a dark corner of the brain
following those peacekeepers' example
and screaming and shouting
"this blood be on us and our children
let us not leave
a single stone standing either
or a single head upon its shoulders"
and then?
is God or is baal the leader of croatians?
stop heaven save at least the young ones
that someone may finish the codex
carve out a cross ignite the crematorium
while the rest of us
will continue to march
along the wall of weeping
ever greater croatians from an ever smaller croatia
by the law of statistics we know that we shall all ...
we are east to the west and west to the east
why have You also abandoned us
we are left with faith love and hopelessness

the chicken are frozen in their eggs
on the easter of our spring
and even the crows abandon our crosses
how many of us are still left
shall we exist when we are no more
except in heaven or hell

reliquiae reliquiarum
olim magni et inclyti
regni Croatiae

and here barrels of acid blood
and maggots that eat the maggots
off their own corpses
and lift each other's masks
and hands that are copying
codex criminalis [22 October 1993]

Croatian easter crucified

she too was hanging by Your side, O Lord,
and after the ninth hour
for another nine centuries
nailed to three crosses
the superscription in a hundred languages
Reliquiae reliquiarum ...
regni Croatiae

why does your harsh angel of death
not bypass our dwelling as well
though we sprinkle our door-posts
with the blood of innocent lambs?

how long
will a tearing dance of screams
from the stones of our temple
rage around her cross along with the shattering of skulls
with the chiming of hour hands pointing at us
while we pant wearily and tread desperately
on others on ourselves
rearing up to the cross of cries
on the way of the cross
crucify her crucify her
cry for her and for your children
hurling our hammers
onto heads onto pegs
ours and others'
on us and on You
forging nailing
both the croanathema and anthem?

how long will Your angels, O Lord,
be pulling out nails from your cross
and hammering them into ours?

will any of them also push off the rock
that we are rolling onto our own grave?

why, O Lord,
are a million judases resurrected
along with her every time
and why is her resurrection
always on good friday? [February 2001]

LAMENTING THE DEAD IN IRAQ AND SOUTH AFRICA: TRANSITIONING FROM INDIVIDUAL TRAUMA TO COLLECTIVE MOURNING PERFORMANCES*

Kimberly Wedeven Segall

There was nobody to cry
There was no body to shatter my silence
I was as lost as a child in the bosom of the universe
And there was nobody guiding me to find my homeland
At the last moment, the flute started to speak....
—Jamal Khambar, Kurdish Iraqi, 27 February 2007

With a major historical shift—as in South Africa after 1994 or in the ongoing turmoil of Iraq after 2003—the political transition out of a terrorized regime-state does not guarantee individuals will automatically shift out of their traumatized states. Decades of terror and war break down cultural structures and individual ideas of self; large numbers of individuals suffer from traumatic stress disorder; all this influences social reconstruction.[1] While many critics analyze political transitions, this article considers cultural forums that could assist militants in transitioning from violent experiences. Specifically, I analyze how poetic laments and stories begin to work out traumatic experiences for former guerilla fighters. My study of cultural performances is limited to two specific groups of resistance fighters who have both faced draconian measures of state terror and torture: the Kurds in northern Iraq and the Xhosa in South Africa. In stark contrast to the helplessness of the experience of torture or severe oppression, public commemorations can break through the individual's traumatized alienation; furthermore, a song or

---

* This is a slightly revised reprint of an article published in *Comparative Studies of South Asia, Africa and the Middle East* 25 (2005): 138–51. My thanks to the *Comparative Studies* editors, to Asad Gozeh for his critical insights and feedback, and to Seattle Pacific University for the Faculty Research Grant.

1. See James Dawes, *The Language of War* (Cambridge: Harvard University Press, 2002), 133.

story—especially through the acting agent's choice of movement, pace, length, and so forth—offers a measure of reassuring control. Thus, this degree of artistic control and this group setting for performed memories of the past offer psychological closure and a public, embodied sign that a shift in context (from former terrorized state to a new transitional state) has occurred.

In Iraq in 1993, many Kurds told me stories of chemical bombings, torture, disappearances. I was given a video of Saddam Hussein's military and secret police gunning down Kurdish men in a public execution. In another scene, a young boy in the video described the way everyone in his village was brought to a large bulldozed pit and shot. He was wounded and buried among the bodies and crept away at night to a neighboring village. These stories, related through oral and media forms, were reworked with ancient legends, emerged in poetic laments at funerals, and were redesigned as songs of Kurdish courage to be played during festive dances. Similarly, in South Africa, stories of the apartheid police raiding and burning homes, arresting and torturing the Xhosa emerged in performances and songs. Working as an ESL teacher and humanitarian aid worker with the Sorani-speaking Kurds in the village of Shaqlawa, Iraq (1993–1994) and directing a play with Xhosa-speaking survivors of apartheid political violence during my Northwestern University Research Fellowship (1999–2000), I found instances in both groups where performances move individuals from debilitating isolation (personal trauma) to communally embraced mourning.

The difficulty of shifting an individual's horrific recollections to a communal form is due to the painful and paradoxical nature of traumatic memory. Presenting a traumatic narrative is to remember and tell what one most desires to forget. Yet once told, these presented memories allow the group to share grief, offering a measure of closure because of the group's embrace of a commonly held narrative. When group members validate each other's stories and songs of past sorrow, it resembles the witness's role in a testimony. In *Testimony*, Dori Laub, M.D., argues: "Bearing witness to a trauma is, in fact, a process that includes the listener. For the testimonial process to take place, there needs to be a bonding, the intimate and total presence of another—in the position of one who hears. Testimonies are not monologues; they cannot take place in solitude."[2] Sharing stories or songs— part of witnessing each other's acts of mourning—defines the performing group's identity and reaffirms their common social bonds of witnessed suffering.

CYCLES OF VENGEANCE OR COMMEMORATIVE CLOSURE?

In considering how cultural performances can work through traumatic memory toward healing, one must first confront Western bias. General Western perceptions of Africa and the Middle East associate these areas with cycles of violence;

---

2. Dori Laub and Shoshana Felman, *Testimony* (New York: Routledge, 1992), 70.

thus, public recollections of tragedy are often conceived of as a mere preface to vengeance. Yet these generalizations fail to consider how years of ethno-genocidal attacks must find a release valve. Public laments incorporate complex emotions—alienation, anger, revenge, repressed silence, guilt, regret, conciliation, and even anxiety over horrific, invasive memories—into a larger narrative, an artistically bound, controlled form that can work toward healing after war's destruction of the social fabric.

In the two case studies of this paper, I find that the songs as well as stories expressing sorrow or protesting injustice act out traumatic memories in two central ways.[3] Because posttraumatic stress disorder is centrally characterized as a disordered sense of time that results in severe anxiety, depression, alienation, and other symptoms, the cultural practices of rituals, songs, public storytelling, and funeral laments that perform the past in a new context emphasize the distinction between the traumatic past and the present moment. For songs of lament, the embodied memory of well-known verses shifts out of the cognitive mode—since cognition is often disrupted by posttraumatic stress disorder—to a physical, rhythmic release of tension, and for narrated memories, the improvisation and spontaneity accompanying storytelling—in juxtaposition to the helpless state of torture and terror—offers a measure of artistic choice and control.

This measure of control helps to reveal that the historical context of the past has changed or shifted, in contrast to a traumatic stress disorder symptom characterized by feeling historically bound, trapped in the traumatic event, or consumed with avoiding its return. In *Drama and Healing*, Roger Grainger argues that performances that emotionally engage us draw upon common experiences and a sense of "losing" ourselves; by acting out and reflecting on the process of performance, there is a "movement of withdrawal and detachment" that separates the artifice of the play to provide reflective distance on the associated "reality" of our lives.[4] It is this immersion into performance, followed by a reflective withdrawal and detachment that can offer psychological healing with positive social consequences.

The role of improvisation in poetic laments or storytelling offers a second telling of a traumatic event in a very different form and context from the original experience. This difference between the two forms and contexts fosters a reflective distance, similar to the roles that Robert Landy describes in therapeutic theater. Landy argues that the "individual as actor lives simultaneously in two realities ...

---

3. See Kai Erikson, ed., and introduction to *Sociological Visions* (New York: Rowman & Littlefield, 1997). for clarification on the way that, despite individual uniqueness, there are also patterns within groups: "The social forces of which sociologists speak operate in such a way as to affect the likelihood that aggregates of people will behave in a certain way: we are dealing here with drifts, tendencies, probabilities, not with how particular individuals will act" (4).

4. Roger Grainger, *Drama and Healing* (London: Kingsley, 1990), 27.

present and past, rehearsal and performance, the studied moment and the spontaneous moment, every day life and the imagination … actor and role."[5] Individuals can examine how they act out roles in life because of this "dramatic paradox."[6] Landy characterizes various levels of intensity for the playing of roles in life or in acting: (1) "overdistance" as a highly cognitive distance; (2) accordingly, "underdistance" as a flooding of sentiment and experience; and (3) "aesthetic distance" as a moderation of sentiment and rationality. Using this model, I argue that for posttraumatic stress disorder, the intensity of emotion often floods the individual or is kept carefully repressed in a state of "underdistance." The use of improvisation and of a witnessing audience for the Kurds and the introduction of roles and rehearsal scenes for the Xhosa offers "aesthetic distance"—psychological distance on the event to provide rationality and relief after the horror of the past. This psychological distance through public performances is both individually healing and socially constructive because of positive detachment and creative change.

ORAL STORIES, POETIC LAMENTS, AND THE IRAQI KURDS

In northern Iraq, in interviews with Kurdish freedom fighters in 1993–1994 and recently with Kurdish refugees in the United States, I found that many of them did not have time to mourn as they fled in the mountains and engaged in subversive tactics. They talked about how painful it was to quickly bury a dead companion and then move on to the next military engagement or hideout. "There was no time to grieve when we were in the mountains; we often had to flee the site of the attack, especially because of Saddam's use of poison gas," one individual contended. After Saddam Hussein's rule of terror, individuals who had not been allowed to mourn publicly because of the regime can now mourn.

When I asked them about public forms of mourning, they remembered various rituals that were common in times of peace, such as one of the kinswoman composing poetic laments about a dead person. The tradition of ululating to grieve and publicly to proclaim laments for the dead is associated largely as a role for women. The laments remember heroic acts and personal attributes and family connections of the lost loved ones. The women's laments are usually not political protests but rather a process of recollecting positive attributes and specific memories about the lost beloved. This cultural form problematizes general occidental perceptions that traumatic memories always lead to political vendettas. Also, the renaming of positive characteristics of the dead is a very different practice than silence. If there is silence, if the dead are not collectively mourned, then the repressed memories of terror and violence will live on in the survivors and filter into traumatic stress disorder symptoms that the second generation will

---

5. Robert Landy, *Persona and Performance* (New York: Guilford, 1993), 11.
6. Ibid., 12.

feel indirectly. Laments place a historical context on violence and add a community framework. The double context—imagined moment of death and moments of vibrant life—dilutes the terror of the haunted memory and adds fullness to the traumatic memory, extending the narrative in a similar manner as arrived at by therapists who use narrative therapy. In discussing postwar Iraq with the Kurds, I asked if it would relieve some of the frustration and anger of the past to have commemorative ceremonies for the dead. This option was commonly embraced.

Varying from public laments, the dance songs or *shiyee* combine joyful celebrations of bravery with recognition of past sorrow. As one common song states: "if you are not sharing my sad as well as my happy days, then I will not visit you on any day." The idea is that individuals and families help one another; for instance, during the three days of the funeral, community members visit and bring food to console the family. The bonding of the community is also present in the line dancing where men and women respond to the songs and form a line to do a series of steps with linked hands in a circle. Through singing and dancing, isolated obsessions with traumatic images and personal violation are now acted out with more expressive, physical interactions.

Popular songs and dances appear to be ever-changing artistic responses and also habit-based exercises. In *How Societies Remember*, Paul Connerton argues that forms of habitual recollection are distinct from personal or cognitive memories.[7] Habitual practices such as songs and dances access another form of recollection that enables the processing of traumatic memories in stress disorders. The well-known patterning of a song may interrupt, replace, or impede the traumatic images; thus, these traumatic images are rendered less invasive, less likely to deaden other incoming senses.

In interviews, I asked, "Have songs ever brought you consolation?" One of the most moving answers described how a popular song provided comfort after the chemical bombings during 1987–1988:

> An eerie silence enveloped me as I walked through the village of Sheikh Wasan in Iraqi Kurdistan early that morning, it resembled a ghost village.... The day before there had been several hundred people living here. Now, dead animals and chickens were lying everywhere. The few [people] that were still alive were blind and crying for each other. The artillery shells began falling on the village and I could hear the roar of approaching tanks. A strange, fruity smell began to overwhelm me.... Mustard gas.... An hour after the attack the noise of 36 helicopters filled the dark sky. Saddam was setting out to kill all survivors. The choppers dropped gas bombs on every mountain passage that people might take later. Everyone was trapped. Within hours the incubation period was over. The real horror was just beginning. The symptoms appear on everyone. Everyone lost

---

7. Paul Connerton, *How Societies Remember* (Cambridge: Cambridge University Press, 1989), 23.

their sight. Their lungs and every exposed part of the skin began to burn.… Panic deepened quickly with news of a military incursion into the valley, and everyone tried to escape.… A number of people made it to the towns to be with their relatives and get treatment; however the secret police rounded them up the next day and murdered them all. We found their mass graves after the Gulf War.[8]

This event occurred eleven months after Saddam Hussein had bombed Halabja, and a popular song mourning the thousands of deaths in Halabja had already been created by Shiavan Peperwer. As one group of fourteen survivors made their way through the mountains trying to escape the mustard gas, they sang Peperwer's song. "I see the bombs, I hear the noise of a plane above. On the ground you see women and children dying because of the gas. Halabja. Halabja." One of the *peshmergas*—a Kurdish word for those who fight in the face of death—commented that he had tears in his eyes when singing the song in the mountain, and for a long time whenever he heard the song it would remind him of how he helped save his brother and how they escaped the gas. As a public form of mourning, they could continue on as a group despite the despairing sights they had seen. The song fostered group courage and solidarity in their search to escape the chemical weapons. While cognitive processes may break down in the face of such traumatic sights, the *embodied memory* of a popular song offers an alternative venue, a healing release. No longer limited as an individual burden of memory, there is also relief as it becomes a group act of singing.

Equally popular are the Kurdish songs broadcast over the radio, played during the 2003 U.S.–Iraq war. While songs of mourning have been a source of identity and community strength for the Kurdish people for some time, during the 2003 war the Kurdish radio programs frequently played a mourning song as a call for resistance. How did the Halabja song, written during the 1980s, "I see the bombs, I hear the noise of a plane above," now influence a 2003 context? When Pamela Constable returned to Halabja fifteen years after the bombing in 2003, she notes that,

> Despite the revitalizing effect that the fall of Hussein has had on Halabja, the town is still very much in mourning. Virtually every family here lost a relative in the gassing, and the main cemetery is full of large, grassy hills where entire clans are buried.… The town's major landmark is a stark white monument to the dead. Inside is a plaster tableau of lifelike victims frozen as they fell, covered with chemical ash and cradling their children for protection. The center is a rotunda in which some 5,000 victims' names are carved in black stone.[9]

---

8. Asad Gozeh, "Images of Poison Gas Still Haunt People in Kurdistan" (online: http://www.kurdishmedia.com [4 June 2003]).

9. Pamela Constable, "Cloud over Halabja Begins to Dissipate," *The Washington Post* (7 August 2003): A10.

The town's memorial of the event resembles the commemorative effect of the song "Halabja" and of a poem called "Halabja: Another Sad Kurdish Song?" by Shahin Sorekli (2000), which marks Halabja as a central mnemonic event in what the Kurds call the Anfal genocide. The poem ends:

> And the Kurds of the south:
> In the thirteen years that passed
> Were they able to reconcile,
> Have they learned a lesson meanwhile?
> Or is Halabja just another sad song
> In the folklore of our tragic survival?[10]

Folklore and historic songs are memory keepers for group identity and Kurdish perseverance. The song of Halabja, as the poem implies, is one method "to reconcile" with the traumatic events of the past. The song, poem, and memorial of Halabja all embody secondary forms that detach from the original horror of the incident.

Another song—played every hour during the war, both on the television and on radio stations—urged resistance to Saddam Hussein. This song reminded the Kurds of how other dictators have historically been defeated in Iraq.

> But Saddam Hussein, go and build your castles, but you will not stay there! … You have tried to build castles where Alexander the Great failed! My country is like wood and fire, for every enemy that comes is burnt up. Your life and your freedom are of equal value, and I will fight even unto death for Kurdistan.

The televised images focused less on the singer than on images of Kurdish fighters advancing toward Baghdad. The song of protest encourages the people to identify with a common history and motivates continued political resistance.

Also haunting local songs and memories was the fate of the many "disappeared," those arrested and never heard from again.[11] The Qosh Tepe women in a Barzani village faced persecution because its political leader, Mulla Mustafa Barzani, resisted Saddam Hussein; the village was destroyed, and the people were relocated in the south. Later the people were relocated to the north. In 1983, the military arrived and arrested every boy and man over the age of twelve, and these

---

10. Shahin Sorekli, "Halabja: Another Sad Kurdish Song?" (online: http://www.kurdishmedia.com [15 March 2000]).

11. Nir Rosen, "Uncovering the Dead" (online: http://www.kurdishmedia.com [28 May 2003]). In May 1993, Nir Rosen reported, "Eleven men from the al-Musawi family were arrested. In prison they tied Husayn's hands behind his back and hung him from them, dislocated his shoulders and tortured him with electricity. They beat him with cables and metal rods until he was drenched in his own blood…. The al-Musawis did not know if the lost sons were dead or alive until they received the [new] information."

men were never heard from again. As Christine Allison argues, the women's lament shifts between songs recalling the dead and hopeful desire that the men of the village are in prison and remain alive.[12] In this unique form of communal lament, "a single voice would sing, usually in stanzas of three lines, pausing to weep between them. Other women would take up the song, or interject when they felt moved."[13] The songs expressed both grief and hope in a community forum.

While most Kurdish stories are based on personal memories, historical legends also extend back generations. This tradition of telling legends of the past resists the consuming terror of the present. In effect, the legends subvert oppressive power, as is evident during the 21 March New Year holiday, Nao Roz, where fires are lit on hilltops.[14] The lit fires announced the death of an ancient King Zohhak, who killed Kurdish men and women. The tyrant was assassinated by a Kurdish blacksmith who killed the king with his hammer and lit a fire to signal the liberation.[15] Yet this story of resistance is followed by a time of reconciliation.[16] The week after Nao Roz, according to Mehrdad Izady, is the time when old feuds are to be settled within communities.[17] Nao Roz not only recognizes the culture's fight against terror through a story; it is also a time when a centralizing story encourages internal divisions to be reconciled.

Just as the popular songs and laments express grief, build group solidarity, and add a reflective distance to the past, so also the oral tradition of storytelling enhances hope and a sense of community during desperate times. During the early 1990s, many Kurds would tell me heart-rending stories of oppression, on the condition that "you must never forget" the plight of the Kurds. The storytelling was a protest against Saddam Hussein in the sense that outsiders were being

---

12. Christine Allison, "Old and New Oral Traditions in Badinan," in *Kurdish Culture and Identity* (ed. Christine Allison and Philip Kreyenbroek; London: Zed, 1996), 43.

13. Ibid.

14. Mehrdad Izady, *The Kurds* (London: Russak, 1992). Izady spells the event "New Ruz," 242.

15. The Kurdish legend has another more fanciful version: the tyrant is a cannibal with snake heads who eats young Kurdish boys and girls. Local leaders, wanting to save the Kurds, used sheep parts as a substitute, in order to save Kurdish children. This myth of origin fosters an identity of resistance in the midst of persecution and reflects how the Kurdish people have fought against being geographically, culturally, and physically consumed by foreign kings for centuries.

16. The way feuds are settled—based in community rituals and stories of common oppressors—is important when considering the recent Kurdish feud that escalated into a civil war between two Kurdish groups, beginning in 1994. When I asked Asad Gozeh about amnesty, Asad responded that there should be war courts, yet amnesty should be granted to most of the military, because the military were forced through conscription to participate. Later he added: "We need to forget about the crimes of the past" (November 2003).

17. Izady, *The Kurds*, 242.

told so that they would become responsible for passing on these stories of injustice to others. Since the Kurds did not have passports to travel freely, hope trekked through stories, shared with outsiders who could relay their message. Members of the largest ethnic group without a homeland, many of the Kurds described not only the destruction of their village but also their relocation to concentrated living quarters and their desire to rebuild their homes: in total, around four thousand villages and towns were bulldozed. The traumatic stories passed on to outsiders, in my case to a teacher or *mamosta*, served to rekindle a sense of hope.

During the reign of Saddam Hussein, the Kurds were not allowed to grieve publicly. To prohibit mourning silences the community, further increasing the isolation and atmosphere of terror against the Kurds. Narrating traumatic memory, a complex process of disclosing and evading the past, relies on external clues from the audience about whether the public will ostracize or accept such a story of atrocity. When an event is reflected upon or told to another person, connections are engendered between this event, interpretive links, and the audience. "A public space of trauma provides a consensual reality and collective memory through which the fragments of personal memory can be assembled, reconstructed, and displayed with a tacit assumption of validity."[18] Where memories of injustice are recognized, memory bonds and attachments occur in this shared space.

Public performances that expose the horrific truths as unjust allow for a shared interpretation, yet also allow a measure of distance and release from isolated, personal emotions. The songs and stories that recognize injustice allow the participant to commemorate, to focus on one interpretive selection, and thus release other interpretive fragments associated with traumatic memories. As Antze and Lambek argue: "By closure, then, we do not mean a simple forgetting. We mean, if anything, the reverse, a preoccupation with a particular fragment of the past, a hypostatization via excessive commemoration."[19]

Improvisational Stories, Protest Songs, and Xhosa Survivors

Similarly, in South Africa songs and personal stories were used for comfort during the protest movement and for transition from the state of terror to a new national state. For both the Xhosa and the Kurds, it is evident how embodied memory bonds with witnessing audiences and artistic improvisation offers a measure of control and a visible relief from the helplessness of the past. The differences, of course, are not only in the cultural specificity of languages and regions but also in the degree of transition after regimes of terror. While the Iraqi context is still

---

18. Laurence Kirmayer, "Landscapes of Memory: Trauma, Narrative, and Dissociation," in *Tense Past: Cultural Essays in Trauma and Memory* (ed. Paul Antze and Michael Lambek; New York: Routledge, 1996), 190.

19. Antze and Lambek, *Tense Past,* xxi.

in labor with severe transitional pains, South Africa has had more of a temporal and contextual development. My work examines a case study on the role of South African songs and improvisation in performance to move from individual trauma to collective mourning and to redefine the present context through the embodied control of these cultural forms. While protest songs influenced how people formed groups and raised consciousness in the apartheid context, as shown in the film documentary *Amandla* (2003), current songs and stories in local performance can also aid the social and personal *transitions* away from apartheid.

In South Africa, after 21,000 victims of human-rights violation told their stories to the Truth and Reconciliation Commission, survivors continued to tell their stories in theater. I was asked by Erik Harper, one of the counselors at the Trauma Center in Cape Town, South Africa, to direct and facilitate a group of twelve survivors who wanted to perform their memories.[20] After giving their testimony at the Commission, why did they want to re-enact their stories again? After having attended many of the Truth and Reconciliation Commission hearings, I observed how the testimonies of the victims of human-rights violations provided a catharsis, a healing release of emotion, with public acknowledgment of their suffering by the commissioners and audience. Yet the stories solicited by the Commission focused only on the moment of victimization. In the subsequent play, survivors went further; they told how they survived, how they had political purpose, how they acted in a heroic, not just a victimized, fashion. These extended narratives along with the inclusion of song and improvisation created a very different context and form than the Truth Commission.

To understand how songs in improvisational theater influenced the *Khumbulani/Remembrance* group, it is important to examine the development of the drama workshop. Calling from a faulty phone line in the township of Philippi, a trauma survivor answered my question about why she wanted to stage a performance: "There are many victims of violation who have not told their stories. By speaking out, we give them courage to break through their shame." After this conversation, I agreed to facilitate a drama workshop, in consultation with a psychologist, recognizing that the ethics of intervention must be grounded in a facilitating role that listens to local needs. When asked why they wanted to narrate their stories, a survivor responded, "Together as *Khumbulani* drama we remember because there are still many people who do not speak of the past." On the first day, the survivors conceived of their audience as other survivors of violence and township community members; later they wanted to perform at public schools. The first performance was at the Trauma Center (8 December 2000) with fifty invited guests; the second performance was at Philippi Township Community Hall on the Day of Reconciliation (16 December 2000) for two hundred

---

20. The names of *Khumbulani* members have been omitted or changed to protect their identities, since the workshop is a therapeutic venue.

survivors, community members, and local leaders; the third performance was downtown at the District Six Museum (May 2001). After the second day of the theater workshop, a survivor commented, "There are important comrades, people elected on the township board, who are losing hope. We must remind them of what we did in the past, our victory. We must continue to hope." For this group, the stories offered hope, refused shame, and broke through the stifling silence felt by their township community.

How did the group develop this performance? After the performance warm-ups, I facilitated storytelling activities by giving the group choices about what type of storytelling exercise to do: drawing pictures, singing songs, sharing one memory, writing a memory, physically embodying a memory image. The group wanted to start with pictures that depicted the story they wanted to tell. From the outset, the group was formed by individuals who came because they wanted to tell their story, and I emphasized that they should think of a story that they felt safe telling to an audience. To have control over one's own story, especially by keeping it unscripted, subject to improvisational change, reverses the original context of the traumatic story—the shocking experience of extreme vulnerability.

When our group told each other the stories that they wanted to perform, I wrote down the main event narrated in each story. After they had told their stories, I sat down on the floor in the middle of the group beside a large blank paper and wrote down the three main events on which the stories focused: fire, arrest, imprisonment. These events, located in the jail or the township, became the basis for three separate scenes in the play. The jail and the township—what Pierre Nora calls "sites of memory"—took former traumatic sites and replayed them in a dramatic setting.[21] The inclusion of theatrical techniques such as memory statues and songs reinforced how the traumatic story was being told in a new context. Since traumatic stress disorder is primarily characterized by a *dislocation of time*—"the pathology consists of the past invading the present in re-experiences and re-enactments"[22]—the performance further heals by organizing the past, separating out the present from the past. The theatrical rendition of the past, like the Kurds' singing of the 1980s song "Halabja" in 2003, emphasized a changed historical context.

After having told their stories in small groups, the group began telling individual stories on stage, and the first person who told his story spoke of being tortured:

> I was imprisoned under the Communist Security Act for fifteen years. They moved me around to six different prisons. I was not allowed any contact with

---

21. Pierre Nora, *Rethinking France = Les lieux de mémoire* (trans. Mary Trouille and Pierre Nora; Chicago: University of Chicago Press, 2001).

22. Allan Young, "Bodily Memory and Traumatic Memory," in Antze and Lambek, *Tense Past*, 97.

my family or friends. I could not have a lawyer. They tortured me, beating and electrocuting me everywhere, even my private parts.

The tall Xhosa man who had spoken dropped his eyes to the floor and hung his head, suffocating in the memory of the torture. The silence afterwards was deafening. None of the members of the group moved. My intentions to be a fairly nonintervening facilitator began to feel unethical in the face of this man drowning in traumatic memory. Eventually I walked a few steps closer to the stage and said, "Thank you for your story." The group broke into applause. Then I asked him, "What were you doing before you were arrested?" He spoke of the death of his father, the financial struggles of his family, the difficulty of finding enough to eat, and he described how he fought with the military wing of the African National Congress. I asked him if he wanted to extend the scene by showing how he fought before being arrested. He liked that idea, and the group agreed with him. Guiding through questions, I preserved choice and a sense of agency to assist the survivors.

Another survivor offered to play the part of the apartheid police. So I placed the two men who wanted to speak of their torture at the back of the audience seating area and asked them to enter as resistance fighters. I also suggested that the police look for the fighters but not find them; then the police select four audience members (actually workshop actors sitting in the audience) to arrest and bring on stage, setting them up in a line to look like human bars of a jail cell. Later the fighters, crouched on stage, would stand in between and behind these human bars to tell their prison stories. The inclusion of resistance memories transposed the horrific scene of torture by adding a framework of political resistance.

After asking the two Xhosa men if they wanted to push past the human bars after their stories and tell what happened after prison, both survivors chose to extend their stories:

> [He pushes through the staged jail bodies.] Now I have been released. I am free because of the CODESSA negotiations. I considered suicide when I was released. Since I was tortured and electrocuted all over my body, I thought that I would never be able to have children. Now I am married and have a son. And I am free. [He begins singing a song of resistance. The group joins in.]

This spontaneous song transformed this scene and the play process. After this, songs became an improvisational tool for the actors. Since songs celebrating the resistance guerrillas were well known to this group, such songs greatly influenced the survivors' interpretative performance of their traumatic memories. These Xhosa songs performed before the group, similar to the Kurdish songs of lament or protest, furthered the release from traumatic alienation.

While survivors only occasionally added songs to the end of their story, the improvisation through song also occurred when survivors broke into tears during the storytelling. When a storyteller wept at the remembrance of a traumatic event, there was always a member of the group who would begin a song and move to embrace the mourning survivor. The rest of the group would take up the song and circle around the one who wept and the one who comforted. Unlike the first time a story was told, when there was silence afterwards, the addition of songs changed the group dynamics and the form of remembrance. The alienating memory of violation was transposed with a community experience of singing, a movement from the individual to the communal.

After several more rehearsals, certain songs served as transition scenes. For instance, "Thina Sizwe" ("We the Nation Weep for Our Land") provided a mournful, yet hopeful hymn, and the song became another interpretive narrative to accompany the individual's story of loss. In this song, the "we" of collective remembrance of suffering—where "We the Nation Weep for Our Land"— is placed next to the individual's tears and heart-wrenching stories—the "I" of testimony. The "we" has an envisioned commonality, or, as Ehrlmann comments about Zulu songs, "the metonymic inclusion of the self in an imagined collectivity distant from the chaos and isolation of the here and now" can bring a measure of comfort.[23] One survivor commented on the singing: "The songs are well known to us. They remind us of how we fought in the past and how we continue to fight against poverty." The songs previously sung in funerals, marches, and rallies to spur on comrades in a battle against apartheid now symbolized present struggles, and the larger framework of "Thina Sizwe" remembered national loss, not individual alienation.

Celebratory protest dances (like the Kurdish form of *shiyee*) brought great joy to the group, which on the first day appeared quite depressed. In my initial interviews with the psychologist Erik Harper at the Trauma Center, he mentioned that many of his clients struggled with suicidal impulses as the devastating lack of control of being tortured was compounded by the desperation of poverty.[24] In our subsequent meetings Harper noted how his clients valued the drama group, and many of the therapists sent their clients to the workshop to observe and to join in the singing of the songs. Often after a more meditative song such as "Nkosi Sikel IAfrica," ("God bless Africa")—a song that is both hymn and now the first part of the national anthem—they chose a fight song/dance (called *toyi-toying*) for the guerilla fighters: "Hey guerrilla! Hey, hey, guerrilla man!" The group would hold their imaginary weapons and dance down the aisles. While a binary relationship (between us and them) is prevalent in many of the protest song lyrics, these songs with dance movements acted out and released the pain of the past.

Many members of the audience in the township of Philippi could relate to experiences of police inspections and arrests. I wanted the audience to become

---

23. Veit Erlmann, *Nightsong: Performance, Power, and Practice in South Africa* (Chicago: University of Chicago Press, 1996), 211.

24. Erik Harper, Interview by Kimberly Segall, October 5, 1999.

part of performing the historic experience. So for the police inspections, audience members were asked for ID cards. Also because many Xhosa knew these songs, hundreds of people in the audience joined in the singing. Like the Kurdish festival of Nao Roz, this event became a time of shared cultural knowledge while reconciling common past suffering. The audience became both witness and participant with the survivors, who acted as cultural agents, performing personal memory, mourning, and local history.

The group chose to end the play as a commemorative event, after considering multiple options. One member said: "We want to enact reparation claims in a second play." Another member said: "This play is about us, about our memories. The next play can be on reparations." They wanted to light a candle to remember their loved ones who had died. After the ritual of lighting candles and naming their lost loved ones, they sang "Senzeni Na?" a mournful chant of "what have we done, what have we done? Our only crime was being black." The song recaptured how they were brutalized for no reason other than the color of their skin. This song often brought group members to tears. If performances of recovery have a process, for this group, the first step was to have control over traumatic memories and to position them in selected rituals and songs to mourn the past.

Following the song, they each told the reason why they were doing this play and thanked the directors. In contrast to the insecurity expressed at the first drama workshops, the group was confident at the last drama (2000): "We are *Khumbulani*. We remember, and we are strong." Another said, "we must remember what the Boer police did to us and remember that what has happened is in the past. It has passed." Another repeated Nelson Mandela's words, "We will forgive, but not forget." The forgiveness of the past came through commemoration. This refrain was repeated by others. "We are doing this play to remember the past and for reconciliation. We will forgive, but never forget." Remembrance is a process by which sensory information is sorted out and evaluated in a very personal way, and past memories are also sorted out in relation to feedback from one's social group. Memory is not a computer archive where the same information in the same order is drawn every time. Memory itself is not a perfect record of events; it is "perspectival and the perspective is a continuously shifting one."[25] Thus, the process of returning to the past memory is part of a selection of fragments that are then used in the present—fragments that are placed into a contemporary context, story, interpretation, purpose. Forgiveness selects a fragment to commemorate and thus does not accentuate other pieces, in a sense forgetting or downplaying the more extreme, obsessive, vengeful, traumatizing pieces.

---

25. Michael Lambek, "The Past Imperfect: Remembrance as Moral Practice" in Antze and Lambek, *Tense Past*, 242.

COMPARISONS AND FOLLOW-UP INTERVIEWS

This paper argues that Xhosa and Kurdish cultural performances, such as the lament, allow for individual healing. Because South Africa is politically at a further transitional point than Iraq in terms of the negotiated justice mechanism of the Truth and Reconciliation Commission, I conclude by asking how the public performances of lament vary from a state mechanism such as the Commission or a public monument such as the Iraqi Halabja memorial.

Many individuals at the Truth and Reconciliation Commission noted that testifying provided a release of tension, yet for some Archbishop Tutu's framework of forgiveness felt overwhelming when they considered the rapists and torturers who had violated them. For instance, after ten years of silence, Thandi Shezi, one of the survivor-actors, first spoke at the Truth and Reconciliation Commission of being gang-raped by four security policemen. Afterward she decided to tell her story on the dramatic, local stage of *The Story I Am about to Tell*. She describes why she restaged her trauma:

> Every time I stand up there in front of the audience at six p.m., a piece of my anger goes away. By next week, I'll be left with none at all! When [Desmond] Tutu talked about forgiveness I used to mock him and say he's mad.... Now I know how anger and grudges and hatred grow inside you like a tumor. Now I'm beginning to become human again.[26]

The Story I Am about to Tell is similar to *Khumbulani*; it is in the restaging of traumatic events that a deeper perspective about the event occurs, a transposed recognition with other survivors/actors and an audience. While the Truth and Reconciliation Commission formed a critical vehicle for sharing stories of the past, cultural performances, in contrast, are played out multiple times with varying audiences to bring healing over time.

Cultural performances also adapt themselves to local audiences and tell community histories, whether Kurdish or Xhosa. The Commission aimed to find out about historical events, especially violations of persons. Yet the *Khumbulani* group wanted also to speak of heroism and resistance in their communities. One survivor showed me a small book that described the heroes and battles and events in the Cape Town Townships. She told the stories and pointed out the local leaders and emphasized, "this is why we must do this play. There are only a few copies of this book. This one is not mine, but I borrowed it to show you, so you will remember our history." Untold histories of local heroes, not accented by the state

---

26. Mark Gevisser, "Setting the Stage for a Journey into South Africa's Heart of Darkness," *Sunday Independent* (10 August 1997): 4.

forum for memory, emerged in the play and allowed for heroic identities necessary for community development and individual healing.[27]

Cultural performances, as was witnessed in the Kurdish and Xhosa studies, are memory vehicles to pass on second-generation memories after years of terror and tragedy. Survivors of atrocity are often individually silent about their past; "the stories are not passed on to their children," according to one therapist at the Cape Town Trauma Center. If given a safe, public medium, then survivors pass on their stories to their children. One *Khumbulani* member expressed concern about the omission of second-generation memories:

> The youth are not being told the stories of the struggle by their parents. These youth don't know their past and are forgetting who they are, joining gangs and getting into trouble.... We must perform for schools, because the youth are forgetting. And the white children don't know what happened at all. We must tell our stories to build reconciliation.

Similar to the Kurd's tradition of Nao Roz, this Xhosa group's desire to perform at schools reveals the importance of stories for fostering reconciliation in the next generation and for crossing cultural lines of difference. One member commented on the mournful or protest songs saying:

> When we sing, it reminds us what we fought for. It is important to tell our stories. For a second play, I know many comrades who cannot speak of exile. No one knows what happened to us when we were sent to Angola. It was lonely and difficult. We were fighting a war over there. People here don't understand that experience.

In performing for one's community, there are varied experiences of the war and exile, expressed to a larger audience for greater understanding of the past. After traumatic experience, individuals attempt "to reconstitute various broken threads of their lives."[28] Combined with control of personal storytelling, these activities reshape one's self as a public figure and one's current context. One group member commented, "In this drama, I became aware that if you speak to someone about your pain, you become free and heal."

---

27. See also Robert Cover, *Narrative, Violence and the Law* (Ann Arbor: University of Michigan Press, 1995). Law exists and locates itself through justifying narratives, as Cover argues: "No set of legal institutions or prescriptions exists apart from the narratives that locates it and give it meaning" (95–96). Narratives and nation building are bonded through legal structures. Law's center stage concentrates on individual ownership and healing; thus, law's narrative is limited to individual problems, obscuring the severe ways entire communities were devastated.

28. Jacob Lindy and Robert Lifton, eds. and introduction in *Beyond Invisible Walls: The Psychological Legacy of Soviet Trauma* (New York: Brunner-Routledge, 2001), 3.

The lament as a performance form also suggests a social bond of reciprocity. The past is honored by those who choose to attend the mourning event. When local leaders and people of varying economic status gather together, it accentuates how a larger community has testified to the injustice of the past. When the injured can speak of injustices and when political leaders honor the dead, it is a form of reparative justice, which, Teresa Godwin Phelps argues, satisfies the need for vengeance.[29] Unlike the oral performance of the lament, a memorial becomes a fixed site and over time, depending on relationships in the community, can create ambivalence. At the Halabja memorial, Colin Powell, former U.S. secretary of state, attended the opening in 2003, followed by numerous foreign, state, and local Kurdish leaders. While many leaders pledged economic restitution to this city, the promises were not kept. Khadar Karim Mohammed, the council chairman, stated: "We got lots of empty promises from visitors. The only money we got was to build two schools."[30] Staged at the memorial, local students protested the lack of development, including the absence of running water, power, or sewage in Halabja: "Why don't they build power stations here, so we don't have constant cuts?" asked one student. Whether foreign or state monies disappeared or never came in, the economic promises made were associated with the honoring of victims symbolized by the monument; the two were intertwined, suggesting that the social bonds of mourning must continually be respected by an ongoing commitment to development.

CONCLUSIONS

So why are these cultural performances still important? Since traumatic memories remember what one most desires to forget, performing them is a painful process that is worked out in communities as well as in state institutions. Initially survivors tend to repeat short obsessive fragments of their past. Cultural performances, on the other hand, like therapeutic performance goals, do not stay in this shell-shocked state of repeating the short traumatic episode; rather, the public process leads to extending the narrative associations to add a sense of closure. While we recognize that countries need ceremonies after political transitions, we often forget that community groups have ceremonies and cultural traditions that can also assist individuals in transitioning out of the terrorized state of the past.

Performed embodiments—improvisations with poetic laments, stories, songs, dance—add a sense of control after the unexpected violations that define terror. Traumatic memories not only make everyday activities difficult in the present,

29. Teresa Godwin Phelps, *Shattered Voices* (Philadelphia: University of Pennsylvania Press, 2004) 12–13.

30. Jonathan Steele, "Saddam Can't Be Blamed for Halabja's Latest Convulsions," *The Guardian* (2 March 2007).

but also traumatic images block out many portions of the past. Thus, traumatic memories, in effect, can erase other forms of memory. Social adjustments after periods of terror are difficult when past memories dominate present responses. For instance, Akila al-Hashemi, an Iraqi woman serving on the Governing Council, stated that she and her particular party were often silent because "we are still under the shock, we are still afraid"; when she was fifteen, the Baath Party gained control. "Now I'm fifty. You see? You can imagine—can I change in two days, in two months, in two years? We need to be re-educated, rehabilitated."[31] A returning exile reports on the Iraqis, "They are so normalized to the Baath and the fear and the death and the terror that they can't see the advantages now."[32] Cultural performances, especially songs and stories that give agency to their actors, are an important part of releasing the terror of the past, so that individuals can recover from the shock and begin imagining change. Songs and stories of the past influence a group's outlook and identification. Cultural performances help shift and solidify public memory, and public memory, as Michael Kammen argues, "is ideologically important because it shapes a nation's ethos and sense of identity."[33] Cultural performances work as important nation-building tools.

James Dawes argues that "war dismantles the cultures that constitute the individual; it violates the boundaries that structure social meaning."[34] In effect, cultural performances register the historical and political shift on a social and personal level to ease and awaken communities to the transition out of terror. When we identify the importance of these local rituals, we may find, as Victor Turner argues, "cultural performances are not simple reflectors or expressions of culture or even of changing culture but may themselves be active agencies of change."[35]

---

31. Reported by George Packer, "Letter from Baghdad: War after the War," *New Yorker* (24 November 2003), 82.

32. Ibid., 82.

33. Michael Kammen, *Mystic Chords of Memory: The Transformation of Tradition in American Culture* (New York: Knopf, 1991), 13.

34. Dawes, *The Language of War*, 133.

35. Victor Turner, *The Anthropology of Performance* (New York: Performing Arts Journal, 1987), 24.

The Poetry of Job as a Resource for the Articulation of Embodied Lament in the Context of HIV and AIDS in South Africa

Gerald West

Introduction

The work that forms the basis of reflection in this essay comes from actual collaboration between socially engaged biblical scholars, organic intellectuals, and ordinary "readers" of the Bible who are living with HIV and AIDS. This work has structural form, arising as it does from the ongoing alliance between the Ujamaa Centre for Community Development and Research (a community-based project within the School of Religion and Theology) and Siyaphila Support Groups (community-based organizations in civil society in the KwaZulu-Natal province of South Africa).

A great deal could be said about both these organizations, but for the purposes of this essay it will be sufficient to introduce them succinctly. The Ujamaa Centre took institutional shape in the late 1980s in apartheid South Africa, as an attempt by socially engaged biblical scholars, organic intellectuals, and ordinary black South Africans (most of whom were poor, working class, and marginalized, and among whom the majority were women) to read the Bible in a context of massive social upheaval and violence. Funerals and displaced people's camps were the sites in which these three parties initially encountered each other, but soon we shifted to other sites in which we read the Bible together in an attempt to hear God speak into our context amidst the turmoil.

Over the years we have established an institutional base—the Ujamaa Centre—within the School of Religion and Theology at the University of KwaZulu-Natal; we have developed a collaborative Bible reading process—the Contextual Bible Study method, and we have entered into collaborative action with particular local projects.[1] Among these projects is the Siyaphila Support

---

1. Gerald O. West, "Contextualized Reading of the Bible," *Analecta Bruxellensia* 11 (2006): 131–48.

Group network. Responding to a request from one of our large, predominantly black, hospitals, we offered our offices and our personnel to those who were testing positive for HIV but for whom there were no support structures. In the early years of the epidemic there were no support structures whatsoever, not even basic counseling, for those who were courageous enough to test. Our offices became a safe site and the first stop of those, mostly women, who had tested and were HIV-positive. As is our usual practice, we offered to work with this emerging sector to help them organize themselves. We also offered them the opportunity to participate in our weekly rhythms of Contextual Bible Study. Both offers were accepted, and out of this emerged an autonomous community-based organization called the Siyaphila Support Group.[2] "Siyaphila" means "we are well/alive/positive" in Zulu, and although a formal organization now recognized and financially supported by our local municipality and the health system in our province, many of its features are those of a social movement.

The Ujamaa Centre, through its Solidarity Programme for People Living with HIV and AIDS, coordinated by Bongi Zengele, maintains regular contact and collaborates with the Siyaphila Support Group network. Among the things we do together is Contextual Bible Study.

HIV AND AIDS: THE CURRENT CONTEXT

Before I say more about Contextual Bible Study and the particular Bible studies that form the basis of this essay, it is important to say something briefly about nature and scope of the HIV and AIDS pandemic in South Africa. This is not easy to do, however, for the pandemic constantly changes its profile. Fortunately, a major study was published in 2007, based on data from the South African National HIV Prevalence, HIV Incidence, Behaviour and Communication Survey, 2005.[3]

This study reports on HIV incidence and prevalence. Incidence is a measure of the number and distribution of new infections. This is important because "incidence is the key indicator of the rate of HIV transmission and provides the most direct means of assessing the impact of HIV prevention programmes."[4] Furthermore, "Incidence data provide critical new insights into the dynamics of the HIV epidemic and is a more appropriate measure to correlate biological data with recent behaviours or recent behavioural changes."[5] Prevalence measures

---

2. Gerald O. West, "Reading the Bible in the Light of HIV/Aids in South Africa," *Ecumenical Review* 55 (2003): 335–44.

3. Thomas Rehle, Olive Shisana, Victoria Pillay, Khangelani Zuma, Adrian Puren, and Warren Parker, "National HIV Incidence Measures: New Insights into the South African Epidemic," *South African Medical Journal* 97 (2007): 194–99.

4. Ibid., 194.

5. Ibid., 199.

"the result of cumulative new infections over time minus the cumulative deaths among HIV-infected persons."[6]

There is an estimated 1.4 percent incidence per year of HIV in the population aged two years or older, with an estimated 571,000 new HIV infections for 2005. The incidence of HIV in the child population aged two to fourteen years is 0.5 percent a year, with an estimated 69,000 new infections in this very young age group. The HIV incidence for youth fifteen to twenty-four years of age is 2.2 percent (192,000 new infections), and for those above twenty-five years of age it is 1.7 percent (310,000 new infections) a year. For these age ranges together, fifteen to forty-nine years of age, the HIV incidence is 2.4 percent, meaning that there are an estimated 500,000 new infections a year.[7]

The high incidence in children is deeply worrying, as is the high incidence among the youth. Even more alarming are the study's gender-based findings. The incidence of HIV among females was highest in the twenty- to twenty-nine-year age range, at 5.6 percent, more than six times the incidence found in twenty- to twenty-nine-year-old males (0.9 percent). Among youth aged fifteen to twenty-four, females account for 90 percent of the recent HIV infections. So the differences in HIV incidence between males and females are especially large in the younger age groups under thirty years of age. While HIV incidence among females rises fast and peaks in the twenty- to twenty-nine-year age band, the incidence of HIV among males increases much more slowly than in females and peaks at a lower level in the thirty- to thirty-nine-year age group (2.7 percent).[8]

As the study goes on to argue, "These differential HIV transmission dynamics between males and females are reflected in the HIV prevalence profiles."[9] Again, HIV prevalence increases sharply among young females and peaks at 28.2 percent in the twenty- to twenty-nine age range. In males HIV prevalence increases slowly between the ages of twenty and twenty-nine, then rises more sharply, but not as sharply as among females, peaking at 23.3 percent ten years later in the thirty to thirty-nine age group.[10]

HIV also has a race and socioeconomic profile. "HIV incidence in the black race group is nine times higher than the incidence found in the other race groups [whites, indians, and coloureds]."[11] "Persons living in urban informal settlements have by far the highest incidence rates (5.1 percent) compared with those living in rural formal areas (1.6 percent), rural informal areas (1.4 percent), and urban formal areas (0.8 percent)."[12]

---

6. Ibid., 198.

7. Ibid., 196.

8. Ibid., 196–97.

9. Ibid., 197.

10. Ibid.

11. Ibid., 196.

12. Ibid.

Sociobehavioral factors also play a role in our HIV profile. So HIV prevalence and incidence are higher for those who were single (16.6 percent prevalence, 3.0 percent incidence) than for those who are married (14.3 percent, 1.3 percent). The most alarming finding, however, is that the most at-risk group is those individuals (mainly women, 79.6 percent) who have been widowed (whose median age was forty-three years old). Their HIV prevalence and incidence was considerably higher (34 percent, 5.8 percent) than either those who were single or married.[13]

Finally, there is an increased risk of HIV acquisition during pregnancy. Within the age range of fifteen to forty-nine, females who were pregnant were found to have an HIV incidence of 5.2 percent compared with the 3.8 percent of those who were not pregnant.[14]

The study concludes that the "incidence rates among young females in their prime childbearing age are especially alarming,"[15]as is the high incidence among widows[16]and women generally. Women are particularly at risk of HIV infection, especially those, such as widows, who are particularly vulnerable socioeconomically. In general, there is a high risk among those who are socio-economically vulnerable. "Although only 8.7 percent of the total South African population aged 2 years and above lives in urban informal settlements, 29.1 percent (166,000/571,000) of the total estimated number of new HIV infections in South Africa are found in this residence geotype."[17]

Another worrying indication in this study is the high incidence of "new nonvertical infections" among children in South Africa. "These infections," the researchers argue, "in children between 2 and 14 years are probably not linked to mother-to-child transmission, and infection would therefore have occurred through other modes of transmission, potentially including child sexual abuse, scarification practices and health care services."[18]The study ends on a pessimistic note, stating that "the highly resourced plethora of prevention programmes in South Africa has failed to address HIV incidence in these high-risk categories sufficiently, and more efficient and targeted interventions are clearly urgently required."[19]

More starkly, based on an interpretation of studies such as the above and other forms of statistical information, the Treatment Action Campaign, the activist and advocacy Non-governmental Organisation at the forefront of HIV and AIDS work in South Africa, argues that at least 600,000 people have died from AIDS-related illnesses (such as tuberculosis, pneumonia, and diarrhea) between

---

13. Ibid., 197.
14. Ibid., 199.
15. Ibid., 198.
16. Ibid., 199.
17. Ibid., 198.
18. Ibid.
19. Ibid., 199.

1998 and 2003. Among these it is "young adults [twenty to forty years] who are dying disproportionately of AIDS."[20]Life expectancy is currently about fifty-one years of age.

About 10.8 percent of our population above the age of two is HIV-positive, meaning that more than six million South Africans are HIV-positive. At least one in ten of all of us is HIV-positive; three out of every ten women who attend a public antenatal clinic are HIV-positive,[21]and, unfortunately, there is no clear evidence that the epidemic is stabilizing.

Especially when one considers that with appropriate antiretroviral treatment (ART), AIDS is a chronic but manageable disease, equally alarming are the small numbers of HIV-positive South Africans on antiretroviral treatment. This is an indication of both a continued "lack of national leadership and pervasive AIDS denialism."[22]By January 2006 the total number of people on antiretroviral treatment "totaled about 200,000 to 220,000," with less than half of these accessing ART in the public sector and the rest receiving it in the private and not-for-profit sectors.[23]This total figure is less than half those who need ART.

Significantly, about 60 percent of patients receiving publicly funded ART are women.[24]Women clearly are far less prone to AIDS denialism and take more responsibility, publicly, for their own health and that of their communities than men. But in the private sector men outnumber women on treatment, probably because "workplace treatment programmes are generally more available to male workers." Very few patients access ART at rural and remote sites,[25]indicating how difficult it is to "associate" oneself with HIV and AIDS in such communities.

A worrying feature of ART is how few children benefit from government and private-sector programs, with children making up only 10–15 percent of those currently accessing ART.[26]The problem here is that fewer ARTs are registered for pediatric use, partially because of "ethical concerns about conducting clinical trials on children," but also partially because "the market in developed countries is small because prevention measures mean that few infants are infected with HIV via their mothers." Consequently, while "[i]n the United States about 98 percent of HIV-positive children are expected to live to adulthood, and to have life

---

20. Nathan Geffen, "What Do South Africa's Aids Statistics Mean? A TAC Briefing Paper" (online: http://www.tac.org.za/aidsstats.html).

21. Ibid.

22. International Treatment Preparedness Coalition, "Missing the Target: Off Target for 2010: How to Avoid Breaking the Promise of Universal Access (Update to ITPC's AIDS Treatment Report from the Frontlines)" (online: http://www.aidstreatmentaccess.org/itpcupdatefinal.pdf), 33–34.

23. Ibid., 33.

24. Ibid.

25. Ibid., 34.

26. Ibid., 33.

spans close to those of their uninfected peers," in some areas of Africa, "half of HIV-positive infants are expected to die before they turn two."[27]

Finally, in this brief profile of the pandemic in South Africa, what further compounds the problem is the stigma and discrimination that accompany it. Indeed, the executive director of UNAIDS stated in 2000 that the most pressing item on the agenda for the world community in combating HIV and AIDS was the need for a "renewed effort to combat stigma."[28]In the words of Nelson Mandela, "Many who suffer from HIV and AIDS are not killed by the virus, but by stigma."[29]Our journey so far with HIV and AIDS shows us that we still have a long way to go in understanding how and why stigma and discrimination "attach" themselves to HIV and AIDS. That they do is uncontested. In a recent study by Beverley Haddad among church leaders in a peri-urban area on the outskirts of Pietermaritzburg, South Africa, she found that even those ministers, pastors, and priests who did want to engage publicly with the pandemic chose not to because they felt constrained by their ecclesial-cultural contexts not to offend their congregations. In the words of one of these church leaders:

> It is not easy to speak about this disease because many people only want you to speak to them about God and not things on the side. Do not tell them about this thing because it frightens them. Because if you speak about this thing openly, they are going to complain that you are being rude in church because you are talking about secretive things because even though this disease is known, even though they know that there is a killer disease, they do not want to be told about it to their faces. Because when you are at church it is believed that you are a holy person. So now when you preach about how people contract the disease, they know that they are out of line if they do something like that.[30]

But we must go beyond acknowledging the reality of stigma and discrimination; we must also search for new conceptual frameworks to understand its grasp on us. The dominant framework to date has drawn on the pioneering work of Erving Goffman,[31]in which he defined stigma as "an attribute that is significantly discred-

---

27. Belinda Beresford, "Where Research Has Brought Us," *Mail & Guardian* (13–19 April 2007): 14.

28. Richard Parker and Peter Aggleton, "HIV and AIDS-Related Stigma and Discrimination: A Conceptual Framework and Implications for Action," *Social Science & Medicine* 57 (2003): 13–24.

29. "Stop Blaming Government for Aids Research, Says Mandela," *Mail & Guardian* (1 January 2002): 21.

30. Beverley G. Haddad, "'We Pray but We Cannot Heal': Theological Challenges Posed by the HIV/AIDS Crisis," *JTSA* 125 (2006): 84–85.

31. Erving Goffman, *Stigma: Notes on the Management of a Spoiled Identity* (New York: Simon & Schuster, 1963).

iting," and the stigmatized individual is thus seen to be a person who possesses "an undesirable difference."[32] But as Parker and Aggleton have argued more recently,

> Useful and important as Goffman's formulations of this problem were, a fuller understanding of stigmatization, at least as it functions in the context of HIV/AIDS, requires us to unpack this analytic category—and to rethink the directions that it has pushed us in our research and intervention work. Above all, the emphasis placed by Goffman on stigma as a "discrediting attribute" has led to a focus on stigma as though it were *a kind of thing* (in particular, a cultural or even individual value)—a relatively static characteristic or feature, albeit one that is at some level culturally constructed.[33]

Instead, Parker and Aggleton want to move beyond the individualistic emphasis that has characterized so much of the work on stigma and discrimination, toward a notion—influenced by Michel Foucault's emphasis on the cultural production of difference—of stigmatization and discrimination "as part of the political economy of social exclusion present in the contemporary world."[34] In order to do this, they argue, "it is imperative to situate the analysis of HIV/AIDS historically, and to remember that the epidemic has developed during a period of rapid globalization linked to a radical restructuring of the world economy," characterized by "rapidly accelerating processes of social exclusion, together with an intensified interaction between what might be described as 'traditional' and 'modern' forms of exclusion."[35] Not surprisingly, among the most vivid of these processes of exclusion "has been the rapidly increasing feminization of poverty together with the increasing polarization between rich and poor in both the so-called developed as well as the so-called developing worlds."[36] In their view, and we in the Ujamaa Centre would agree with this analysis, "This intensifying interaction between multiple forms of inequality and exclusion offers a general model for an analysis of the interaction between multiple forms of stigma that has typified the history of the HIV and AIDS epidemics." We would also agree that "by examining the synergy between diverse forms of inequality and stigma, we may be better able to untangle the complex webs of meaning and power that are at work in HIV and AIDS-related stigma, stigmatization and discrimination."[37]

---

32. Parker and Aggleton, "HIV and AIDS-Related Stigma," 14.

33. Ibid. For an initial theological engagement with this discussion, see Denise M. Ackermann, "From Mere Existence to Tenacious Endurance: Stigma, HIV/AIDS and a Feminist Theology of Praxis," in *African Women, Religion, and Health: Essays in Honor of Mercy Amba Ewudziwa Oduyoye* (ed. Isabel Apawo Phiri and Sarojini Nadar; Pietermaritzburg: Cluster, 2006), 221–42.

34. Parker and Aggleton, "HIV and AIDS-Related Stigma," 19.

35. Ibid.

36. Ibid.

37. Ibid.

This is the context in which we in the Ujamaa Centre collaborate and work with those infected and affected by HIV and AIDS, such as the Siyaphila Support Groups.

Among the many activities and interventions undertaken by Siyaphila Support Groups, many of which are designed to affirm dignity and develop resilience, Contextual Bible Study with the Ujamaa Centre is a regular, fortnightly, feature. The affirmation and practice of agency and dignity are central tenets of our participatory Contextual Bible Study methodology, and the kinds of biblical texts chosen by Siyaphila Support Group facilitators themselves are often those in which Jesus stands with marginalized individuals and sectors, over against dominating and discriminating sectors.[38]

Alongside these affirming biblical texts, the Ujamaa Centre offers more unfamiliar texts, understanding that such texts have the potential to provide additional lines of connection between faith communities in our current contexts and faith communities behind and within the biblical texts. We also offer literary and sociohistorical modes of reading (in a noninvasive question-based format) to supplement the modes of reading already operative within the group. However, the Contextual Bible Study is framed, beginning and ending, with what we call "community consciousness questions," questions that overtly depend and draw on local resources.

The following Bible study (using NRSV), which forms the basis for the reflection in this essay, will illustrate the above points.

1. Job 1:21, "The LORD gave, and the LORD has taken away; blessed be the name of the LORD," is a biblical text often read at funerals. What does this text say about people who have died of AIDS-related illnesses, and what does it say to people living with HIV and AIDS?

2. Read Job 3 together at least twice. What is Job trying to say in this text? What images or metaphors does Job use in his lament?

3. How does this text resonate with people living with HIV and AIDS? Which of Job's images or metaphors are particularly relevant?

4. What would be your own version of Job 3? Share it with those in the group.

5. What is God's view of how Job has spoken in chapter 3 (and elsewhere)? Read Job 42:7.

6. How can you share your version of Job 3 with your local church or community or family?

---

38. West, "Reading the Bible in the Light of HIV/AIDS," 335–44.

Questions 1, 3, 4, and 6 are all what we call "community consciousness" questions, drawing as they do on the local knowledge and experience of the community. Questions 2 and 5 are what we call "critical consciousness" questions, drawing as they do on aspects of biblical scholarship, in this case the literary dimensions of the book of Job.

As the Bible study indicates, we chose this text because parts of the book of Job are familiar to those who attend the many funerals on Saturdays in our communities. Job 1:21 is a favorite funeral text. Indeed, it is just about the only portion of the book of Job that is familiar to most churchgoers in our region. But because biblical scholars know that this is not the whole story (or argument), we wondered how Siyaphila members would respond to engaging more substantially with the book of Job. When I told Bongi Zengele, who is the organic intellectual (although not a biblical scholar) who helped found and now coordinates our work with the Siyaphila Support Group network, that there were other parts of Job that might resonate with the experience of members of Siyaphila, she immediately suggested that we try to construct a Bible study on Job 3 that could be used at one of the fortnightly meetings of one of the Siyaphila groups.

The Bible study, based on the questions above, was traumatic and transformative.[39]Those present, slowly at first, and then in rush, identified with elements of Job 3 and used this resource, both in its metaphorical detail and in its rhetorical mode, to vent their lament. My own initial response to this outpouring of lament was one of alarm, but Bongi Zengele, who is a regular companion of this particular Siyaphila group, reassured me, so we kept the Contextual Bible Study process moving. She was right; the outpouring of lament led to a sense of healing calm some hours later. Duration is an important aspect of the Contextual Bible Study process; time is needed for what is inchoate, embodied, and incipient to find forms of articulation.[40]

In this case what came to articulation were forms of lament. In response to question 4 in the Bible study, members of the group each produced their own "version" of Job 3. We gave no direction as to how they should do this. We simply gave pen, paper, and time and space for the exercise, for those who wanted to participate. All chose to do this. What follows are the individual laments of the participants. They were written by the participants, who want to be named but not linked directly with a particular lament. Bongi Zengele translated their laments into English. I use them here with the permission of the group: Ntombenhle Ngcobo, Thembi Ndawo, Nonhlanhla Zuma, Mduduzi Mshengu, Hlengiwe Zulu,

---

39. Gerald O. West and Bongi Zengele, "Reading Job 'Positively' in the Context of HIV/AIDS in South Africa," *Concilium* 4 (2004): 112–24.

40. Gerald O. West, "Indigenous Exegesis: Exploring the Interface between Missionary Methods and the Rhetorical Rhythms of Africa; Locating Local Reading Resources in the Academy," *Neot* 36 (2002): 156–57.

Nelly Nene, S'fiso Zuma, Fikile Ngcobo, Jabu Molefe, Xolani Khumalo, S'bongile Shezi, and Phindile Ndlovu.[41]

1. God you have allowed me to feel this painful experience. I don't know whether this is because I am a bad person in your eyes, or because of my sinfulness. You have taken away my husband, I am left alone with four young children to look after and I am unemployed. My prayer is: please help me to raise these children under your guidance, let them do good in your eyes like Job. I am begging you to keep me alive for a longer time so that I can be there for my children. Give me strength to come closer to you, more than before God. I curse the family (my in-laws) I stay with, they are horrible to me!

2. My cry to God.
My God why did you give me such a heavy burden? I thought I was doing well, obeying your laws. I beg you to forgive me if I have sinned against you. Curse this incurable disease in my body. If this is the result of my sins, please guide me in your ways; show me the way I should go. I thank you loving Father and Good Shepherd. Amen.

3. I curse God for allowing me to be HIV-positive. I have obeyed God all my life; I am crying deeply now as I see that God is so far away from me. I will hold onto the cross as things are so difficult for me.

4. My God I cry before you, I am like your servant Job. I am sick of an incurable disease—AIDS. I know I will die and be buried underground because of AIDS. I am not blaming anybody. I put all in the hands of God if this is his will … let it be. As Ecclesiastes says, "There is time for everything." God hear my prayer. Amen.

5. My cry is, "Why have you forsaken me my God!" Is it because I did not know you are there? I know now that you are with me. Getting infected with HIV brought me closer to you and I have taken a commitment to praise you as the Lord and my Saviour.

6. I cry like Job; I am very angry at the person who infected me with this virus. I thought I would never speak to him again, but listening to the story of Job is challenging me to change my perception. My own

---

41. This is the first time these individual laments have been shared in a published form. Those who produced them hope that you the reader will use them in contexts where they will make a difference.

parents have rejected me and I had thought I would never speak to them either. But now I am challenged to go back home. I want to work for the community, helping those who are like me, infected with HIV. Give me strong faith....

7. My God my God why did you allow me to have AIDS!!! Why did you give me this one child, when you know that my life-span is short? I will soon die and leave him with no parent! I wish I were not even born into this world! I am an orphan and unemployed. It would be better if I did not even exist in this world!

8. Dear God, pour your Holy Spirit into us who are living with HIV and AIDS; we are hoping in your strength to conquer AIDS!

9. God I do accept that I am a sinner; that is why I am HIV positive. I did not do your will; please give me life for longer now so that I can raise my only child you gave me. Help me to show others who are living with HIV that it is possible to live longer, doing your will. Help me to face challenges that come with my HIV status.

10. God the Father, you can see the trials and tribulations we are faced with in our daily lives. We are sick and tired; we ask you to diminish HIV/AIDS, let it not spread inside our bodies, so that your people are able to live longer, prosperous lives. Our Father God, you see our anger, pain and suffering; we have no power. We ask you Lord to suppress HIV so that it will not spread, and that more people will live healthy lives.

11. Oh Lord, why me; why have you deserted me; what have I done to deserve such punishment?

12. My God, why is it so difficult for me to accept that I am HIV positive? I do try, but it is so hard to accept; this is so difficult to deal with in my mind. I am the only one left in my family; they have all gone to you. Why is it Lord that this remains so difficult in my mind? I curse the day I first heard that I was HIV positive. If I knew how to care for myself I would have gained weight by now. I repeat again, God why don't you give me more freedom to live positively in my HIV status?

This is not the place to analyze these laments, except to say that they carry in their form both the liturgical traditions of the participants, elements of the contours of Job's lament in chapter 3, and the patterns of embodied pain that suffering generates. What I do want to point to from these laments is the emergence of lament as a mode of theological discourse in South Africa.

Religion has always been a vital part of our life in South Africa, although ambiguous. It has been used both to construct and sustain colonial and racial domination and to resist them. In the struggle for liberation, lament has had a limited but important role, particularly in hymn-like liberation songs such as "Senzeni na?" ("What Have We Done?"). Funerals were significant sites for such forms of lament. But not today. As I have already said, funerals are now occasions for an insistent silence around HIV and AIDS or, worse, moralizing preaching against the sin that brings on God's punishment of AIDS.

From a quite different context, that of the United States, another socially engaged biblical scholar, Ken Stone, notes with dismay a similar cooption of the Bible as part of a wider religious response to AIDS in which the victims are blamed. Citing Michael Clark's "scripture-phobia," induced in Clark by the reality in his context where "the Bible has been used, over and over again … as the ideological justification not only for excluding gay men and lesbians, but also for blaming the victims in the AIDS health crisis,"[42]Stone goes on to acknowledge that "it is not difficult to think of biblical passages which state or imply disaster and distress are divine responses to sinful activities formerly carried out by those who suffer."[43]But Stone then proceeds to "consider the possibility that certain lament psalms can be read in a manner that will encourage resistance to the attitudes towards AIDS that rightly trouble Clark."[44]

In the readings of the Bible that most trouble Clark, those living with HIV and AIDS "are objects of speech, and their distress is focalized by someone other than the sufferer"; they are "treated as objects of authoritative discourses."[45]It is against this reality that Stone sets out "to queer" both the Bible and biblical interpretation. Our reading of Job 3 and Stone's reading of biblical laments set out, therefore, "to reverse the discursive positioning that structures such readings, focusing not on biblical texts that speak *about* the person who suffers but rather on texts in which suffering is focalized by a speaking subject that is, itself, a suffering subject."[46]

Operating within a liberation hermeneutic, the Ujamaa Centre goes further and grants an epistemological privilege to the perspective of the poor,[47]the working-class, and the marginalized, including those living with HIV and AIDS. This epistemological privilege is the basis for our collaborative projects of eman-

---

42. Ken Stone, "Safer Text: Reading Biblical Laments in the Age of Aids," *Theology and Sexuality* 10 (1999): 16.

43. Ibid.

44. Ibid., 16–17.

45. Ibid., 20.

46. Ibid.

47. Per Frostin, *Liberation Theology in Tanzania and South Africa: A First World Interpretation* (Lund: Lund University Press, 1988), 6–11.

cipatory and transformative action. And, as Stone notes, biblical laments (and his focus is the Psalms), "do not generally acquiesce to suffering, do not in most cases try to give it a positive interpretation. Rather, they complain about it; and this complaint offers readers a subject-position from which an end to suffering and distress can be actively pursued." In short, "many of the laments respond to suffering with *resistance*."[48] In the examples of lamenting religion in South Africa that follow, resistance is a significant element.

LAMENT IN ART

Alongside the Bible as a specific site of struggle in itself, we in the Ujamaa Centre have been attentive to other cultural sites in which the Bible (generally) and the book of Job (in particular) appear to have been drawn upon in local lamenting. A powerful example is the work of Trevor Makhoba.

Makhoba was born in KwaZulu-Natal, South Africa in the mid-1950s, and lived for most of his life in one of the large black urban townships of the city of Durban. Having tried his hand at a variety of jobs, Makhoba became a full-time artist in 1987. He died in 2003. Makhoba was a social commentator with strong African traditional and Christian beliefs,[49] so many of his pictures are socioreligious commentary. The above work, a black-and-white linocut on paper, is clearly intended to be read theologically.

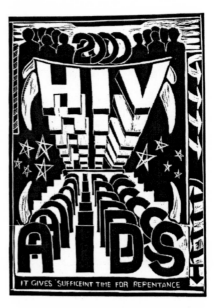

Fig. 1. "IT GIVES SUFFICEINT TIME FOR REPENTANCE: GOD WANTS HIS PEOPLE." A linocut by Trevor Makhoba, 2000. This image is used with the permission of Mrs. G. Makhoba

---

48. Ken Stone, "Safer Text," 21.

49. Juliette C. Leeb-du Toit, "Contextualizing the Use of Biblically Derived and Metaphysical Imagery in the Work of Black Artists from Kwazulu-Natal: c1930–2002" (Ph.D. diss., University of Natal, 2003), 230–32; Valerie T. L. Leigh, "Aspects of Identity in Kwazulu-Natal Art 1980–2000 with Special Reference to the Complexity of Influences Shaping the Work of Andries Botha, Jinny Heath, Derek Leigh and Trevor Makhoba" (M.A. thesis, University of Natal, 2002), 125–28; Gugu Makhoba, interview, 11 June 2005, Gugu Makhoba et al., "Endpiece," in *Trevor Makhoba Memorial Exhibition Catalogue* (ed. Jill Addleson; Durban: Durban Art Gallery, 2004).

This work, produced as part of the "HIV-AIDS Billboard & Print Portfolio: Artists for Human Rights" exhibition in 2000/2001, is Makhoba's first explicit comment on HIV and AIDS. It would be followed by a number of quite different images, namely, oil paintings in rich color that graphically link heterosexual sex, AIDS, and death. These later works seem full of anger and are clearly constructed to shock. The linocut above is also shocking, but in it there does appear to be some resistance and some hope of redemption.

At first glance the work presents the prevailing theological position on HIV/ AIDS in South Africa, which is that this disease is a punishment from God. The mouth of some great beast is waiting (or perhaps advancing) to devour with its twin gaping jaws those who do not repent: HIV (the upper jaw) and AIDS (the lower jaw). Tombstone and coffin-like teeth are posed to crush. Yet the linocut holds out some hope, at the bottom. There is time, it proclaims, for repentance. The jaws have not yet closed; they remain open. "IT GIVES SUFFICEINT TIME" [sic]. The "IT" referred to is unclear but probably refers to this beast, whose millennial nostrils provide an apocalyptic mood. The darkness, Makhoba seems to be saying, of the new millennium and its heraldic disease are almost upon us, but there is still time to repent. The handwritten note in the margin of the print, "GOD WANTS HIS PEOPLE," perhaps reinforces a sense of hope.

While there is much in this image that deserves detailed attention,[50]for the purposes of this essay, I want to suggest that Makhoba is drawing on the book of Job for his primary metaphor, the gaping beast. In so doing, I am also suggesting that Makhoba is less the prophet warning his people than the lamenting victim-subject.

Makhoba's beast is, I think, found in the book of Job, for it is in this book that we encounter Behemoth, sometimes translated as "hippopotamus," as it is in both the old and new Zulu Bible translations (imvubu; Job 40:15–24), and Leviathan, sometimes translated as "crocodile," as it is in the new Zulu Bible translation (ingwenya; 41:1–34). These enigmatic creatures are evoked by God in the concluding God-speech, but quite what their evocation means to accomplish is not that clear. While human beings clearly have no control over these terrifyingly magnificent creatures (which seems to be God's point in the speech), it may be that the poet's point is that even God does not seem fully in control of these particular creatures.[51]Might part of Makhoba's theological reflection on HIV and AIDS be found here, with Behemoth (the hippopotamus) and Leviathan (the crocodile) in the book of Job? "Look at Behemoth," says God, "It is the first of the

---

50. See Gerald O. West, "(Ac)claiming the (Extra)ordinary African 'Reader' of the Bible," in *Reading Other-wise: Social Engaged Biblical Scholars Reading with Their Local Communities* (ed. Gerald O. West; SemeiaSt 62; Atlanta: Society of Biblical Literature, 2007), 29–47.

51. Leo G. Perdue, *Wisdom in Revolt: Metaphorical Theology in the Book of Job* (Sheffield: Almond, 1991).

great acts of God—only its Maker can approach it with the sword" (Job 40:15, 19, NRSV). As for Leviathan, says God,

> were not even the gods overwhelmed at the sight of it?
> No one is so fierce as to dare to stir it up.
> Who can stand before it?
> Who can confront it and be safe?
> —under the whole heaven, who? (Job 41:9b–11)

That even its maker requires a sword when approaching it (Behemoth) and that "no one," perhaps not even God, "is so fierce as to dare to stir it [Leviathan] up" is terrifying indeed, for the HIV/AIDS beast is already upon us, devouring us. Makhoba's beast, like Behemoth and Leviathan, poses the profound theological question of whether God is fully in control. And while one part of Makhoba believes God is in control and therefore must have sent this beast to call to repentance or to punish, another part of Makhoba, the suffering subject, laments a beast that even God seems unable or unwilling to stop.

While Makhoba's beast derives, I think, from or resonates with Behemoth and Leviathan in Job 40–41, the darkened human forms and the night's sky behind the beast's gaping mouth and crushing teeth may derive from or resonate with Job 3. Like Job, I hear Makhoba in this work lamenting the day of his birth and calling for the day to become night. As prophet, Makhoba stands outside the picture, proclaiming the words of the frame to others. As fellow-sufferer, Makhoba stands inside the picture with the darkened figures, with the devouring beast in the darkness of the night, lamenting.

This linocut, a local resource, is itself suggestive for Bible study. The Ujamaa Centre has used this image, with the permission of the late Trevor Makhoba's wife, to construct the following Bible study:

> Input: This Bible study has no biblical text. In fact, it is a Bible study that is in search of a biblical text! Using the art of the late local KwaZulu-Natal artist Trevor Makhoba (with the permission of his wife, Mrs. G. Makhoba), this Bible study attempts to probe what biblical texts we use when we speak theologically about HIV and AIDS.

> Questions:
> 1. In small groups, try to interpret Trevor Makhoba's linocut. What does the linocut say to you?
> 2. Which biblical texts do you think Makhoba is drawing on in this linocut?
> 3. Do you think Makhoba may be drawing on Job 3:1–10, 40:15–24, and 41:1–34?
> 4. What is Makhoba's theology of HIV and AIDS?
> 5. What is your theology of HIV and AIDS?

6. What biblical texts do you draw on to speak theologically about HIV and AIDS?

7. How can we make an impact on the church's theology of HIV and AIDS?

The Ujamaa Centre is committed to using the local resources of ordinary "readers" (whether literate or not) of the Bible in our work, using them as ways into and forms of analysis of biblical texts. In this case, Makhoba's linocut enables us to read unfamiliar texts, such as Job 3 and 40–41. This Bible study juxtaposes biblical and local lament.

LAMENT IN MUSIC

My final example of lamenting religion comes from the poetry and song of Mzwakhe Mbuli, taken from his album "KwaZulu-Natal."[52]

Song of the Spirit
Friday Mavuso, special tribute to the late President of the DPSA—the Disabled People of South Africa—died June 1995, car accident.

When he died I wished I could stage a sit-in in heaven. / Magundulela ngubani oyohaya inkondlo ngawe? / Yini eyakungenza ngikuhloniphe ukufa na? / Lord my God I do not understand./ Pardon me, I am ignorant. / Here I stand in search of thy wisdom. / Is death an idiom, or is death an idiot? / Lord my God, I do not understand.

When are you on duty, and when are you on leave? / Is there a holiday in heaven or not? / Few years ago tragedy deprived us of two great talents. / In one week you took away Arthur—"Fighting Prince"—Mayisela and Paul Ndlovu the singer. / Again, death deprived us of two great talents, legends, Friday Mavuso and Harry Gwala, both paralysed.

Lord my God, I do not understand. / Punish me not, for I am ignorant. / Is there a new commandment? / "Thou shall suffer perpetually" / "Thou shall die more than other races"? / Now I understand why other nations weep when the child is born.

Lord my God, do you care about the poor? / Why then remove the shepherd from the sheep? / Is there a hidden prophecy about the plight of the black people? / Is there a curse bestowed upon us? / Senzeni thina sizwe esimnyama? / Was the bullet that riddled Friday's spinal cord not enough? / Why did you

---

52. Mzwakhe Mbuli, "Song of the Spirit," in *Kwazulu-Natal* (MZ Music, 1996).

remove Friday Mavuso and leave Barend Strydom alone? / I repeat, why did you remove Friday Mavuso and leave Barend Strydom alone?

Lord my God, I cannot fax nor telephone you, but to continue with my provocative poetry…. / Why are there so many more funerals than weddings? / Do you know that our graves are overcrowded? / Is death an idiom, or death an idiot?

Lord my God, why allow people with unfinished projects to enter your kingdom? / When Friday Mavuso finally enters thy kingdom, honour him with a noble crown. / When he enters thy kingdom, ask him who should look after his sheep. / When he enters thy kingdom, ask him what should we do with his wheelchair. / When he enters thy kingdom, tell him I say his departure was too early and too soon for heaven, too soon for burial.

Again, I will not analyze this lament song in any depth; my focus is on recognizing, recovering, and then mobilizing this lament for our work with the Bible in the context of HIV and AIDS. The song stands as a lament in its own right, as does Makhoba's linocut. We co-opt (or collaborate with) them so as to facilitate a more resisting and redemptive reading of the Bible in the context of HIV and AIDS. The rhetoric of this song, I would argue, is that of Job.

Mzwakhe Mbuli is known in South Africa as "the people's poet," for his songs and poetry have long articulated the inchoate embodied experiences of millions of black South Africans struggling for liberation. Now in the context of HIV and AIDS, I suggest, this song continues that prophetic tradition in our society, demonstrating that it is legitimate to talk back to power, including God. The immediate context of this song is the untimely deaths of many black activists and the amnesty granted to Barend Strydom, a white racist murderer, by the Truth and Reconciliation Commission. The wider context, as other tracks on the album indicate, is the HIV/AIDS pandemic. The lines that ask "Why are there so many more funerals than weddings? / Do you know that our graves are overcrowded?" is a direct allusion to this reality of our lives. We attend funerals every weekend, but hardly ever a wedding. Economic issues and associated issues of crime and violence also lurk in the background, including the devastation of global neo-liberal capitalism and our own government's macro-economic buy-in to capitalism and its effects on our context, including massive unemployment.[53] But HIV and AIDS are at the forefront, and this song is a lament about specifically named untimely deaths and untimely deaths in general.

The rhetoric is the rhetoric of the Job character in the book of Job. There is a relentless, respectful-disrespectful questioning of God. Mbuli's lament is resisting discourse, as the struggle form of the song so familiar to millions of South

---

53. Sampie Terreblanche, *A History of Inequality in South Africa, 1652–2002* (Pietermaritzburg: University of Natal Press, 2002).

Africa reminds us. Mbuli wonders if struggle tactics like sit-ins would work in heaven! He acknowledges his ignorance but goes on to ask whether an eleventh commandment has been added to the list he knows so well. He worries that God is racist, punishing blacks disproportionately. Like Job, he longs for more immediate contact with God. And he ends by giving God instructions about how to behave in God's own context, heaven. Surely, Mbuli seems to be saying, if God cannot intervene more justly in our context, God must be able to act justly in God's context!

Throughout the interrogative mood is used. Here, unfortunately, unlike in the book of Job, God does not appear and does not answer. But the lamenting questioning of God has been affirmed and given legitimacy both by the Bible (the book of Job) and by Mbuli (as a political-cultural popular icon who takes up this mode of discourse).

Here, then, is another resource for lamenting religion in South Africa in the context of HIV and AIDS. The following Bible study makes use of this local resource, placing this lament alongside other biblical laments, including the book of Job.

1. Listen to Mzwakhe Mbuli's song, "Song of the Spirit."
2. Listen again, this time following the words of the song (provided on a sheet of paper for each participant).
3. What do you think this song is about?
4. What kind/form of theological discourse is Mbuli using in this song? Are you familiar with this form/kind of theological discourse?
5. Where can you find similar forms/kinds of discourse in the Bible? Are you familiar with any of these? Share your experiences with these texts with the group.
6. Each small group will be allocated one of the following texts: Job 3; Pss 22; 31; 55; 13; 44; 88.[54] Read your text together and then identify the ways in which it speaks (a) about individual physical and social distress; (b) about relationships; and (c) about and to God.
7. Do you identify with your text? In what ways do you identify with it, and in what ways do you not?
8. Write your own song of lament.
9. How can we encourage the church to recognize lament as an important theological discourse in our time?

---

54. These psalms are used by Ken Stone ("Safer Text") in his resisting readings of biblical laments in the context of HIV and AIDS. We will use these experimentally and see how useful they are in our context.

A Religion of Lament

Ken Stone wonders aloud whether his suggested readings of biblical laments might simply perpetuate "traditional theism, a mode of theology whose relevance for the age of AIDS has been rejected by a number of gay theologians."[55]While this worry is not a major concern in our context, Stone's responses to his question are useful for our context as well. His first response is that "this willingness to confront God directly and to accuse God of some sort of complicity in one's suffering helps to constitute part of the radicality of the laments," in that "such complaints against God can be interpreted at least in part as complaints against an unjust social order that uses religious language for legitimation."[56]

His second response is that, "to the extent that the complaints against God acknowledge that suffering can be caused by forces other than human beings, these complaints give readers a precedent for recognizing a tragic dimension to human existence without falling into complacency about suffering." This is important in the context of HIV and AIDS, "for there is a sense in which the AIDS crisis cannot be reduced to human social evil even if it is exacerbated by such evil."[57]

His third and final response, and perhaps the most important for him and us, is that "the willingness of the laments to accuse God of complicity in human suffering underscores the unacceptability of such suffering in an uncompromising and astonishing fashion. It calls into question any theological discourse that is willing to construct a comforting God while refusing to confront the difficult question of evil."[58]

To these I would add a fourth reason why a reading of biblical laments is significant and useful in our context of HIV and AIDS. Our liberation struggle in South Africa did not allow us the space to recognize or respond to the early onset of HIV and AIDS in our country. And with liberation in 1994 we were too busy celebrating our liberation and reclaiming our African identity and our place in the African renaissance of the African continent to seriously acknowledge and deal with "the African disease" ravaging us. Put differently, how could we lament at a time of rejoicing and celebration and reconstruction? And yet lament we must. Religion in general and the church in particular have been on the retreat since our liberation. The church has handed over much of its "struggle" work, appropriately, to the liberation movements, the government, and civil society. Consequently, the church has withdrawn into itself, settling once again for coherent and comfortable theological systems. But as Stone notes, laments "reflect and produce a desire for an end to pain that is even stronger than the desire for a

---

55. Ibid. 24.
56. Ibid.
57. Ibid.
58. Ibid., 25.

coherent and comfortable theological system."[59] A recovery of biblical lament may shake the church from its theological stupor, hopefully calling the church in South Africa afresh to embrace the pain of the excluded.[60]

And, of course, lament must be and is more than an individual act. While the conceptual categories that shape much of our discourse and programmatic interventions with respect to stigma and discrimination have unfortunately been framed individualistically, there is a rich heritage in biblical lament for corporate, communal, public lament. It is this biblical tradition that Denise Ackerman invoked in the context of the Truth and Reconciliation Commission's work in South Africa, calling for public lament.[61] We in the Ujamaa Centre draw on this biblical tradition among the marginalized, including those who have been marginalized by the church. Our hope is that others, including the not-yet-infected and the church-institutional, will take up our lamenting.

Conclusion

The socially engaged biblical scholar is called, I have argued, to place his and her resources at the service of those living with HIV and AIDS. Just as we have been called to work with the Bible collaboratively with local communities of the poor, working-class, and marginalized around issues of race, class, gender, and culture, so now we are being called to collaborate around HIV and AIDS. Among the resources we bring are relatively unfamiliar biblical laments. That these laments are often embedded in larger literary or liturgical contexts in which lamenting voices are repressed or distorted or co-opted by oppressive and life-denying theologies only makes the reading resources that recover and restore lament more significant.

However, we must not imagine that our scholarly resources are sufficient. They are not, so they must be placed alongside other, already present, local community resources. Together we must find a place for lament in the private and public realms of our context as we struggle with the God of life against the idols and forces of death.

---

59. Ibid.

60. Walter Brueggemann, "A Shape for Old Testament Theology: Embrace of Pain," in *Old Testament Theology: Essays on Structure, Theme, and Text* (ed. Patrick D. Miller; Minneapolis: Fortress, 1992), 22–44.

61. Denise M. Ackermann, "Tales of Terror and Torment: Thoughts on Boundaries and Truth-Telling," *Scriptura* 63 (1997): 425–34.

A Lament for New Orleans*

Clyde Fant

How like a widow sits the city once so beautiful!
She weeps bitterly in the night, with tears on her cheeks,
    because there is none to comfort her.
She stretched forth her hands, but none came to her;
    they heard how she was groaning, but none came unto her.
In her streets the flood bereaves;
    in the sodden houses it is like death.
The leaders and elders of the city have fled,
    but the poor are trapped within her levees.
Her friends have dealt treacherously with her;
    those who promised to help are worse than her enemies.
When she cried aloud, none came;
    smooth words promised much,
    but they were empty rhetoric,
    wells without water, phantom bread.
Shame! Shame upon us all.
Who would have believed it!
She who sang even when she mourned,
The people who danced even in their want–
    now they are dying.
Their colorful robes are stained with mud;
    they are gray, all gray, the pallor of the dead.
Weep, weep for the great city!
Orators of platitudes, politicians of promises,
    it is you who betrayed her!

---

* After Prof. Fant composed "A Lament for New Orleans" with the following superscript, it was posted on the Internet by a friend on 14 September 2005: "*I am from Louisiana. In the last days, grief and outrage have held a contest inside me. So I'm writing this. Because I have to.* Clyde Fant, Th.D."

You took from her her safety;
    you neglected her when she reached out to you.
You channeled her rivers and harnessed her waters,
    but for yourselves! for the profits of your friends!
You caused her marshes to dry
    and her wilderness to recede;
You brought the might of the waves
    and the winds to her very doors.
The poor, those who dwelt in the lowest places,
    who lived in miserable shanties of wood,
    termite-ridden and forlorn,
    where none but the hopeless would dwell:
You have murdered them,
    and their corpses drift in the brackish floods,
    but their cries have gone up to God!
Woe to you, Republicans!
For you pumped wealth from their lands
    and sent their sons to die in your wars,
    but they are as nothing to you.
"Who is my neighbor?"
You do not yet know the answer to this ancient question.
Your only neighbors are your friends in the country clubs,
    or the "good old boys" in the redneck bars.
Your grandfathers set the slaves free, and
    you return them to a worse bondage of perpetual poverty!
Your fathers segregated them, but you ghettoize them;
    you redistrict them to take away the few voices they have.
But God will cause the ruined city to cry on their behalf!
Shame! Shame for your hypocritical use of my name
    to lure the unwary.
Woe to you also, Democrats!
You were the fathers of slavery, first sons of the South!
You damned the poor to generations of ignorance and want.
Your fathers segregated them,
    and you promised to bring them into your family.
But where were you when they needed you?
For you lack the courage of your convictions!
You curry the favor of the enemies of your own people!
You have become impotent by your timidity.
You endorsed the wars. You approved
    the miserable crumbs for education and employment.
You courted the indifferent, smug suburbs:
    may you live among them eternally,

bored forever by their white sameness!
Shame! Shame for your graft in the statehouses,
    your selfishness that has turned your people from you in disgust.
Woe to you Christians who take pride in the name Conservative,
    who call all generous spirits and inclusive hearts liberals,
    who see wars as strength and peace as weakness!
The Prince of Peace rebuke you!
Woe to you also, Liberal Christians!
You scorn the common
    and cause the simple to feel inferior in your midst.
Your hearts are ever open,
    but your pocketbooks are always closed!
He who lived among the poor rebuke you!
Woe to you, television preachers and mega-church pastors!
False prophets!
You deceive the people with your bleats of piety
    while you endorse wars and favor your rich benefactors.
Your prophecies of end times have come true
    in your own generation!
Look upon the city! Look upon hell on earth!
See what your leaders have wrought,
    the shame of the earth!
All mock us and call us fools,
    we who send armies across oceans
    but cannot cross the Mississippi to help our own!
Shame, shame upon you!
I hate, I despise your solemn assemblies,
    the self-hypnotic repetitions of your pagan
    praise-hymns are a scandal in my ears.
Come before me no more lifting up unholy hands.
Do not use my name to grow your personal kingdoms,
    or to bless your political ambitions.
What do think I desire? Barrels of oil from Iraq?
Herds of sacred cows from Texas?
Go now and learn what this means:
    I desire mercy and not sacrifice,
Loving kindness, not benign neglect.
Weep, weep for my city,
For my people,
For my children.
For they are dead.

Part 3
Retrospective/Prospective, Continuing Relevance

LAMENT AS WAKE-UP CALL
(CLASS ANALYSIS AND HISTORICAL POSSIBILITY)

Walter Brueggemann

This retrospective on my work on lament (which may function as well as a retrospective on the fine discussions in this volume) concerns a number of *theses* that represent tentative conclusions on my part and *bids* concerning future engagement with the topic of lament.

1.

Here are some theses that are at the edge of my thinking.

1.1. A proper study of lament may well begin with *genre* (although it could begin otherwise with *experience*). The formal work on the genre of lament has been largely completed. Indeed, the completion of that project was already well accomplished by Hermann Gunkel, together with the complementary study of his student Joachim Begrich concerning "the salvation oracle" that illuminates the dynamism of the form.[1] Beyond Gunkel and Begrich, the most important work has been that of Claus Westermann with his articulation of the movement from "plea" to "praise."[2] Of course, the work of Erhard Gerstenberger belongs in the same trajectory as that of Westermann, wherein Gerstenberger has proposed social venues not unlike "house churches" where liturgies of rehabilitation were conducted through the use of laments as transformative scripts.[3] The genre of lament likely reflects the recurring, stylized usage of Israel in some communal

---

1. Hermann Gunkel and Joachim Begrich, *Introduction to Psalms: The Genres of the Religious Lyric of Israel* (trans. James D. Nogalski; Macon, Ga.: Mercer University Press, 1998); Joachim Begrich, "Das priesterliche Heilsorakel," *ZAW* 52 (1934): 81–92.

2. Claus Westermann, *The Praise of God in the Psalms* (trans. Keith R. Crim; Richmond, Va.: Knox Press, 1965).

3. Erhard Gerstenberger, "Psalms," *Old Testament Form Criticism* (ed. John H. Hayes; San Antonio, Tex.: Trinity University Press, 1974), 179–223. See also Gerstenberger, *Psalms, Part 1 with an Introduction to Cultic Poetry* (FOTL 14; Grand Rapids: Eerdmans, 1988); idem, *Psalms, Part 2, and Lamentations* (FOTL 15; Grand Rapids: Eerdmans, 2001).

settings that made possible a new beginning of life with Yʜᴡʜ together with commensurate new social relationships.

When such genre analysis in Old Testament studies was largely completed and settled, our scholarship has become newly aware of the genre study of Mikhail Bakhtin.[4] Bakhtin has understood genre not so much in terms of literary or rhetorical analysis, but as a coding of social relationships, and an articulation and maintenance of a pattern of social power. This much more dynamic understanding of genre will be important in the discussion that follows.

1.2. In terms of genre, praise is the antipode of lament, and lament cannot be properly understood or practiced without an awareness of the way in which praise functions as a coding of social power. Taken by itself without benefit of lament, the practice of praise is most probably an exercise in equilibrium whereby status quo power arrangements are legitimated, nurtured, and celebrated.[5] While there is an honest practice of praise that entails the ceding of self over to another who is to be esteemed and affirmed, the social function of praise is to legitimate and so to collude with "the force of empire" (or the "empire of force"). As James Boyd White has shown compellingly, collusion with the "empire of force" leads to the loss of "vital speech," the numbing of social awareness, and the shriveling of social possibility.[6]

In his most recent exposé of the "shame" of the U.S. public school system, Jonathan Kozol features, as a representative figure, "Mr. Endicott," who runs a very tight ship in his classroom in an inner-city school in which students are expected to perform "objectively" without show of emotion or any personal interaction:

> Mr. Endicott described the system of belief demanded of teachers by the method of text-driven teaching at his school as a "doxology." In the heart of the doxology is the unquestioned faith that there is one right road, and one road only, to be taken and then every stage along the road must be annunciated—stated on the walls, reiterated by the books—in advance.[7]

To be sure, Endicott's use of the term "doxology" is a curious one, yet in a consideration of genre as code, it is exactly the right usage. Doxology is an act of

---

4. On Bakhtin's understanding of genre as it is taken up in Scripture study, see Barbara Green, *How Are the Mighty Fallen? A Dialogical Study of King Saul in 1 Samuel* (JSOTSup 365; Sheffield: Sheffield Academic Press, 2003), 56–74 and *passim*. More broadly, see idem, *Mikhail Bakhtin and Biblical Scholarship: An Introduction* (SemeiaSt 38; Atlanta: Society of Biblical Literature, 2000).

5. On such a function for praise, see Walter Brueggemann, *Israel's Praise: Doxology against Idolatry and Ideology* (Philadelphia: Fortress, 1988).

6. James Boyd White, *Living Speech: Resisting the Empire of Force* (Princeton: Princeton University Press, 2006).

7. Jonathan Kozol, *The Shame of the Nation: The Restoration of Apartheid Schooling in America* (New York: Crown, 2005), 124.

conformity to a settled line of authority and power and, consequently, a settled line of truth. That settled line is accepted without suspicion or resistance by teachers in the system:

> In itself, the naming of an "outcome" or "objective" for each lesson by a classroom teacher, as we've noted earlier, is a familiar practice in most schools. It's hard, indeed, to think of any public schools, even in historically progressive districts, where administrators don't believe that certain outcomes should be stated clearly, that they ought to have some rational connection to the tests their students have to take, and that these goals should be pursued with continuity and firmness by their teachers.[8]

To the extent that ancient Israel or the contemporary church practices uncriticized praise, it is likely to be such a conforming "doxological" operation.

1.3. Lament, set in the context of hymn, is the social code and social gesture of those who refuse to submit readily to settled power and settled truth and who find their own pain, loss, or anger to be more compelling than officially legitimated truth claims.[9] Thus lament, in its very utterance, is an act of resistance and defiance that interrupts doxology, that asserts an alternative reality, and that believes that out of the candid embrace of pain new social alternatives may be generated.

Two clear examples of such lament as interruption of doxology may be cited in the Old Testament. First, in Exod 2:23–25 Israel broke the silence of bondage and voiced its life beyond that exploitative system of Pharaoh. There is no doubt that their "groan and cry" constitutes a lament of protest: "After a long time the king of Egypt died. The Israelites groaned under their slavery, and cried out. Out of the slavery their cry for help rose up to God" (Exod 2:23). That cry, moreover, mobilized the sovereign, delegitimating power of YHWH that, as the narrative unfolds, counters the equilibrium of Pharaoh with a "departure" to a new historical possibility.

Second, in the poem of Job the "friends" articulate settled truth that assumes and maintains moral equilibrium. Job—who still subscribes to this status quo wisdom—voices his pain that leads to the critical encounter of the poem. Claus Westermann has rightly observed that Job's speeches that voice his pain in response to the opinions of his friends are constituted by laments that break settled truth open and that create new possibility, culminating in an encounter with God's own holiness:

---

8. Ibid.

9. It occurs to me that the categories of James C. Scott, *Domination and the Arts of Resistance: Hidden Transcripts* (New Haven: Yale University Press, 1990), are useful for this point. Praise is the public transcript that meets with general approval, but lament is the "hidden transcript" that subverts the public script.

The passages here enumerated are laments in a wider sense; included are elements of petition, wish, motivation, avowal of trust—in other words, every sort of speech that gets addressed to God. The lament in the strict sense, namely, that which corresponds to the real lament portion in the psalms of lamentation, is in itself segmented. In the case of the patent laments in chs. 3 and 30, a standard threefold articulation is immediately apparent: there is lament directed to God (Lament I), self-lament (Lament II), and lament about enemies (Lament III). In the dialogue section the relationship to one another of these three subcategories of the lament, their distribution within the cycles of discourse, the development of each of these subcategories, and the lack of one or another all constitute essential parts of the dramatic composition. The recognition of this threefold articulation of the lament grows out of study in Psalms. It seems to me that this recognition makes the structure of the speeches of Job more intelligible; the "dramatizing of the lament" can really be perceived only when each of the three persons in the drama—God, Job, the friends—is heard as a particular voice being reflected through one of these subcategories of the lament throughout the whole dialogue section.[10]

In both cases, the lament (of Israel, of Job) utilizes this genre of speech to call into question old power arrangements that had long been legitimated and unquestioned.

1.4. *Praise* that colludes with status quo equilibrium and *lament* that refuses such legitimated arrangements give voice, respectively, to settled social realty and new social possibility.[11] Each of them passionately voices a theodicy wherever the exercise of freedom and responsibility are situated in a social arrangement matched by a rhetorical practice. I take my cue on this point from Peter Berger, although I will line the matter out quite differently. Berger opined:

One of the very important social functions of theodicies is, indeed, their explanation of the socially prevailing inequalities of power and privilege. In this function, of course, theodicies directly legitimate the particular institutional order in question. It is important to stress in this connection that such theodicies may serve as legitimations *both* for the powerful *and* the powerless, for the privileged *and* for the deprived. For the latter, of course, they may serve as "opiates" to make their situation less intolerable, and by the same token to prevent them from rebelling against it. For the former, however, they may serve as subjectively quite important justifications of their enjoyment of the power and privilege of their social position. Put simply, theodicies provide the poor with a meaning for their poverty, but may also provide the rich with a meaning for their wealth.

---

10. Claus Westermann, *The Structure of the Book of Job: A Form-Critical Analysis* (Philadelphia: Fortress, 1981), 31–32.

11. On the tension between social reality and social possibility, see Walter Brueggemann, *Old Testament Theology: Essays on Structure, Theme, and Text* (Minneapolis: Fortress, 1992), 1–44, on "structure legitimation" and "embrace of pain."

In both cases, the result is one of world-maintenance and, very concretely, of the maintenance of the particular institutional order. It is, of course, another question whether the *same* theodicy can serve both groups in this way. If so, the theodicy constitutes an essentially sadomasochistic collusion, on the level of meaning, between oppressors and victims—a phenomenon that is far from rare in history. In other cases, there may be two discrete theodicies established in the society—a theodicy of suffering for one group and theodicy of happiness for the other. These two theodicies may relate to each other in different ways, that is, with different degrees of "symmetry."[12]

Berger apparently refers to a "collusion" whereby the *happiness of the powerful privileged* and *the suffering of the powerless denied* are two facets of the same social explanation. With the practice of the genres of praise and lament as exercises in theodicy, however, we have two theodicies that do not *collude* but rather *contradict* each other. *The theodicy of praise* approves and legitimates present power arrangements, disregards those who suffer from that arrangement, and congratulates the beneficiaries of that system of power and meaning. *The theodicy of lament*, by contrast, critiques present power arrangements and the voices that legitimate them and insists that the disadvantaged and unrecognized who speak are themselves entitled to a better social arrangement. That is, the theodicy of lament intends a disruption of the plausibility of the praise theodicy and, as Berger has seen, is "potentially revolutionary in its consequences." This revolutionary potential becomes apparent to Pharaoh and likely to the God of the Whirlwind who goes to some lengths to resist Job's intervention. Thus praise and lament convey thick social realities and are never innocent or innocuous.

1.5. For Jews, in a way reflected in the Hebrew Bible, exile is the primal habitat for lament.[13] The Jews find themselves, always again, in the grip of an exile-producing empire, for it is the way of empires to produce displaced persons and displaced communities. That sixth-century displacement is variously understood in the Bible as a consequence of imperial aggressiveness or as the outcome of divine judgment. The lament, in that context, is an articulation of grief at loss, alienation, and abandonment, and, at the same time, an act of hope that insists upon restoration and homecoming.[14]

---

12. Peter L. Berger, *The Sacred Canopy: Elements of a Sociological Theory of Religion* (Garden City, N.Y.: Doubleday, 1969), 9–10, 59–60.

13. On exile as a theological metaphor, see Walter Brueggemann, *Cadences of Home: Preaching Among Exiles* (Louisville: Westminster John Knox, 1997).

14. On lament in contemporary setting, see Kathleen M. O'Connor, *Lamentations and the Tears of the World* (Maryknoll, N.Y.: Orbis, 2002). As pertains to the Jewish Shoah, see Milton Teichman and Sharon Leder, eds., *Truth and Lamentation: Stories and Poems on the Holocaust* (Chicago: University of Chicago Press, 1994).

When we consider the three great penitential prayers of the postexilic period, moreover, we are able to see that even acts of penitence, while acknowledging guilt, in fact are complaints that anticipate restoration:

> For we are *slaves*; yet our God has not forsaken us in our slavery, but has extended to us his steadfast love before the kings of Persia, to give us new life to set up the house of our God, to repair its ruins, and to give us a wall in Judea and Jerusalem. (Ezra 9:9)

> Here we are, *slaves* to this day—slaves in the land that you gave to our ancestors to enjoy its fruit and its good gifts. Its rich yield goes to the kings whom you have set over us because of our sins; they have power also over our bodies and over our livestock at their pleasure, and we are in great distress. (Neh 9:36–37)

> Incline your ear, O my God, and hear. Open your eyes and look at our desolation and the city that bears your name. We do not present our supplication before you on the ground of our righteousness, but on the ground of your great mercies. O Lord, hear; O Lord, forgive; O Lord, listen and act and do not delay! For your own sake, O my God, because your city and your people bear your name!" (Dan 9:18–19)

While the penitential note is a serious one that is not unfamiliar in laments, it is also plausible that the penitence is a strategic preparation for the petition that follows.[15] Lament is a *protest* against power relations that have left the Jewish community exploited and alienated and an *insistence* that it may (or must) be otherwise in time to come. All subsequent Jewish laments are rooted in this defining paradigm of radical displacement.

1.6. For Christians, the crucifixion of Jesus is the primal habitat for lament. It is for that reason that, on the Friday cross, Jesus recites Ps 22:1 (Matt 27:46; Mark 15:34).[16] In that instant of utterance, Jesus is God-forsaken, abandoned by the very power of life that he had sought to serve. But the church not only confesses that he was "crucified"; the church confesses rather that he was "crucified under Pontius Pilate." And therefore the lament is not only a theological protest against divine abandonment; it is also a political protest against an empire that executes the righteous. The complaint of Jesus, understood theologically and politically, is that he is being executed by an illegitimate power that characteristically eliminates those who do not conform:

---

15. Fredrik Lindström, *Suffering and Sin: Interpretations of Illness in the Individual Complaint Psalms* (ConBOT 37; Stockholm: Almqvist & Wiksell, 1994), sees that prayers addressed to God in God's absence serve to summon God back into play in the present. This would support the intention of the entire prayer, even penitence, to move God to reemerge in the crisis.

16. See Jürgen Moltmann, *The Crucified God: The Cross of Christ as the Foundation and Criticism of Christian Theology* (New York: Harper & Row, 1974), 146–51.

Pilate's honest perplexity about truth was revealed in his puzzlement that power should require truth if it sought to command authority. Pilate was a realist whose chain-of-command conception of power made it impossible for him to understand the lifestyle of Jesus. Confronted by the lifestyle of Jesus, however, the worldly realism of Pilate is exposed as pseudo-realism. Pilate is unable, either by conviction or by role, to exhibit the unity of truth and power and authority. When power is divorced from truth, authority loses its integrity. When truth is divorced from power, the exercise of power is doomed to self-defeat because power can function only under the spurious authority of self-justification and falsehood. Jesus, on the other hand, affirms, both by conviction and by role, that the only authority power has is the authority of truth.[17]

The function of the confrontation between Jesus and Pilate, as Paul Lehmann has seen so well, is the delegitimation of power that had been generally praised and accepted without question or critique. The lament of Jesus is an expectation and insistence about alternative power arrangements.[18] All Christian laments are rooted in this defining, paradigmatic reality of vulnerability and abandonment.

1.7. When lament is taken seriously by Jews and by Christians, the practice issues in a crisis in God's sovereignty. To be sure, genre as a code for social power might more readily evoke a crisis of human power, as in that most prominent case of Pharaoh and in all his ilk that come after him. The Marxian insight, however, that one cannot separate "religion and law," "theology and politics," means that the crisis evoked concerning "earthly" power includes a crisis of "heavenly" power as well.[19] Thus the lament over Israel's exile is a lament about YHWH's action as well as about the action of "my enemies" (Lam 3:52). Indeed, it is the lament of Israel that evokes an admission from YHWH about abandonment:

> For a brief moment I abandoned you,
> but with great compassion I will gather you.
> In overflowing wrath for a moment
> I hid my face from you,
> but with everlasting love I will have compassion on you,
> says the Lord, your Redeemer. (Isa 54:7–8)

In that exchange of lament and divine response, the old certitudes about divine fidelity are put at risk.

---

17. See Paul Lehmann, *The Transfiguration of Politics: The Presence and Power of Jesus of Nazareth in and over Human Affairs* (New York: Harper & Row, 1975), 55.

18. See Richard B. Hays, *The Conversion of the Imagination: Paul as Interpreter of Israel's Scripture* (Grand Rapids: Eerdmans, 2005), 101–18. Hays proposes that Israel's Psalter is the "matrix" for early Christology.

19. See the phrasing of Marx that links "'heaven and earth'" in David McLellan, *The Thought of Karl Marx: An Introduction* (London: Macmillan, 1971), 22.

Mutatis mutandis, the vulnerability of Jesus on the cross (as voiced in Ps 22:1) exposes the divine weakness in which, as Jürgen Moltmann has it, both the Father and the Son are forsaken. The cross—and the derivative "theology of the cross"—exposes as fraudulent all the conventional classic claims for God as omnipotent and omniscient.[20] For both Jews and Christians, the voice of lament has required, and continues to require, a rearticulation of God against any old-fashioned "top-down" formula.[21] The implications of that divine "delegitimation" for legitimated human power are inescapable and enormous. Once the impotent and marginalized find voice enough to cry out, the old patterns of unilateral legitimated power are irretrievably broken. That, of course, is why such power insists upon conforming silence. Once that conforming silence is broken, everything must be redescribed. In the move from the genre of praise to the genre of lament, once lament has been uttered, there is no going back to innocent, uncriticized praise, no going back to uncontested power. Whenever Pharaoh (or God) may regain power, it will be as chastened, questioned power.

That is, such recovered power will be chastened and questioned until a new pharaoh arises who is able to enforce a new season of conforming silence. But even in such a dread season, the recurring Jewish practice of lament and the resounding cry from the cross assure that no new season of silence can be sustained for very long. The cry will sound again, and when it does, power in heaven and on earth will be again reconfigured in response to the cry.[22]

1.8. The practice of lament is a dialogic engagement that acts against conventional monologic power arrangements. The lament in pain is voiced in a way that expects a divine response. While the dominant hypothesis of a reassuring "salvation oracle" is no more than probable, it is clear that some kind of engagement and response on the part of God is enacted that causes the lament, characteristically, to turn to praise.

1.9. The fact of the response (assurance of being heard) indicates that the lament has drawn Yhwh into some kind of dialogic exchange. This would seem to be a recurring pattern, even though there are cases to the contrary, notably Pss 39 and 88. The lamentations of Jeremiah, moreover, at least twice receive divine response, albeit a response very different from the expected salvation oracle (Jer 12:5–6; 15:19–21). The genre per se transforms power relations because the petition draws Yhwh into the circumstance of the psalmist and so repositions Yhwh in the midst of trouble or conflict. In the case of Ps 35:9, 18, 29, to cite a clear case,

---

20. See the classic statement of a "theology of the cross" by Douglas John Hall, *Lighten Our Darkness: Toward an Indigenous Theology of the Cross* (Philadelphia: Westminster, 1976).

21. See especially the acute reflections of Alan E. Lewis, *Between Cross and Resurrection: A Theology of Holy Saturday* (Grand Rapids: Eerdmans, 2001).

22. On "the cry" as pivotal for a biblical articulation of God, see James L. Kugel, *The God of Old: Inside the Lost World of the Bible* (New York: Free Press, 2003), ch. 5.

the reiterated "then" of the psalmist indicates a readiness to extend the dialogic exchange, though the continued interaction depends upon the effective engagement of Yhwh.[23] Most important is the fact that it is the human speaker who initiates the exchange in which Yhwh may participate.[24]

Such a reconfiguration of power in a dialogic mode tells against conventionally monologic power on two counts. First, within the Psalter itself, praise appears to be monologic, a one-way communication that neither expects nor receives response from Yhwh. For all that is transacted, God may be taken as object rather than as subject, for the genre of praise provides for no two-way negotiation. More broadly, dialogic speech that arises from pain witnesses against monologue not only in the Psalter but in any social circumstance in which dominant power is settled and unresponsive. In such a social arrangement, dialogue is inherently subversive, both because it arises "from below" and because the subject is need or pain, a condition that dominant power characteristically prefers to keep unuttered. The God who is object of praise more likely may be imagined as a God who is unengaged and unresponsive to pain, for acknowledgement of such human utterance would indicate a dysfunction in the governance system and, consequently, functions as a critique of power.

1.10. Lament is the raw, direct articulation of pain that becomes a central reality in the social relationship that is being renegotiated through utterance. When Jews take seriously the fact that *exile* is the primal habitat for lament and when Christians take seriously that *crucifixion* is the primal habitat of lament, Jews and Christians together acknowledge that pain—variously as a consequence of assault, loss, alienation, sickness—is a defining reality of social existence. It may well be that Jews and Christians line out the social significance of pain very differently, and Christians have tended at times, through some "theory of atonement," to glorify pain in gratuitous ways. They are, however, agreed with Jews that pain is a defining reality of life, not to be denied or sublimated into a positive, but a bodily reality that concerns faith and that impinges on all social reality. This direct acknowledgement stands over against every seduction that wants to deny or explain away the reality of pain.[25]

Because conventional formulations of theology are of little help for the primal reality and primal speech of Jews and Christians, pain is open to more than one

---

23. The "then" is not explicit in the Hebrew of these verses; there is no doubt, however, that the nrsv rendering that offers three "thens" is a correct reading of the intent of the psalm.

24. Even the speeches of God from the whirlwind in Job 38–41 are to be understood as dialogical, for they are, in a formal way, an answer to Job; on the disputatious quality of wisdom instruction, see Roland E. Murphy, "Qoheleth's 'Quarrel' with the Fathers," in *From Faith to Faith: Essays in Honor of Donald G. Miller on His Seventieth Birthday* (ed. Dikran Y. Hadidian; Pittsburgh: Pickwick, 1979), 219–34.

25. On the cruciality of pain for responsible interpretation, see Kristin M. Swenson, *Living through Pain: Psalms and the Search for Wholeness* (Waco, Tex.: Baylor University Press, 2005).

"explanation." On the one hand, it can be explained as an impingement of willful human agency ... whether aggressive empire, ruffian neighbors, or "evil-doers" who seem possessed of gifts of magic power. On the other hand, conversely, the laments can entertain the dangerous thought that the pain is a direct consequence of the action of the holy God. Such divine action may be intentional or merited punishment, but it can equally be credited to the holy God "without cause":

> Yet you have rejected us and abased us,
> and have not gone out with our armies.
> You made us turn back from the foe,
> and our enemies have gotten spoil.
> You have made us like sheep for slaughter,
> and have scattered us among the nations.
> You have sold your people for a trifle,
> demanding no high price for them.
> You have made us the taunt of our neighbors,
> the derision and scorn of those around us.
> You have made us a byword among the nations,
> a laughingstock among the peoples.
> All day long my disgrace is before me,
> and shame has covered my face
> at the words of the taunters and revilers,
> at the sight of the enemy and the avenger.
> All this has come upon us,
> yet we have not forgotten you,
> or been false to your covenant.
> Our heart has not turned back,
> nor have our steps departed from your way,
> yet you have broken us in the haunt of jackals,
> and covered us with deep darkness. (Ps 44:9–19)

> You have put me in the depths of the Pit,
> in the regions dark and deep.
> Your wrath lies heavy upon me,
> and you overwhelm me with all your waves.
> You have caused my companions to shun me;
> you have made me a thing of horror to them....
> Your wrath has swept over me;
> your dread assaults destroy me.
> They surround me like a flood all day long;
> from all sides they close in on me.
> You have caused friend and neighbor to shun me;
> my companions are in darkness. (Ps 88:6–8a, 16–18)

1.11. In the face of such pain, the lament refuses colluding silence with God who is either the perpetrator of pain or at least the negligent permitter of such pain. Eschewing colluding silence in pain, the cry of lament is an injection of the primal reality of pain into the sinews of social relationship; once injected, it can never be denied again. Thus the cry is an unrestrained resolve to refuse any social relationship that seeks to maintain prepain equilibrium.

Michael Foucault has posed the insistent question about the relationship of *truth and power* and has shown that all truth is compromised when it is allied with or filtered through power. Foucault, of course, extends the fundamental insight of Marx concerning "interest" and social reality. It may be suggested, given Foucault's discernment, that praise—uncorrected by lament—is an exhibit of the alliance of truth and power. The one praised is said to be all-powerful, and the truthfulness of that claim requires an override of all of pain that is to the con-trary. That of course is the general intent of "theodicy."[26]

Alongside Foucault's tense calculus of "truth and power," the lament invites an alliance between "truth and pain" that is voiced as testimony from below. Power speaks "from above," a practice reflected in praise. But "truth and pain" attest to irreducible bodily reality that is uncompromised by any collusion with power. Thus laments claim, against the formulae of Job's friends, that pain cannot be denied or explained away in the interest of any old certitude. Such pain, against old formulations, has its own intrusiveness that must be voiced and taken seriously. Were one to pursue this line of thought, it may lead to the conclusion that prepain claims of truth, voiced by those who are so far immune to pain, are inherently suspect and not to be taken uncritically.

The alliance of truth with pain—that waits for no external legitimation—invites the recognition that YHWH—to whom laments are addressed—is a God peculiarly responsive to the cry. It is as though YHWH is the legitimator of the social reality of pain by taking the cry seriously, engaging those who cry, and responding with transformative succor. Thus the beginning of Israel's narrative of rescue attests to YHWH as the one attends to the cry: "God heard their groaning, and God remembered his covenant with Abraham, Isaac, and Jacob. God looked upon the Israelites, and God took notice of them" (Exod 2:24–25).

In that terse exchange, it is clear that YHWH, on the face of it, accepts Israel's cry of faith as legitimate and truthful and moves promptly against Pharaoh and his pain-producing social apparatus. James Kugel has elegantly exposited the way in which the God of Israel who hears cries is exactly the right partner for the truthfulness of the cry of pain.[27]

---

26. See Terence W. Tilley, *The Evils of Theodicy* (Eugene, Ore.: Wipf & Stock, 2000).

27. Kugel, *The God of Old*, 124, 135–36, in commenting on Ps 82, writes: "but we ought not to lose sight of our particular focus. It says that hearing the victim's cry is a god's duty and God's duty. It says that if that job is not properly performed, the very foundations of the earth will shake.... Now, what God actually says to Moses about His being merciful is really not news—as we saw in Psalm 82, it was simply any god's job to be compassionate and merciful, and this truth was so universally assumed in the Bible that, as we have seen, it underlies the dozens of passages

1.12. Praise and lament genres that code social power and social relationships construct and legitimate class identity. While the genres are not precisely commensurate to those of Karl Mannheim, they are illuminated by his famous juxtaposition of "ideology and utopia."[28] "Ideology" in Mannheim's usage is an interpretive practice that substantiates and wants to absolutize the present status quo. Hymns that voice full confidence in present power rearrangements over which a benign sovereign God presides function to freeze social power in status quo arrangements. This is especially the effect of hymns that are on the lips of those who are at risk in the status quo, for such singing indicates a signing on for present power arrangements and thus a collusion at their own expense.[29]

Conversely Mannheim's "utopia" is an interpretive act that looks beyond present power arrangements and that anticipates a transformed social reality. Lament in a proper sense may be an act of resignation, but it carries within it a profound yearning for a transformation that will end the unbearable reality of present arrangements. And certainly "complaint" with its characteristic series of imperative petitions is an act of hope that fully expects a response from a hearing God who is capable and who may be willing to intervene in effective ways to make all things new. It is for good reason that African American churches historically and characteristically have featured dirge-like, slow-moving lament that are in fact acts of hope.

1.13. Praise as a genre that codes legitimation of the status quo envisions or proposes no new historical possibility. The only imperatives in such a genre are repeated summons to join the doxology. There are no petitions in such a genre, no expectation of new action, no resolve that anything could be other than it is. Indeed the hymn functions to legitimate and keep things as they are.

1.14. Conversely history-makers arise from sustained practice of laments.[30] The work of lament is to give voice to the unbearable condition of present power arrangements that are theologically understood in terms of the absence, indifference, or negligence of God. The speech that summons God back into action is speech that trusts that when God is newly recruited, everything may change. Because human persons participate in such coded actions of insistence and expectation, it is more than likely that such laments, in situations of genuine need, will evoke responsible engagement on the part of human agents, not simply evoke

---

that speak of the victim's cry. Yet here, in Exodus, this cliché is presented as a revelation. God's ultimate self-revelation to Moses: I am by nature *ḥannun* and *raḥum* (despite all evidence to the contrary). I hear the cry of the victim; I can't help it."

28. Karl Mannheim, *Ideology and Utopia* (New York: Brace, Harcourt, 1936).

29. For contemporary evidence of the capacity to sign on for such status quo claims against one's own interest, see Thomas Frank, *What's the Matter with Kansas? How Conservatives Won the Heart of America* (repr., New York: Owl Books, 2005).

30. On such "history-makers," see Walter Brueggemann, *Hope within History* (Atlanta: Knox, 1987), 49–71.

passive abdication that waits on the action of God. Of course, when laments are uttered in situations that are not contexts of acute crisis, a lament may produce no human history-makers, but only complacent appeal to God's actions.

1.15. Recovery of lament as a characteristic and recurring speech practice in an interpretive community constitutes a profound shift in world-paradigm, not simply an incidental liturgical maneuver. An interpretive community that regularly voices lament is a community that *acknowledges present pain* and that *anticipates transformation*. There is an inherently revolutionary restlessness in the voicing of lament, when lament is connected to bodily pain or the pain of the body politic. Such use of the genre amounts to a protest against doxological legitimation of present arrangements and exposes present arrangements (and commensurate liturgical legitimation) as disconnected from lived, bodily reality. Lament is a resolve in the interpretive community to connect bodily reality and voiced reality in intentional and intense ways.

2.

The current recovery of lament as an interpretive exercise in church communities is surely reflective of a freshly perceived social crisis that will no longer settle for ideological doxology. The well-known crises of 9/11, Iraq, Afghanistan, Katrina, and the unraveling of the fabric of health care, education, and judicial operation make it abundantly clear that the United States is in a deep crisis, a crisis that eventually will require and generate a liturgical practice that is congruent with lived reality. The theses indicated above suggest that a *lyrical practice* congruent with *social circumstance* in U.S. society will have at its center the practice of lament that is an important genre in all of the ways I have indicated above. This analysis suggests, then, that every "constituency" of a healthy community may well consider the work of lament as it pertains to our social emergency. It is convenient to reflect on the public use of lament by appeals to David Tracy's "Three Publics of Theology."

2.1. David Tracy identifies three dimensions of the "public of society": (a) the technoeconomic structure; (b) the realm of polity concerned about social justice and the use of power; and (c) the realm of culture, art, and religion.[31] It is clear that all of these dimensions of the "public society" readily gravitate toward status quo legitimation if not interrupted by the voice of pain. Even "the realm of culture," because it largely depends upon public funding, runs the risk, in a postindustrial economy, to submit to economic pressure that has a stake in silence. The health of society clearly depends upon the capacity to voice pain as it protests and imagines otherwise. To work against the easy drift toward narcoticization in the

---

31. David Tracy, *The Analogical Imagination: Christian Theology and the Culture of Pluralism* (New York: Crossroad, 1981), 7.

face of pain, public leadership must engage with a practice of lament, the primal strategy for resisting the absolutizing of present power arrangements.

2.2. The "technoeconomic structure" refers to the reality of an aggressive expansionism allied with a political oligarchy, devoted to the exploitation of cheap labor around the globe and the pursuit of market for the enhancement of wealth. Its means is a near economic monopoly that seeks to control the available sources of energy. Tracy, in his identification, offers no critical judgment but only names that public sector. Since Tracy, however, the unrestrained aggressiveness of this structure has become everywhere visible. Indeed, that system of domination has taken on life of its own that co-opts well-meaning slogans in pursuit of antineighborly policies.

In such a social environment, the practice of lament honors the voice of pain that is everywhere in our society becoming urgent. It is certain that the growing number of poor and disadvantaged people (even without mention of immigrants) is not an accident in our society but is a seemingly inescapable outcome of a manipulative political-economic enterprise that increasingly fences out all but "the chosen few." The assumption that such a "technoeconomic structure" is mechanistic and rational and even-handed without notice of the social interests and passions that drive it needs to be called into question. It is credible that the practice of lament may shatter such assumptions.

2.3. The "polity" that cares about justice refers to a political culture that manages, limits, and legitimates social influence and social access. It is clear that a democratic polity depends especially upon an independent judiciary and an independent media. The judiciary is necessary to present advocacy for the sake of the excluded. The media is necessary to exhibit. beyond "official truth." the human reality that comes in, with, and under policy. It is clear that both an independent judiciary and an independent media are in jeopardy in our society. And as they are in jeopardy, the "technoeconomic structure" can proceed unfettered in its ruthless bent for monopoly.

There is, of course, present in our national history evidence that the judiciary may function as a venue for the protection of the rights of those who cannot protect their own rights. And there is a long history of a fearless media that engages in truth-telling even when it offends.[32] But political tampering with the courts and media deference to power (especially when large concentrations of media power are owned and controlled by corporate interests) create a social environment of compliance, interrelation, and willing censorship in which voices of pain are muted. And when pain goes unuttered, truth disappears. The recovery of the cry of the outsider as a political datum is urgent among us.

---

32. I write this in the immediate wake of the death of David Halberstam. His life and his death remind us in a forceful way what a difference a fearless, independent media can make to the proper functioning of a democracy.

2.4. The realm of "culture" refers especially to the arts and religion. There is of course a long history of the arts as a venue for the voice and reality of the outsider, and there are still works of art and music and theater among us that continue to give such voice. We may be glad for art that remains outside the certification of the "technoeconomic structure." But at the same time, we may notice that the "dumbing down" of U.S. culture in general results in a loss of "edge" in artistic articulation so that, instead of *advocacy*, too much artistic expression is required to be *entertainment* of the most vulgar kind.

One would expect, moreover, that a religious venue would be a place for the demanding voices "from below." So totalizing is the narrative of the "technoeconomic structure" that occupies our "polity," however, that it is exceedingly difficult in the religious community to sustain an alternative narrative outside the "imperial doxology" that can bear witness to the raw suffering in the world.

Perhaps I overstate the point. If overstated, I do so because I believe an ideology of doxology, a celebration of the goodness and virtue of our society, goes along without a critical countervoice. If this judgment is right, then the recovery of lament as a primal theological practice and as an act of theological-political subversion is an urgent happening among us that is to be welcomed. I believe that the lament figured in ancient Israel as a wake-up call to established power and as a wake-up call to the God of Israel who did on occasion "slumber or sleep."[33]

I take it that, broadly construed, attentiveness to lament, in study and in practice, might be a wake-up call to a society that is too long on self-congratulations. The utterance of pain and expected succor is indeed a wake-up call to a "technoeconomic structure" that has become socially irresponsible and humanly indifferent. The lament is a wake-up call to a "polity" that has watched, without much notice, the erosion of dialogic transactions that make democracy possible. And surely it is a wake-up call to the religious communities to become critical of "praise" and to the arts community wherein it is tempted to pander to establishment tastes.

But finally, I submit, the matter is a wake-up call to those of us in the scholarly field whose responsibility it is to pay attention to these textual matters. Here it is likely that the culprit in neglect has been the passion for "objectivity" in which we have imagined we could study these ancient texts and ancient practices at a distance, without a summons issued even to us. The virtue of objectivity, against easy advocacy and the work of historical criticism against every easy religious ideology, is easy enough to recognize and appreciate. It may also be, however, that the shoe is now on the other foot, that objective scholarship may not notice

---

33. On such a "wake-up call to established power," see Gerald T. Sheppard, " 'Enemies' and the Politics of Prayer in the Book of Psalms," in *The Bible and the Politics of Exegesis: Essays in Honor of Norman K. Gottwald on His Sixty-Fifth Birthday* (ed. David Jobling, Peggy Lynne Day, and Gerald T Sheppard; Cleveland: Pilgrim, 1991), 61–82.

that the material we study is profoundly related to the revolution now happening in the world wherein old power and old certitude fail. What is required now, I suspect, is what Gramsci termed "organic intellectuals" who are in the service of the revolution. The revolution is not liberal or conservative, not of the right or of the left. It is rather the recovery of the elemental bodily reality of the human enterprise. It is not sufficient, in such a horizon, that our scholarship should consider the ancient texts of lament unless we also honor the echoes of those ancient laments now voiced among the dispossessed in the present world economy.[34] Scholarship concerning such texts cannot finally avoid such a social reality. The work of the scholars represented in this volume is a powerful testimony to the way in which scholarship matters. It could be argued that the recovery of lament, that most elemental human discourse, is too urgent to be left to scholars. But it can also be insisted that it is too important not to be the proper work of scholars who have a critical role to play in connecting *ancient texts* to *contemporary crises*. Without this text to the forefront, we run the risk of "laughing now," only to "weep later." Alternatively, the work is to take up the texts of weeping now, with reference to the hurt of the world, in order that there might be laughter later when all may laugh together (see Luke 6:21, 25). It is the lament that evokes the "fear not" of God. And it is for that "fear not" that the world waits, a divine utterance issued in response to human insistence, a human insistence that hurts and hopes, and refuses silence.

---

34. For a splendid example of "contemporary echoes," see Nancy C. Lee, *The Singers of Lamentations: Cities under Siege, from Ur to Jerusalem to Sarajevo* (BibInt 60; Leiden: Brill, 2002).

Bibliography

Ackermann, Denise M. "Tales of Terror and Torment: Thoughts on Boundaries and Truth-Telling." *Scriptura* 63 (1997): 425–34.

———. "From Mere Existence to Tenacious Endurance: Stigma, HIV/AIDS and a Feminist Theology of Praxis." Pages 221–42 in *African Women, Religion, and Health: Essays in Honor of Mercy Amba Ewudziwa Oduyoye.* Edited by Isabel Apawo Phiri and Sarojini Nadar. Pietermaritzburg: Cluster, 2006.

Aggleton, Peter and Richard Parker. "HIV and AIDS-Related Stigma and Discrimination: A Conceptual Framework and Implications for Action." *Social Science & Medicine* 57 (2003): 13–24.

Albertz, Rainer. *A History of Israelite Religion in the Old Testament Period.* Translated by J. Bowden. 2 vols. Louisville: Westminster John Knox, 1994.

Albrektson, Bertil. *Studies in the Text and Theology of the Book of Lamentations.* Studia Theologica Lundensia. Lund: Gleerup, 1963.

Alexiou, Margaret. *The Ritual Lament in Greek Tradition.* Cambridge: Cambridge University Press, 1974.

Allen, William Francis, Charles Pickard Ware, and Lucy McKim Garrison, eds. *Slave Songs of the United States.* Bedford, Mass.: Applewood, 1867.

Allison, Christine. "Old and New Oral Traditions in Badinan." Pages 29–47 in *Kurdish Culture and Identity.* Edited by Christine Allison and Philip Kreyenbroek. London: Zed, 1996.

Alonso-Schökel, Luis. *A Manual of Hebrew Poetics.* Rome: Pontifical Biblical Institute, 1988.

Alster, Bendt. "Edin-na ú-sag-gá: Reconstruction, History, and Interpretation of a Sumerian Cultic Lament." Pages 19–31 in *Keilschriftliche Literaturen: ausgewählte Vorträge der XXXII. Rencontre assyriologique internationale, Münster, 8.–12.7.1985.* Edited by Karl Hecker and Walter Sommerfeld. BBVO 6. Berlin: Reimer, 1986.

———. "Inanna Repenting: The Conclusion of 'Inanna's Descent.'" *Acta Sumerologica* 18 (1996): 1–18.

———. "The Mythology of Mourning." *Acta Sumerologica* 5 (1983): 1–16.

Anderson, Gary. *A Time to Mourn, a Time to Dance: The Expression of Grief and Joy in Israelite Religion.* University Park: Pennsylvania State University Press, 1991.

Arnett, Paul, Joanne Cubbs, and Eugene W. Metcalf Jr., eds. *Gee's Bend: The Architecture of the Quilt.* Atlanta: Tinwood Books, 2006.

Bakhtin, Mikhail M. *The Dialogic Imagination: Four Essays.* Edited by Michael Holquist. Translated by Caryl Emerson and Michael Holquist. Austin: University of Texas Press, 1981.

Bautch, Richard J. *Developments in Genre between Post-exilic Penitential Prayers and the Psalms of Communal Lament.* SBLAcBib 7. Atlanta: Society of Biblical Literature, 2003.

Bending, Lucy. *The Representation of Bodily Pain in Late Nineteenth-Century English Culture.* Oxford: Clarendon, 2000.

Benjamin, Walter. "The Task of the Translator." Pages 70–82 in *Illuminations.* Edited by Walter Benjamin. Translated by Harry Zohn. New York: Schocken, 1968.

Benthien, Claudia. *Skin: On the Cultural Border between Self and the World.* Translated by Thomas Dunlap. New York: Columbia University Press, 2002.

Beresford, Belinda. "Where Research Has Brought Us." *Mail & Guardian* (13–19 April 2007): 14.

Berger, Peter L. *The Sacred Canopy: Elements of a Sociological Theory of Religion.* Garden City, N.Y.: Doubleday, 1969.

Bergler, Siegfried. "Threni V—Nur ein alphabetisierendes Lied? Versuch einer Deutung." *VT* 27 (1977): 304–20.

Berlin, Adele. *Lamentations: A Commentary.* OTL. Louisville: Westminster John Knox, 2002.

———. "On Reading Biblical Poetry: The Role of Metaphor." Pages 25–36 in *Congress Volume: Cambridge, 1995.* VTSup 66. Leiden: Brill, 1997.

———. "Psalms and the Literature of Exile: Psalms 137, 44, 69, and 78." Pages 65–86 in *The Book of Psalms: Composition and Reception.* Edited by Peter W. Flint and Patrick D. Miller. Leiden: Brill, 2005.

Billman, Kathleen D., and Daniel L. Migliore. *Rachel's Cry: Prayer of Lament and Rebirth of Hope.* Cleveland: United Church Press, 1999.

Black, Jeremy A. "A-se-er Gi₆-ta, a Balag of Inana." *Acta Sumerologica* 7 (1985): 11–87.

Blassingame, John W., ed. *Slave Testimony: Two Centuries of Letters, Speeches, Interviews and Autobiographies.* Baton Rouge: Louisiana State University Press, 1977.

Boda, Mark J. "Confession as Theological Expression: Ideological Origins of Penitential Prayer." Pages 21–50 in *Seeking the Favor of God, Volume 1: The Origins of Penitential Prayer in Second Temple Judaism.* Edited by Mark J. Boda, Daniel K. Falk, and Rodney A. Werline. SBLEJL 21. Atlanta: Society of Biblical Literature; Leiden: Brill, 2006.

———. "Form Criticism in Transition: Penitential Prayer and Lament, *Sitz im Leben* and Form." Pages 181–92 in *Seeking the Favor of God, Volume 1: The Origins of Penitential Prayer in Second Temple Judaism.* Edited by Mark J.

Boda, Daniel K. Falk, and Rodney A. Werline. SBLEJL 21. Atlanta: Society of Biblical Literature; Leiden: Brill, 2006.

———. "From Complaint to Contrition: Peering through the Liturgical Window of Jer 14,1–15,4." *ZAW* 113 (2001): 186–97.

———. "Lamentations, Book of." *Dictionary of the Old Testament: Wisdom, Poetry and Writings.* Edited by Tremper Longman III, Peter Enns, and Daniel G. Reid. Downers Grove, Ill.: InterVarsity Press, 2007.

———. *Praying the Tradition: The Origin and Use of Tradition in Nehemiah 9.* BZAW 277. Berlin: de Gruyter, 1999.

———. "Zechariah: Master Mason or Penitential Prophet." Pages 49–69 in *Yahwism after the Exile: Perspectives on Israelite Religion in the Persian Era.* Edited by Bob Becking and Rainer Albertz. Studies in Theology and Religion. Assen: Van Gorcum, 2002.

Boda, Mark J., Daniel K. Falk, and Rodney A. Werline, eds. *Seeking the Favor of God, Volume 2: The Development of Penitential Prayer in Second Temple Judaism.* SBLEJL 22. Atlanta: Society of Biblical Literature; Leiden: Brill, 2007.

Bowen, Nancy R. "The Daughters of Your People: Female Prophets in Ezekiel 13:17–23." *JBL* 118 (1999): 417–33.

Brandscheidt, Renate. *Gotteszorn und Menschenleid: Die Gerichtsklage des leidenden Gerechten in Klgl 3.* TTS. Trier: Paulinus, 1983.

Brogan, Terry V. F., and Clive Scott. "Enjambment." In *The New Princeton Encyclopedia of Poetry and Poetics.* Edited by Alex Preminger and Terry V. F. Brogan. 3rd ed. Princeton: Princeton University Press, 1993.

Brown, Sally A., and Patrick Miller, eds. *Lament: Reclaiming Practices in Pulpit, Pew, and Public Square.* Louisville: Westminster John Knox, 2005.

Brown, William P. "*Creatio Corporis* and the Rhetoric of Defense in Job 10 and Psalm 139." Page 107–24 in *God Who Creates: Essays in Honor of W. Sibley Towner.* Edited by William P. Brown and S. Dean McBride Jr. Grand Rapids: Eerdmans, 2000.

———. *Seeing the Psalms. A Theology of Metaphor.* Louisville: Westminster John Knox, 2002.

Broyles, Craig C. *The Conflict of Faith and Experience in the Psalms: A Form-Critical and Theological Study.* JSOTSup 52. Sheffield: JSOT Press, 1989.

Brueggemann, Walter. *Cadences of Home: Preaching Among Exiles.* Louisville: Westminster John Knox, 1997.

———. "The Costly Loss of Lament." *JSOT* 36 (1986): 57–71.

———. "The Formfulness of Grief." *Int* 31 (1977): 263–75.

———. "Four Indispensable Conversations among Exiles." *ChrCent* 114 (1997): 630–32. Repr. as pages 59–68 in *Deep Memory, Exuberant Hope: Contested Truth in a Post-Christian World.* Edited by Patrick D. Miller. Minneapolis: Fortress, 2000.

———. *Hope within History.* Atlanta: Knox, 1987.

————. *Israel's Praise: Doxology against Idolatry and Ideology.* Philadelphia: Fortress, 1988.

————. *The Message of the Psalms: A Theological Commentary.* Augsburg Old Testament Studies. Minneapolis: Augsburg, 1984.

————. *Old Testament Theology: Essays on Structure, Theme, and Text.* Minneapolis: Fortress, 1992.

————. "A Shape for Old Testament Theology: Embrace of Pain." Pages 22–44 in *Old Testament Theology: Essays on Structure, Theme, and Text.* Edited by Patrick D. Miller. Minneapolis: Fortress, 1992.

————. "Summons to New Life: A Reflection." Pages 347–69 in *Repentance in Christian Theology.* Edited By Mark J. Boda and Gordon T. Smith. Collegeville, Minn.: Liturgical Press, 2006.

————. *Theology of the Old Testament: Testimony, Dispute, Advocacy.* Minneapolis: Fortress, 1997.

Bruhm, Steven. *Gothic Bodies: The Politics of Pain in Romantic Fiction.* Philadelphia: University of Pennsylvania Press, 1994.

Brunet, Gilbert. *Les lamentations contre Jérémie: Réinterprétation des quatre premières Lamentations.* Paris: Presses universitaires de France, 1968.

Buccellati, Giorgio. "Gli Israeliti di Palestina al tempo dell'esilio." *BeO* 2 (1960): 199–209.

Buss, Martin J. *Form Criticism in Its Context.* JSOTSup 274. Sheffield: Sheffield Academic Press, 1999.

Caputo, John D. *On Religion.* London: Routledge, 2001.

Childs, Brevard S. *Introduction to the Old Testament as Scripture.* Philadelphia: Fortress, 1979.

————. *Memory and Tradition in Israel.* SBT 37. London: SCM, 1962.

Cohen, Mark E. *The Canonical Lamentations of Ancient Mesopotamia.* 2 vols. Potomac, Md.: Capital Decisions, 1988.

————. *Sumerian Hymnology: The Eršemma.* HUCASup 2. Cincinnati: Hebrew Union College, 1981.

Collins, John J. *The Bible after Babel.* Grand Rapids: Eerdmans, 2005.

Connerton, Paul. *How Societies Remember.* Cambridge: Cambridge University Press, 1989.

Cook, Stephen L. *Prophecy and Apocalypticism: The Postexilic Social Setting.* Minneapolis: Fortress, 1995.

Cover, Robert. *Narrative, Violence and the Law.* Ann Arbor: University of Michigan Press, 1995.

Craven, Toni. *The Book of Psalms.* Collegeville, Minn.: Liturgical Press, 1992.

Cross, Frank Moore. "4QLam." Pages 229–37 in *Qumran Cave 4.XI: Psalms to Chronicles.* Edited by Eugene C. Ulrich et al. DJD XVI. Oxford: Clarendon, 2000.

Crüsemann, Frank. *Studien zur Formgeschichte von Hymnus und Danklied in Israel.* WMANT 32. Neukirchen-Vluyn: Neukirchener, 1969.

Csordas, Thomas, ed. *Embodiment and Experience: The Existential Ground of Culture and Self.* Cambridge: Cambridge University Press, 1994.

Cunningham, Graham. *"Deliver Me from Evil": Mesopotamian Incantations 2500–1500 B.C.E.* Studia Pohl Series maior 17. Rome: Pontifical Biblical Institute, 1997.

Damrosch, David. *The Narrative Covenant: Transformations of Genre in the Growth of Biblical Literature.* San Francisco: Harper & Row, 1987.

Dawes, James. *The Language of War.* Cambridge; Harvard University Press, 2002.

Day, John. *Psalms.* OTG. Sheffield: JSOT Press, 1992.

Del Vecchio Good, Mary-Jo, et al., eds. *Pain as Human Experience: An Anthropological Perspective.* Berkeley and Los Angeles: University of California Press, 1992.

Derrida, Jacques. "Des Tours de Babel." *Semeia* 54 (1991): 3–34

Detweiler, Robert. "Overliving." *Semeia* 54 (1991): 239–55.

Dever, William G. *What Did the Biblical Writers Know and When Did They Know It?* Grand Rapids: Eerdmans 2001.

Dobbs-Allsopp, F. W. "Brief Comments on John Collins's *The Bible after Babel*." *JHS* 6 (2006): 16–17.

———. "Darwinism, Genre Theory, and City Laments." *JAOS* 120 (2000): 625–30.

———. *Lamentations: A Bible Commentary for Teaching and Preaching.* IBC. Louisville: Westminster John Knox, 2002.

———. "Late Linguistic Features in the Song of Songs." Pages 27–77 in *Perspectives on the Song of Songs—Perspektiven der Hoheliedauslegung.* Edited by Anselm C. Hagedorn. BZAW 346. Berlin: de Gruyter, 2005.

———. "Linguistic Evidence for the Date of Lamentations." *JANES* 26 (1998): 1–36.

———. "Psalms and Lyric Verse," Pages 346–79 in *The Evolution of Rationality: Interdisciplinary Essays in Honor of J. Wentzel van Huyssteen.* Edited by F. Leron Shults. Grand Rapids: Eerdmans, 2006.

———. "Rethinking Historical Criticism." *BibInt* 7 (1999): 235–71.

———. "Tragedy, Tradition, and Theology in the Book of Lamentations" *JSOT* 74 (1997): 36–40.

———. *Weep, O Daughter of Zion: A Study of the City-Lament Genre in the Hebrew Bible.* BibOr 44. Roma: Pontifical Biblical Institute, 1993.

Donne, John. *The Complete Poetry of John Donne.* Edited by J. T. Shawcross. New York: Doubleday, 1967.

Dorsey, David A. "Lamentations: Communicating Meaning Through Structure." *EJ* 6 (1988): 83–90.

Doyle, Brian, trans. *Lamentations.* Historical Commentary on the Old Testament. Leuven: Peeters, 1998.

Driver, Samuel R. *An Introduction to the Literature of the Old Testament.* 8th ed. Edinburgh: T&T Clark, 1909.

Egmond, Florike, and Robert Zwijnenberg, eds. *Bodily Extremities: Preoccupations with the Human Body in Early Modern European Culture.* Burlington, Vt.: Ashgate, 2003.

Ehrensvärd, Martin. "Once Again: The Problem of Dating Biblical Hebrew." *SJOT* 11 (1997): 29–40.

Erikson, Kai, ed. *Sociological Visions.* New York: Rowman & Littlefield, 1997.

Erlmann, Veit. *Nightsong: Performance, Power, and Practice in South Africa.* Chicago: University of Chicago Press, 1996.

Fan, Ni. *Yu Zishan Ji.* Taipei: Taiwan Commercial Press, 1968.

Farber-Flügge, Gertrud. *Der Mythos Inanna und Enki unter besonderer Berücksichtigung der Liste der me.* Studia Pohl 10. Rome: Biblical Institute Press, 1973.

Farley, Wendy. *Tragic Vision and Divine Compassion: A Contemporary Theodicy.* Louisville: Westminster John Knox, 1990.

Featherstone, Mike, et al., eds. *The Body: Social Process and Cultural Theory.* London: Sage, 1990.

Feher, Michel, et al., eds. *Fragments for a History of the Human Body.* 3 vols. New York: Zone, 1989.

Finnegan, Ruth. *Oral Literature in Africa.* Oxford: Clarendon, 1970.

Flückiger-Hawker, Esther. *Urnamma of Ur in Sumerian Literary Tradition.* OBO 166. Göttingen: Vandenhoeck & Ruprecht, 1999.

Foley, J. M. *Singer of Tales in Performance.* Bloominton: Indiana University Press, 1995.

Foucault, Michel. *Discipline and Punish: The Birth of the Prison.* Translated by Alan Sheridan. New York: Vintage, 1979.

Frank, Thomas. *What's the Matter with Kansas? How Conservatives Won the Heart of America.* New York: Owl Books, 2005.

Fritz, Volkmar. "Tempel II: Alter Orient und Altes Testament." *TRE* 33 (2002): 46–54.

Frostin, Per. *Liberation Theology in Tanzania and South Africa: A First World Interpretation.* Lund: Lund University Press, 1988.

Fuchs, Ottmar. *Die Klage als Gebet: Eine theologische Besinnung am Beispiel des Psalms 22.* Munich: Kösel, 1982.

Gates, H. L., ed. *The Classic Slave Narratives.* New York: Signet, 2002.

Geller, Stephen A. *Parallelism in Early Biblical Poetry.* HSM 20. Missoula, Mont.: Scholars Press, 1979.

Gerstenberger, Erhard. *Der bittende Mensch.* WMANT 51 Neukirchen-Vluyn: Neukirchener, 1980.

———. "Psalms." Pages 179–223 in *Old Testament Form Criticism.* Edited by John H. Hayes. San Antonio, Tex.: Trinity University Press, 1974.

———. *Psalms, Part 1.* FOTL 14 Grand Rapids: Eerdmans, 1988.

———. *Psalms, Part 2, and Lamentations.* FOTL 15. Grand Rapids: Eerdmans, 2001.

Gillmayr-Bucher, Susanne. "Body Images in the Psalms." *JSOT* 28 (2004): 301–26.

Godwin, Teresa Phelps. *Shattered Voices*. Philadelphia: University of Pennsylvania Press, 2004.

Goffman, Erving. *Stigma: Notes on the Management of a Spoiled Identity*. New York: Simon & Schuster, 1963.

Gordis, Robert. "Commentary on the Text of Lamentations [Part Two]." *JQR* 58 (1967): 14–33.

———. "The Conclusion of the Book of Lamentations (5:22)." *JBL* 93 (1974): 289–93.

———. *The Song of Songs and Lamentations: A Study, Modern Translation and Commentary*. Rev. ed. New York: Ktav, 1974.

Gottlieb, Hans. *A Study on the Text of Lamentations*. Aarhus: Aarhus Universitet, 1978.

Gottwald, Norman K. *Studies in the Book of Lamentations*. SBT 14. Chicago: Allenson, 1954.

———. *Studies in the Book of Lamentations*. Rev. ed. SBT 14. London: SCM, 1962.

Gozeh, Asad. "Images of Poison Gas Still Haunt People in Kurdistan." Online: http://www.kurdishmedia.com.

Graham, William T. *The Lament for the South—Yu Hsin's Ai Chiang-nan Fu*. Cambridge: Cambridge University Press, 1980.

———, trans. "Yü Hsin and *The Lament for the South*." *HTAS* 36 (1976): 82–113.

Grainger, Roger. *Drama and Healing*. London: Kingsley, 1990.

Green, Barbara. *Mikhail Bakhtin and Biblical Scholarship: An Introduction*. SemeiaSt 38 Atlanta: Society of Biblical Literature, 2000.

Greenstein, Edward L. *Essays on Biblical Method and Translation*. BJS 92. Atlanta: Scholars Press, 1989.

———. "Qinah 'al hurbam 'ir umiqdaš besifrut hayisra'elit ha-qedumah." Pages 88–97 in *Homage to Shmuel: Studies in the World of the Bible* [Hebrew]. Edited by Zipora Talshir, Shamir Yonam and Daniel Sivan. Jerusalem: Ben Gurion University, 2001.

Gunkel, Hermann. "Klagelieder Jeremiae." *RGG* 3:1049–52.

Gunkel, Hermann, and Joachim Begrich. *Einleitung in die Psalmen: Die Gattungen der Religiösen Lyrik Israels*. 3rd ed. Göttingen: Vandenhoeck & Ruprecht, 1975.

———. *Introduction to the Psalms: The Genres of the Religious Lyric of Israel*. Translated by James D. Nogalski. Mercer Library of Biblical Studies. Macon, Ga.: Mercer University Press, 1998.

Gurewicz, S. B. "The Problem of Lamentations 3." *ABR* 8 (1960): 19–23.

Habel, Norman C. *Concordia Commentary: Jeremiah, Lamentations*. St. Louis: Concordia, 1968.

Haddad, Beverley G. " 'We Pray but We Cannot Heal': Theological Challenges Posed by the HIV/AIDS Crisis." *JTSA* 125 (2006): 80–90.

Hall, Douglas John. *Lighten Our Darkness: Toward an Indigenous Theology of the Cross*. Philadelphia: Westminster, 1976.

Hallo, William W., and Johannes J. A. van Dijk. *The Exaltation of Inanna*. YNER 3. New Haven: Yale University Press, 1968.

Halpern, Baruch. *David's Secret Demons: Messiah, Murderer, Traitor, King*. Grand Rapids: Eerdmans, 2001.

Hawkes, David. *The Songs of the South: An Ancient Anthology of Poems by Qu Yuan and Other Poets*. Harmondsworth: Penguin, 1985.

Hawtrey, Kim. "The Exile as a Crisis for Cultic Religion: Lamentations and Ezekiel." *RTR* 52 (1993): 74–83.

Hays, Rchard B. *The Conversion of the Imagination: Paul as Interpreter of Israel's Scripture*. Grand Rapids: Eerdmans, 2005.

Heater, Homer. "Structure and Meaning in Lamentations." *BibSac* 149 (1992): 304–15.

Heim, Knut M. "The Personification of Jerusalem and the Drama of Her Bereavement in Lamentations." Pages 129–69 in *Zion, City of Our God*. Edited by Richard S. Hess and Gordon J. Wenham; Grand Rapids: Eerdmans, 1999.

Heinemann, Joseph. *Prayer in the Talmud: Forms and Patterns*. SJ 9. Berlin: de Gruyter, 1977.

Herman, Judith. *Trauma and Recovery*. New York: Basic, 1992.

Higginson, Thomas Wenworth. "Negro Spirituals." Online: http://afroamhistory. about.com/library/blthomas_higginson_spirituals.htm.

Hillers, Delbert. *Lamentations*. AB 7A. Garden City, N.Y. : Doubleday, 1972.

———. *Poets before Homer: Collected Essays on Ancient Literature*. Edited by F. W. Dobbs-Allsopp. Winona Lake, Ind.: Eisenbrauns, forthcoming.

Hock, Hans Henrich. *Principles of Historical Linguistics*. Berlin: de Gruyter, 1986.

Holladay, William. "Style, Irony, and Authenticity in Jeremiah." *JBL* 81 (1962): 44–54.

Houk, Cornelius. "Acrostic Psalms and Syllables." Pages 54–60 in *The Psalms and Other Studies on the Old Testament*. Edited by Jack C. Knight and Lawrence A. Sinclair. Nashotah, Wis.: Forward Movement Publications, 1990.

———. "Multiple Poets in Lamentations." *JSOT* 30 (2005): 111–25.

Hughes, Langston. "Wake." Page 327 in *The Oxford Anthology of African American Poetry*. Edited by Arnold Rampersad. New York: Oxford University Press, 1995.

Hunter, Jannie. *Faces of a Lamenting City: The Development and Coherence of the Book of Lamentations*. Frankfurt am Main: Lang, 1996.

Hurvitz, Avi. "The Historical Quest for 'Ancient Israel' and the Linguistic Evidence of the Hebrew Bible: Some Methodological Observations." *VT* 47 (1997): 301–15.

———. *A Linguistic Study of the Relationship between the Priestly Source and the Book of Ezekiel*. CahRB 20. Paris: Gabalda, 1982.

Izady, Mehrad. *The Kurds*. London: Russak, 1992.

Jahnow, Hedwig. *Das hebräische Leichenlied im Rahmen der Völkerdichtung.* BZAW 36. Giessen: Töpelmann, 1923.

Johnson, Bo. "Form and Message in Lamentations." *ZAW* 97 (1985): 58–73.

Johnson, James Weldon, and J. Rosamond Johnson. *The Books of American Negro Spirituals.* New York: Viking, 1925. Repr., New York: Da Capo, 1969.

Jones, Serene. "'Soul Anatomy': Calvin's Commentary on the Psalms." Pages 265–84 in *Psalms in Community: Jewish and Christian Textual, Liturgical, and Artistic Traditions.* Edited by Harold W. Attridge and Margot E. Fassler. SBLSymS 25. Atlanta: Society of Biblical Literature, 2003.

Joosten, Jan. "The Distinction between Classical and Late Biblical Hebrew as Reflected in Syntax." *HS* 46 (2005): 327–39.

Joyce, Paul "Lamentations and the Grief Process: A Psychological Reading." *BibInt* 1 (1993): 304–20.

Kadushin, Max. *The Rabbinic Mind.* 3rd ed. New York: Bloch, 1972.

Kammen, Michael. *Mystic Chords of Memory: The Transformation of Tradition in American Culture.* New York: Knopf, 1991.

Karlgren, Bernhard. *The Book of Odes.* Stockholm: Museum of Far Eastern Antiquities, 1950.

Kemble, Frances Anne. *Journal of a Residence on a Georgian Plantation in 1838–1839.* 1863. Repr., Athens: University of Georgia Press, 1984.

King, Philip J., and Lawrence E. Stager. *Life in Biblical Israel.* Louisville: Westminster John Knox, 2001.

Kirmayer, Laurence. "Landscapes of Memory: Trauma, Narrative, and Dissociation." Pages 173–98 in *Tense Past: Cultural Essays in Trauma and Memory.* Edited by Paul Antze and Michael Lambek. New York: Routledge, 1996.

Klein, Ralph W. *Israel in Exile: A Theological Interpretation.* OBT. Philadelphia: Fortress, 1979.

Kleinman, Arthur. *The Illness Narratives: Suffering, Healing, and the Human Condition.* New York: Basic Books, 1988.

———. *Social Origins of Distress and Disease: Depression, Neurasthenia, and Pain in Modern China.* New Haven: Yale University Press, 1986.

Knoppers, Gary. "The Vanishing Solomon: The Disappearance of the United Monarchy from Recent Histories of Ancient Israel." *JBL* 116 (1997): 19–44.

Kozol, Jonathan. *The Shame of the Nation: The Restoration of Apartheid Schooling in America.* New York: Crown, 2005.

Kraemer, David. *Responses to Suffering in Classical Rabbinic Literature.* New York: Oxford University Press, 1995.

Kramer, Samuel N. "Lamentation over the Destruction of Nipur." *Acta Sumerologica* 13 (1991): 1–26.

———. *Two Elegies on a Pushkin Museum Tablet: A New Sumerian Literary Genre.* Moscow: Izd-vo vostochnoĭ lit-ry, 1960.

Krašovec, Jože. "The Source of Hope in the Book of Lamentations." *VT* 42 (1992): 224–30.

Kraus, Han-Joachim. *Klagelieder (Threni)* 2nd ed. BKAT. Neukirchen: Kreis Moers, 1960.

Kuan, Jeffrey. "Asian Biblical Interpretation." Pages 70–77 of vol. 1 in *Dictionary of Biblical Interpretation*. Edited by John H. Hayes. 2 vols. Nashville: Abingdon, 1999.

Kugel, James L. *The God of Old: Inside the Lost World of the Bible*. New York: Free Press, 2003.

Kuschel, Karl-Joseph. "Ist Gott verantwortlich für das Übel: Überlegungen zu einer Theologie der Anklagen." Pages 228–31 in *Angesichts des Leids an Gott Glauben? Zur Theologie der Klage*. Edited by Gotthard Fuchs. Frankfurt am Main: Knecht, 1996.

Lanahan, William. "The Speaking Voice in the Book of Lamentations." *JBL* 93 1974: 41–49.

Landes, George M. "Linguistic Criteria and the Date of the Book of Jonah." *ErIsr* 16 (1982): 147–70.

Landy, Robert. *Persona and Performance*. New York: Guilford, 1993.

Larkin, Katrina J. *The Eschatology of Second Zechariah: A Study of the Formation of a Mantological Wisdom Anthology*. CBET. Kampen: Kok, 1994.

Laub, Dori, and Shoshana Felman. *Testimony*. New York: Routledge, 1992.

Laytner, Anson. *Arguing with God: A Jewish Tradition*. Northvale, N.J.: Aronson, 1990.

Lee, Archie C. C. "The Chinese Creation Myth of Nu Kua and the Biblical Narrative in Gen 1–11." *BibInt* 2 (1994): 312–24.

———. "Cross-Textual Hermeneutics on Gospel and Culture." *AJT* 10 (1996): 38–48.

———. "Death and the Perception of the Divine in Zhuangzi and Koheleth." *Ching Feng* 38 (1995): 68–81.

———. "Exile and Return in the Perspective of 1997." Pages 97–108 in *Reading from This Place: Social Location and Biblical Interpretation in Global Perspective*. Edited by Fernando F. Segovia and Mary Ann Tolbert. Minneapolis: Fortress, 1995.

———. "Feminist Critique of the Bible and Female Principle in Culture." *AJT* 10 (1996): 240–52.

———. "The Recitation of the Past: A Cross-Textual Reading of Psalm 78 and the Odes." *Ching Feng* 38 (1996): 173–200.

Lee, Nancy. "Prophet and Singer in the Fray: the Book of Jeremiah" Pages 190–209 in *Uprooting and Planting: Essays on Jeremiah for Leslie Allen*. Edited by John Goldingay. Library of Hebrew Bible/Old Testament Studies 359. London: T&T Clark, 2007.

———. *The Singers of Lamentations: Cities under Siege, from Ur to Jerusalem to Sarajevo*. BibInt 60. Leiden: Brill, 2002.

———, ed. *Between Despair and Lamentation*. Translated by Ivana Pozajić Jerić. Elmhurst, Ill.: Elmhurst College, 2002.

Lehmann, Paul. *The Transfiguration of Politics: The Presence and Power of Jesus of Nazareth in and over Human Affairs*. New York: Harper & Row, 1975.

Leigh, Valerie T. L. "Aspects of Identity in Kwazulu-Natal Art 1980–2000 with Special Reference to the Complexity of Influences Shaping the Work of Andries Botha, Jinny Heath, Derek Leigh and Trevor Makhoba." M.A. thesis. University of Natal, 2002.

Levine, Herbert J. *Sing unto God a New Song*. Indianapolis: Indiana University Press, 1995.

Lewis, Alan E. *Between Cross and Resurrection: A Theology of Holy Saturday*. Grand Rapids: Eerdmans, 2001.

Limbeck, Meinard. "Die Klage—Eine verschwundene Gebetsgattung." *TQ* 157 (1977): 13–16.

Linafelt, Tod. "The Refusal of a Conclusion in the Book of Lamentations." *JBL* 120 (2001): 340–43.

———. "Surviving Lamentations." *HBT* 17 (1995): 45–61.

———. *Surviving Lamentations: Catastrophe, Lament and Protest in the Afterlife of a Biblical Book*. Chicago: University of Chicago Press, 2000.

Lindström, Fredrik. *Suffering and Sin: Interpretations of Illness in the Individual Complaint Psalms*. ConBOT 37. Stockholm: Almqvist & Wiksell, 1994.

Lindy, Jacob, and Robert Lifton, eds. *Beyond Invisible Walls: The Psychological Legacy of Soviet Trauma*. New York: Brunner-Routledge, 2001.

Longman, Tremper, III. "Form Criticism, Recent Developments in Genre Theory, and the Evangelical." *WTJ* 47 (1985): 46–67.

Lord, Albert B. *The Singer of Tales*. New York: Atheneum, 1968.

Lowth, Robert. *Isaiah: A New Translation*. London, 1778. Repr., London: Routledge, 1995.

———. *Lectures on the Sacred Poetry of the Hebrews* Rev. and enl. ed. London, 1788. Repr., London: Routledge, 1995.

Makhoba, Gugu, et al. "Endpiece." In *Trevor Makhoba Memorial Exhibition Catalogue*. Edited by Jill Addleson. Durban: Durban Art Gallery, 2004.

Mandolfo, Carleen. *Daughter Zion Talks Back to the Prophets*. SemeiaSt 58. Atlanta: Society of Biblical Literature; Leiden: Brill, 2007.

———. "A Generic Renegade: A Dialogic Theological Reading of Job and Lament Psalms" Pages 45–66 in *Diachronic and Synchronic: Reading the Psalms in Real Time, Proceedings of the Baylor Symposium on the Book of Psalms*. Edited by Joel S. Burnett, W. Dennis Tucker, and W. H. Bellinger. Library of Hebrew Bible/Old Testament Studies 488. New York: T&T Clark, 2007.

———. *God in the Dock: Dialogic Tension in the Psalms of Lament*. JSOTSup 357. London: Sheffield Academic Press, 2002.

———. "Psalm 88 and the Holocaust: Lament in Search of a Divine Response." *BibInt* 15 (2007): 151–70.

Mannheim, Karl. *Ideology and Utopia*. New York: Brace, Harcourt, 1936.

Maul, Stefan M. *Die sumerisch-akkadischen Eršahunga-Gebete.* Wiesbaden: Harrassowitz, 1988.

———. *Zukunftsbewältigung: Eine Untersuchung altorientalischen Denkens anhand der babylonisch-assyrischen Löserituale (Nam-bur-bi).* BaghF 18. Mainz: Zabern, 1994.

McCann, Lisa, and Laurie A. Pearlman. *Psychological Trauma and the Adult Survivor: Theory, Therapy and Transformation.* Brunner/Mazal Psychosocial Stress Series 21. New York: Brunner/Mazal, 1990.

McDaniel, Thomas F. "Philological Studies in Lamentations, I and II." *Bib* 49 (1968): 27–53, 199–220.

McKenzie, Steven L. "Deuteronomistic History." *ABD* 2:160–68.

McLellan, David. *The Thought of Karl Marx: An Introduction.* London: Macmillan, 1971.

Merritt, Carole. *Homecoming: African-American Family History in Georgia.* Atlanta: African American Family History Association, 1982.

Meyers, Carol. "Miriam the Musician." Pages 207–30 in *A Feminist Companion to Exodus to Deuteronomy.* Edited by Athalya Brenner. Sheffield: Sheffield Academic Press, 1994.

Michalowski, Piotr. *The Lamentation over the Destruction of Sumer and Ur.* Winona Lake, Ind.: Eisenbrauns, 1989.

Middlemas, Jill. *The Troubles of Templeless Judah.* Oxford: Oxford University Press, 2005.

Mintz, Alan. *Hurban: Responses to Catastrophe in Hebrew Literature.* New York: Columbia University Press, 1984.

———. "The Rhetoric of Lamentations and the Representation of Catastrophe." *Prooftexts* 2 (1982): 1–17.

Moltmann, Jürgen. *The Crucified God: The Cross of Christ as the Foundation and Criticism of Christian Theology.* New York: Harper & Row, 1974.

Moore, Michael S. "Human Suffering in Lamentations." *RB* 90 (1983): 534–55.

Morris, David B. *The Culture of Pain.* Berkeley and Los Angeles: University of California Press, 1991.

———. "The Languages of Pain." Pages 89–99 in *Exploring the Concept of the Mind.* Edited by Richard M. Caplan. Iowa City: University of Iowa Press, 1986.

Morrow, William. *Protest against God: The Eclipse of a Biblical Tradition.* Hebrew Bible Monographs 4. Sheffield: Sheffield Phoenix Press, 2006.

Morson, Gary Saul, and Caryl Emerson, *Mikhail Bakhtin: Creation of a Prosaics.* Stanford, Calif.: Stanford University Press, 1990.

Mowinckel, Sigmund. *The Psalms in Israel's Worship.* Translated by D. R. Ap-Thomas. 2 vols. Nashville: Abingdon, 1962.

Mueller, Janel M. "Pain, Persecution, and the Construction of Selfhood in Foxe's Acts and Monuments." Pages 161–87 in *Religion and Culture in Renaissance*

England. Edited by Claire McEachern and Debora Shuger. Cambridge: Cambridge University Press, 1997.

Murphy, Roland E. "Qoheleth's 'Quarrel' with the Fathers." Pages 219–34 in *From Faith to Faith: Essays in Honor of Donald G. Miller on His Seventieth Birthday*. Edited by Dikran Y. Hadidian. Pittsburgh: Pickwick, 1979.

Nasuti, Harry P. *Defining the Sacred Songs: Genre, Tradition and the Post-critical Interpretation of the Psalms*. JSOTSup 218. Sheffield: Sheffield Academic Press, 1999.

Nelson, Hilde. *Damaged Identities, Narrative Repair*. Ithaca, N.Y.: Cornell University Press, 2001.

Newman, Judith H. "Nehemiah 9 and the Scripturalization of Prayer in the Second Temple Period." Pages 112–23 in *The Function of Scripture in Early Jewish and Christian Tradition*. Edited by Craig A. Evans and James A. Sanders. JSNTSup 154. Sheffield: Sheffield Academic Press, 1998.

———. *Praying by the Book: The Scripturalization of Prayer in Second Temple Judaism*. SBLEJL 14. Atlanta: Scholars Press, 1999.

Newsom, Carol A. *The Book of Job: A Contest of Moral Imaginations*. Oxford: Oxford University Press, 2003.

———. "Response to Norman K. Gottwald, 'Social Class and Ideology in Isaiah 40–55.'" *Semeia* 58 (1992): 73–78.

Nora, Pierre. *Rethinking France: Les lieux de mémoire*. Translated by Mary Trouille and Pierre Nora. Chicago: University of Chicago Press, 2001.

O'Connor, Kathleen M. "Lamentations." Pages 178–82 in *The Women's Bible Commentary: Expanded Edition with Apocrypha*. Edited by Carol A. Newsom and Sharon H. Ringe. Louisville: Westminster John Knox, 1998.

———. *Lamentations and the Tears of the World*. Maryknoll, N.Y.: Orbis, 2002.

O'Connor, Michael P. *Hebrew Verse Structure*. Winona Lake, Ind.: Eisenbrauns, 1980.

O'Donovan-Anderson, Michael, ed. *The Incorporated Self: Interdisciplinary Perspectives on Embodiment*. New York: Rowan & Littlefield, 1996.

Ozick, Cynthia. *The Shawl: A Story and Novella*. New York: Knopf, 1989.

Parker, Simon B. "Toward Literary Translations of Ugaritic Poetry." *UF* 22 (1991): 257–70.

Perdue, Leo G. *Wisdom in Revolt: Metaphorical Theology in the Book of Job*. Sheffield: Almond, 1991.

Petersen, David L., and Kent Harold Richards, *Interpreting Hebrew Poetry*. Minneapolis: Fortress, 1992.

Petuchowski, Jakob J. *Theology and Poetry: Studies in the Medieval Piyyut*. Littman Library of Jewish Civilization. London: Routledge & Kegan Paul, 1978.

Pincikowski, Scott E. *Bodies of Pain: Suffering in the Works of Hartmann von Aue*. New York: Routledge, 2002.

Plaskow, Judith. *Standing Again at Sinai: Judaism from a Feminist Perspective*. San Francisco: Harper & Row, 1991.

Porteous, Norman W. "Jerusalem-Zion: The Growth of a Symbol." Pages 335–52 in *Verbannung und Heimkehr. [Rudolph Festschrif].* Edited by Arnulf Kuschke. Tübingen: Mohr Siebeck, 1961.

Porter, Roy. "History of the Body." Pages 206–32 in *New Perspectives on Historical Writing.* Edited by Peter Burke. University Park: Pennsylvania State University Press, 1992.

Prazniak, Roxann. *Dialogues across Civilizations: Sketches in World History from the Chinese and European Experiences.* Boulder, Colo.: Westview, 1996.

Prince, Mary. *The History of Mary Prince, a West Indian Slave.* London: Westley & Davis, 1831. Repr. in *The Classic Slave Narratives.* Edited by Henry Louis Gates Jr. New York: New American Library, 2002.

Pröbstl, Volker. *Nehemia 9, Psalm 106 und Psalm 136 und die Rezeption des Pentateuchs.* Göttingen: Cuvillier, 1997.

Provan, Iain. *Lamentations.* NCBC. Grand Rapids: Eerdmans, 1991.

———. "Past, Present and Future in Lamentations III 52–66: The Case for the Precative Perfect Re-examined." *VT* 41 (1991): 164–75.

———. "Reading Texts against an Historical Background: The Case of Lamentations 1." *SJOT* 1 (1990): 130–43.

Rad, Gerhard von. *Gesammelte Studien zum Alten Testament.* TBü. Munich: Kaiser, 1956.

———. *The Problem of the Hexateuch and Other Essays.* London: Oliver & Boyd, 1966.

Rehle, Thomas, et al. "National HIV Incidence Measures: New Insights into the South African Epidemic." *South African Medical Journal* 97 (2007): 194–99.

Renkema, Johan. *Lamentations.* Translated by Brian Doyle. HCOT Leuven: Peeters, 1998.

———. "The Literary Structure of Lamentations (I–IV)." Pages 294–396 in *The Structural Analysis of Biblical and Canaanite Poetry.* Edited by Willem van der Meer and Johannes C. de Moor. JSOTSup 74. Sheffield: Sheffield Academic Press, 1988.

Rey, Roselyne. *The History of Pain.* Cambridge: Harvard University Press, 1995.

Römer, Willem H. Ph. *Hymnen und Klagelieder in sumerischer Sprache.* AOAT 276. Münster: Ugarit-Verlag, 2001.

———. *Die Klage über die Zerstörung von Ur.* AOAT 309. Münster: Ugarit Verlag, 2004.

Rooker, Mark F. *Biblical Hebrew in Transition: The Language of the Book of Ezekiel.* JSOTSup 90. Sheffield: JSOT Press, 1990.

Rosen, Nir. "Uncovering the Dead." Online: http://www.kurdishmedia.com.

Rosenfeld, Abraham, ed. *The Authorized Kinot for the Ninth of Av.* London: Labworth, 1965.

Rosmarin, Adena. *The Power of Genre.* Minneapolis: University of Minnesota Press, 1985.

Rudolph, W. *Das Buch Ruth, Das Hohe Lied, Die Klagelieder.* 2nd ed. KAT 17. Gütersloh: Mohn, 1962.

———. "Der Text der Klagelieder." *ZAW* 56 (1938): 101–22.

Saebø, Magne. "Who Is 'the Man' in Lamentation 3? A Fresh Approach." Pages 294–306 in *Understanding Poets and Prophets: Essays in Honour of George Wishart Anderson.* Edited by A. Graeme Auld; Sheffield: Sheffield Academic Press, 1993.

Sakenfeld, Katharine Doob. *Faithfulness in Action: Loyalty in Biblical Perspective.* OBT. Philadelphia: Fortress, 1985.

Scarry, Elaine. *The Body in Pain: The Making and Unmaking of the World.* New York: Oxford University Press, 1985.

Schwarcz, Vera. "In the Shadows of the Red Sun: A New Generation of Chinese Writers." *Asian Review* 3 (1989): 4–16.

———. "'Memory and Commemoration': The Chinese Search for a Livable Past." Pages 170–83 in *Popular Protest and Political Culture in Modern China.* Edited by Jeffery N. Wasserstrom and Elisabeth J. Perry. 2nd ed. Boulder, Colo.: Westview, 1994.

Scott, James C. *Domination and the Arts of Resistance: Hidden Transcripts.* New Haven: Yale University Press, 1990.

Seidman, Naomi. "Burning the Book of Lamentations," Page 178–88 in *Out of the Garden: Women Writers on the Bible.* Edited by Christina Buchmann and Celina Spiegel. New York: Fawcett Columbine, 1992.

Shea, William H. "The Qinah Structure of the Book of Lamentations." *Bib* 60 (1979): 103–7.

Sheppard, Gerald T. "'Enemies' and the Politics of Prayer in the Book of Psalms." Pages 61–82 in *The Bible and the Politics of Exegesis: Essays in Honor of Norman K. Gottwald on His Sixty-Fifth Birthday.* Edited by David Jobling, Peggy Lynne Day, and Gerald T. Sheppard. Cleveland: Pilgrim, 1991.

Shilling, Chris. *The Body and Social Theory.* London: Sage, 1993.

Singer, Peter. "Unspeakable Acts." Review of Elaine Scarry, *The Body In Pain: The Making and Unmaking of the World,* and Edward Peters, *Torture. New York Review of Books* (27 February 1986): 3.

Sladek, William R. *Inanna's Descent to the Netherworld.* Ann Arbor, Mich.: University Microfilms, 1974.

Soloveitchik, Joseph B. *The Lord Is Righteous in All His Ways: Reflections on the Tish'ah be-Av Kinot.* Edited by Jacob J. Schacter. Jersey City, N.J.: Ktav, 2006.

Sommer, Benjamin D. *A Prophet Reads Scripture: Allusion in Isaiah 40–66.* Stanford, Calif.: Stanford University Press, 1998.

Sorekli, Shahin. "Halabja: Another Sad Kurdish Song?" Online: http://www.kurdishmedia.com.

Stanley, Brian. *The Bible and the Flag: Protestant Missions and British Imperialism in the Nineteenth and Twentieth Centuries.* Leicester: Apollos, 1990.

Stone, Ken. "Safer Text: Reading Biblical Laments in the Age of AIDS." *Theology and Sexuality* 10 (1999): 16–27.

Stout, Jeffrey. *Democracy and Tradition*. Princeton: Princeton University Press, 2004.

Sugirtharajah, R. S. *Asian Biblical Hermeneutics and Postcolonialism: Contesting the Interpretations*. Maryknoll, N.Y.: Orbis, 1998.

——. *The Bible and the Third World: Pre-colonial, Colonial, and Postcolonial Encounters*. Cambridge: Cambridge University Press, 2001.

Suško, Mario, ed. *Contemporary Poetry of Bosnia and Hercegovina*. Sarajevo: International Peace Center, 1993.

Swenson, Kristin M. *Living through Pain: Psalms and the Search for Wholeness*. Waco, Tex.: Baylor University Press, 2005.

Synnott, Anthony. *The Body Social: Symbolism, Self and Society*. London: Routledge, 1993.

Teichman, Milton, and Sharon Leder, eds., *Truth and Lamentation: Stories and Poems on the Holocaust*. Chicago: University of Chicago Press, 1994.

Terreblanche, Sampie. *A History of Inequality in South Africa, 1652–2002*. Pietermaritzburg: University of Natal Press, 2002.

Tilley, Terence W. *The Evils of Theodicy*. Eugene, Ore.: Wipf & Stock, 2000.

Tinney, Steve. *The Nippur Lament*. Occasional Publications of the S. N. Kramer Fund 16. Philadelphia: University Museum, 1996.

Toit, Juliette C. Leeb-du. "Contextualizing the Use of Biblically Derived and Metaphysical Imagery in the Work of Black Artists from Kwazulu-Natal: c1930–2002." Ph.D. diss. University of Natal, 2003.

Tongqun, Lu. *A Special Study of Yu Xin*. Tianjin: Tainjin People's Press, 1997.

Turner, Bryan S. *The Body and Society*. New York: Basil Blackwell, 1984.

Turner, Victor. *The Anthropology of Performance*. New York: Performing Arts Journal, 1987.

Tracy, David. *The Analogical Imagination: Christian Theology and the Culture of Pluralism*. New York: Crossroad, 1981.

Venuti, Lawrence, ed. *The Translation Studies Reader*. London: Routledge, 2000.

Volk, Konrad. *Die Balag-Komposition Uru Am-ma-ir-ra-bi*. Freiburger altorientalistische Studien 18. Stuttgart: Steiner, 1989.

Watson, Wilfred G. E. *Classical Hebrew Poetry*. JSOTSup 26. Sheffield: Sheffield Academic Press, 1984.

Weinfeld, Moshe. *Deuteronomy and the Deuteronomic School*. Oxford: Clarendon, 1972.

Weinhouse, Linda. "Faith and Fantasy: The Texts of the Jews." *Medieval Encounters* 5 (1999): 391–408.

Weiss, Andrea. *Figurative Language in Biblical Prose Narrative*. Leiden: Brill, 2006.

Weiss, Meir. *The Bible from Within*. Jerusalem: Magnes, 1984.

Werline, Rodney A. *Penitential Prayer in Second Temple Judaism: The Development of a Religious Institution*. SBLEJL 13. Atlanta: Scholars Press, 1998.

West, Gerald O. "(Ac)claiming the (Extra)ordinary African 'Reader' of the Bible." Pages 29–47 in *Reading Other-Wise: Socially Engaged Biblical Scholars Reading with Their Local Communities*. Edited by Gerald O. West. SemeiaSt 62. Atlanta: Society of Biblical Literature, 2007.

———. "Contextualized Reading of the Bible." *Analecta Bruxellensia* 11 (2006): 131–48.

———. "Indigenous Exegesis: Exploring the Interface between Missionary Methods and the Rhetorical Rhythms of Africa; Locating Local Reading Resources in the Academy." *Neot* 36 (2002): 147–62.

———. "Reading the Bible in the Light of HIV/AIDS in South Africa." *Ecumenical Review* 55 (2003): 335–44.

West, Gerald O., and Bongi Zengele. "Reading Job 'Positively' in the Context of HIV/AIDS in South Africa." *Concilium* 4 (2004): 112–24.

Westermann, Claus. *Lamentations: Issues and Interpretation*. Minneapolis: Fortress, 1994.

———. *Praise and Lament in the Psalms*. Translated by Keith R. Crim and Richard N. Soulen. Atlanta: Knox, 1981.

———. *The Praise of God in the Psalms*. Translated by Keith R. Crim. Richmond, Va.: Knox, 1965.

———. *The Structure of the Book of Job: A Form-Critical Analysis*. Philadelphia: Fortress, 1981.

White, James Boyd. *Living Speech: Resisting the Empire of Force*. Princeton: Princeton University Press, 2006.

———. *When Words Lose Their Meaning: Constitutions and Reconstitutions of Language, Character, and Community*. Chicago: University of Chicago Press, 1984.

Willey, Patricia Tull. *Remember the Former Things: The Recollection of Previous Texts in Second Isaiah*. SBLDS 161. Atlanta: Scholars Press, 1997.

Williams, Simon J., and Gillian Bendelow, eds. *The Lived Body: Sociological Themes, Embodied Issues*. London: Routledge, 1998.

Wire, Antoinette Clark. "Chinese Biblical Interpretation since Mid-century." *BibInt* 4 (1996): 101–23.

Wright, G. E. *God Who Acts*. SBT 8. London: SCM, 1952.

Yerushalmi, Yosef H. *Jewish History and Jewish Memory*. Seattle: University of Washington Press, 1982.

Yin-k'o, Ch'en. "Reading *The Lament for the South*." *Journal of Ch'ing-hua* 13 (1941): 11–16.

Zgoll, Annette. *Die Kunst Betens*. AOAT 308. Münster: Ugarit-Verlag, 2003.

———. *Der Rechtsfall der En-ḥedu-Ana im Lied nin-me-šara*. AOAT 246. Münster: Ugarit-Verlag, 1997.

Zvi, Ehud Ben, and Marvin A. Sweeney, eds. *The Changing Face of Form Criticism for the Twenty-First Century*. Grand Rapids: Eerdmans, 2003.

Zwickel, Wolfgang. "Tempel." Pages 799–810 in *Neues Bibel-Lexikon*. Edited by Manfred Görg and Bernard Lang. Zürich: Benziger, 1988.

———. *Der Tempelkult in Kanaan und Israel*. FAT 10. Tübingen: Mohr Siebeck, 1994.

CONTRIBUTORS

Borislav Arapović is the Honorary President of the Institute for Bible Translation, after having served as its Director from 1973 to 1997. The focus of his research is Croatian literature, especially its prowar and antiwar rhetoric, and the historical aspects of Bible translation into the Croatian language, as well as indigenous languages under the former Russian Empire and the Soviet Union. He has also published, in Croatian, four collections of poems.

Wilma Ann Bailey is Associate Professor of Hebrew and Aramaic Scripture at Christian Theological Seminary in Indianapolis. In recent years she has focused her study on the lament tradition in the Hebrew Bible and the African American experience, women's stories, prepubescent marriage in ancient Israel, and peace texts. Her latest book is *"You Shall Not Kill"? Or "You Shall Not Murder"? The Assault on a Biblical Text* (Liturgical Press, 2005).

Adele Berlin, the Robert H. Smith Professor of Biblical Studies at the University of Maryland, is particularly interested in biblical narrative and poetry and in the interpretation of the Bible. Author or editor of seven books, including *The Jewish Study Bible* (Oxford University Press) and a commentary on Lamentations, she is now at work on Psalms. Berlin is a Fellow of the American Academy for Jewish Research and a past President of the Society of Biblical Literature (2000). She has held fellowships from the National Endowment for the Humanities, the John Simon Guggenheim Foundation, the American Council of Learned Societies, and the Center for Advanced Judaic Studies at the University of Pennsylvania.

Mark J. Boda is Professor of Old Testament at McMaster Divinity College and Professor, Faculty of Theology, at McMaster University, Hamilton, Ontario. His key areas of interest include Old Testament theology, prayer and penitence in the Old Testament and Christian theology, Babylonian period Hebrew books and history, and the Book of the Twelve. He has authored or edited thirteen books, including the recent three-volume SBLEJL series on penitential prayer (*Seeking the Favor of God*, ed. with Daniel Falk and Rodney Werline, 2006–2008), the Liturgical Press volume on *Repentance in*

Christian Theology (ed. with Gordon T. Smith, 2006), and the forthcoming *A Severe Mercy: Sin and Its Remedy in the Old Testament* (Eisenbrauns).

Walter Brueggemann has completed forty-seven years of seminary teaching and continues in retirement to think about the biblical text in relation to church and society. He has long been interested in the laments as a countertheme to triumphalist religion and is pleased to count among his students some of the leaders in current lament research. He has recently published a book on preaching, *The Word Militant* (Fortress) and a book of prayers, *Prayers for a Privileged People* (Abingdon). He continues to find the biblical text more interesting and more compelling than most of the alternatives.

Amy Cottrill is Assistant Professor of Religion at Birmingham-Southern College in Birmingham, Alabama, where she teaches a wide range of courses in biblical studies. Professor Cottrill completed her Ph.D. in Hebrew Bible at Emory University in 2006, and the current focus of her scholarly research is the use of texts in the construction of cultural identities. Reflective of that interest is her book, *Language, Power, and Identity in the Lament Psalms of the Individual* (T&T Clark, 2008).

F. W. Dobbs-Allsopp is Associate Professor of Old Testament at Princeton Theological Seminary (Ph.D., Johns Hopkins University, 1992). His research and teaching interests include Hebrew poetry (especially Lamentations, Psalms, Song of Songs), integration of literary and historical methods of interpretation, postmodern thought and theory, Semitic languages and linguistics, and comparative study of biblical literature within its ancient Near Eastern context. His recent publications include two co-edited volumes—*Hebrew Inscriptions* (Yale University Press, 2005) and *Two Early Alphabetic Inscriptions from the Wadi el-Ḥôl* (AASOR 59.2, 2005)—and various essays and articles, such as "I Am Black and Beautiful: The Song, Cixous, and Écriture Féminine"; "Psalms and Lyric Verse"; and "(More) Thoughts on Performatives." He is currently at work on a monograph-length study of biblical Hebrew poetry, tentatively entitled *"Verse, Properly So Called": Essays on Biblical (Hebrew) Poetry*.

Clyde E. Fant is the O. L. Walker Professor of Christian Studies Emeritus, Stetson University, DeLand, Florida. His other writings include *Bonhoeffer: Worldly Preaching* (Nelson, 1975); *The Misunderstood Jesus* (Peake Road, 1996); *An Introduction to the Bible* (Abingdon, 2001); *A Guide to Biblical Sites in Greece and Turkey* (Oxford University Press, 2003); and *Lost Treasures of the Bible: Biblical Objects in World Museums* (co-author; Eerdmans, 2008).

Erhard S. Gerstenberger, who has been retired since 1997, was born in the Lower Rhine area, Germany, and received his theological education at Marburg, Tübingen, Bonn, and Wuppertal. He was a parish minister and served as an assistant professor at Yale Divinity School and a professor of Old Testament in Brazil, subsequently at Giessen and Marburg Universities. Publications include *Yahweh the Patriarch* (Fortress, 1996); *Theologies in the Old Testament* (Fortress, 2002); and *Israel in the Persian Period* (Society of Biblical Literature, forthcoming).

Archie Chi Chung Lee is Dean of Faculty of Arts and Professor in the Cultural and Religious Studies Department at The Chinese University of Hong Kong. He has been interested in the interaction and interplay between the Bible and other religio-cultural as well as sociopolitical texts in Asia. He has published in the area of cross-textual reading of the Bible. His recent publications include "East Asian Theology," *Modern Theologians* (2004); and "Mothers Bewailing: Reading Lamentations" (in *Her Master's Tools? Feminist and Postcolonial Engagements of Historical-Critical Discourse* [Society of Biblical Literature, 2005]). He is also the associate editor of the *Global Bible Commentary* (2004).

Nancy C. Lee is Associate Professor of Religious Studies and the founding director of the Niebuhr Center at Elmhurst College in Chicago through the Lilly Endowment. Besides lament, her work focuses on biblical prophets, including women, social justice, and these elements in cultures and religious traditions as they intersect with society. She is founding co-chair of the SBL Lament group, a Fulbright Fellow to Croatia, author or editor of six books and contributor to eight books, most lately a poem in *Prayers for a New Social Awakening* (Westminster John Knox). She is currently writing a popular study, *Lyrics of Lament: Cultures and Faiths Facing Tragedy, Transforming Rituals and Society* (Fortress), and co-authoring a textbook on classical and contemporary prophetic figures across cultures, *The Enduring Prophets: Visions and Voices of Social Justice*. She has co-led a service-learning course in South Africa for a number of years, volunteering at the Chris Hani Independent School in Langa, and is doing grant work and research on educational strategies for at-risk children in Chicago and international contexts.

Tod Linafelt is Associate Professor of Biblical Literature at Georgetown University in Washington, D.C. His work has focused on reading the Bible in conversation with literary theory and criticism, as well as on the cultural history of the Bible. He is the author of *Surviving Lamentations: Catastrophe, Lament, and Protest in the Afterlife of a Biblical Book* (2000) and of a commentary on the book of Ruth (Berit Olam, 1999). He is editor or co-editor of four books, including most recently *Mel Gibson's Bible* (with Timothy K.

Beal, 2005), and has written over two dozen scholarly articles or essays for journals such as the *Journal of Biblical Literature, The Journal of Religion,* and the *Journal of the American Academy of Religion.* He is a recent past president of the Mid-Atlantic region of the Society of Biblical Literature.

Carleen Mandolfo is Associate Professor of Religious Studies at Colby College in Waterville, Maine. Her work on biblical lament literature includes *God in the Dock: Dialogic Tension in the Psalms of Lament* (Continuum, 2002) and *Daughter Zion Talks Back to the Prophets: A Dialogic Theology of the Book of Lamentations* (Society of Biblical Literature; Brill, 2007), as well as various articles on lament psalms, the book of Lamentations, and the book of Job.

William S. Morrow, Ph.D. (University of Toronto), is Associate Professor of Hebrew and Hebrew Scriptures at Queen's Theological College and Head of the Department of Religious Studies at Queen's University, Kingston, Ontario. His publications deal with biblical law in its ancient Near Eastern context and the effects of violence on the development of biblical religion. His latest book is *Protest against God: The Eclipse of a Biblical Tradition* (Sheffield Phoenix Press, 2006).

Kathleen M. O'Connor holds the William Marcellus McPheeters Chair in Old Testament at Columbia Theological Seminary in Decatur, Georgia. She is currently writing a book on Jeremiah drawing from studies of trauma and disaster. O'Connor received a Henry Luce III Fellowship for 2004–2005 to do this work and finds in Jeremiah theological tools for communal rebuilding after national catastrophe. Her previous book, *Lamentations and the Tears of the World* (Orbis, 2002), was awarded first prize by the Catholic Press Association for a book on scripture. She has written and co-edited books and articles on feminist interpretation, wisdom literature, and the prophets for scholarly and popular audiences. Her editorships include *Catholic Biblical Quarterly, Journal of Biblical Literature*, and, currently, *Feasting on the Word, a Lectionary*. She serves as current Vice-President of the Catholic Biblical Association of America and sits on the Council of the Society of Biblical literature.

Kimberly Wedeven Segall specializes in cultural and postcolonial studies and is an Associate Professor of English at Seattle Pacific University. After receiving a research grant from Northwestern University, she directed the play *Khumbulani/Remembrance*, first performed by and for Xhosa survivors of political violence in Cape Town, South Africa, in December 2000. She teaches courses on Middle Eastern writers in exile, postcolonial African literature, and introduction to postcolonial writing from India, Africa, and the Caribbean. Her current book project is called *Over My Dead Body: Imagining Identity after*

Violence, from South Africa to Iraq. She has published in *Comparative Studies of South Asia, Africa and the Middle East*; *Public Culture*; and *Research in African Literatures.*

Gerald West is Professor of Old Testament and Biblical Hermeneutics at the School of Religion and Theology at the University of KwaZulu-Natal, Pietermaritzburg, South Africa. He is also the Director of the Ujamaa Centre for Community Development and Research, which provides an interface between academic biblical scholarship and Bible reading in local churches and communities of the poor, working-class, and marginalized. He has published a number of books and articles, among which is the volume he edited with Musa Dube on *The Bible in Africa: Transactions, Trajectories and Trends* (Brill, 2000); *The Academy of the Poor: Towards a Dialogical Reading of the Bible* (Cluster, 2003), and an edited volume on *Reading Other-Wise: Socially Engaged Biblical Scholars Reading with Their Local Communities* (Semeia Studies, Society of Biblical Literature, 2007).

Robert Williamson Jr. teaches biblical studies at Hendrix College in Conway, Arkansas. He specializes in wisdom literature, Qumran studies, and the history of biblical interpretation. His recent work appears in *Dead Sea Discoveries* and *The Dictionary of Major Biblical Interpreters.* His current project is a study of the symbolizations of life in Second Temple Hebrew wisdom literature.

Index of Ancient Sources

INDEX OF MODERN AUTHORS

Printed in the United States
204146BV00002B/106-210/P